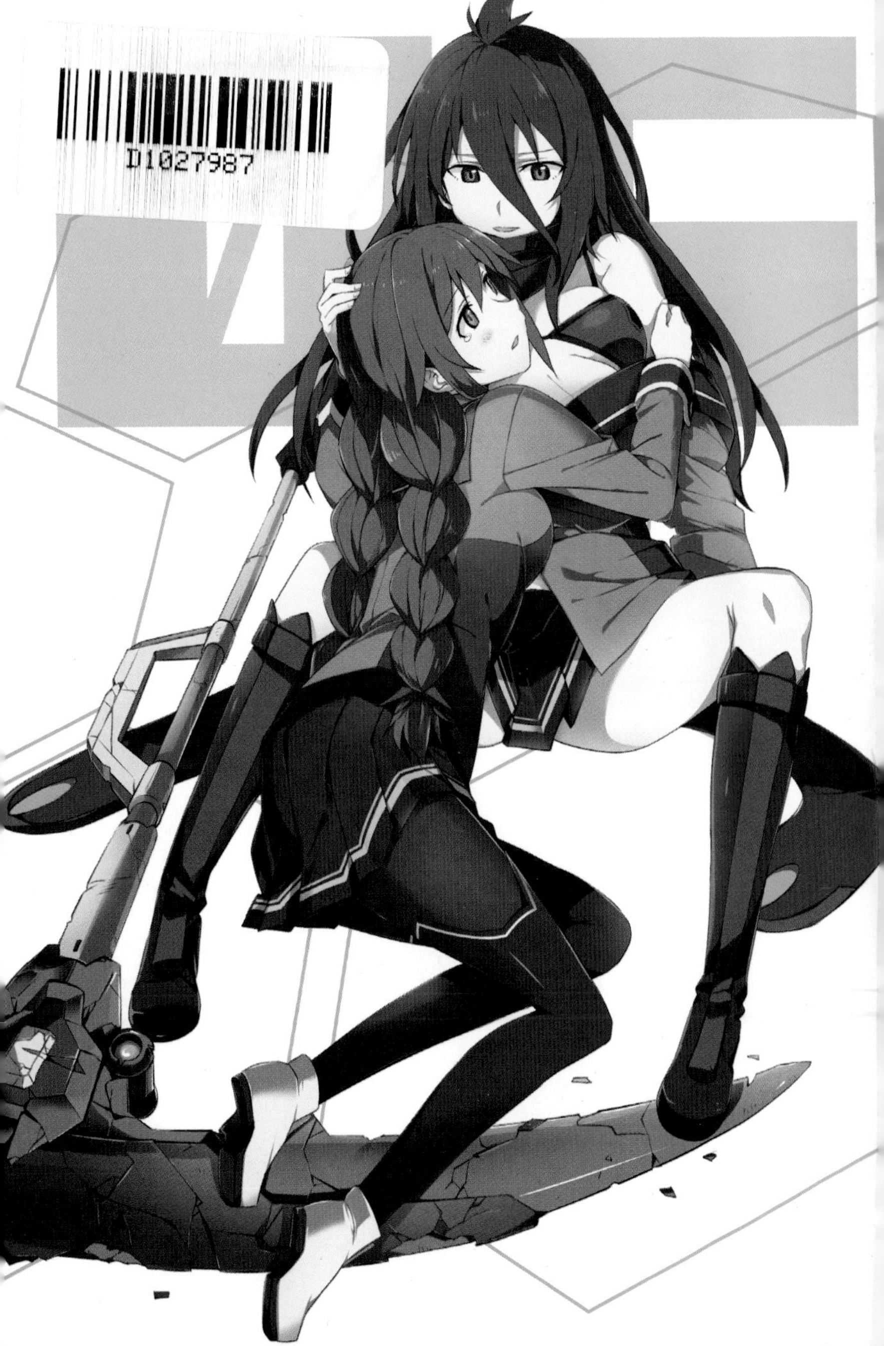

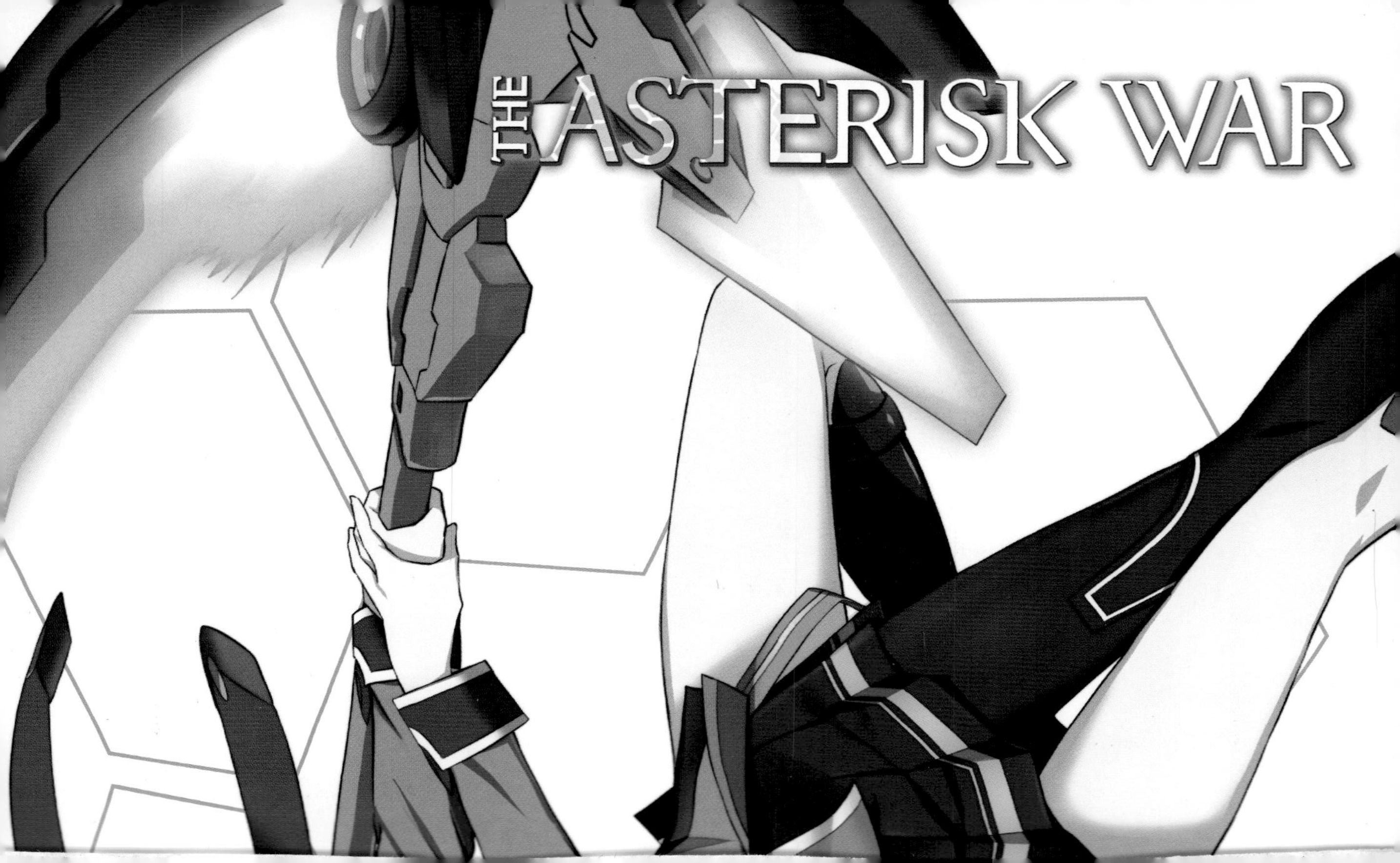
THE ASTERISK WAR

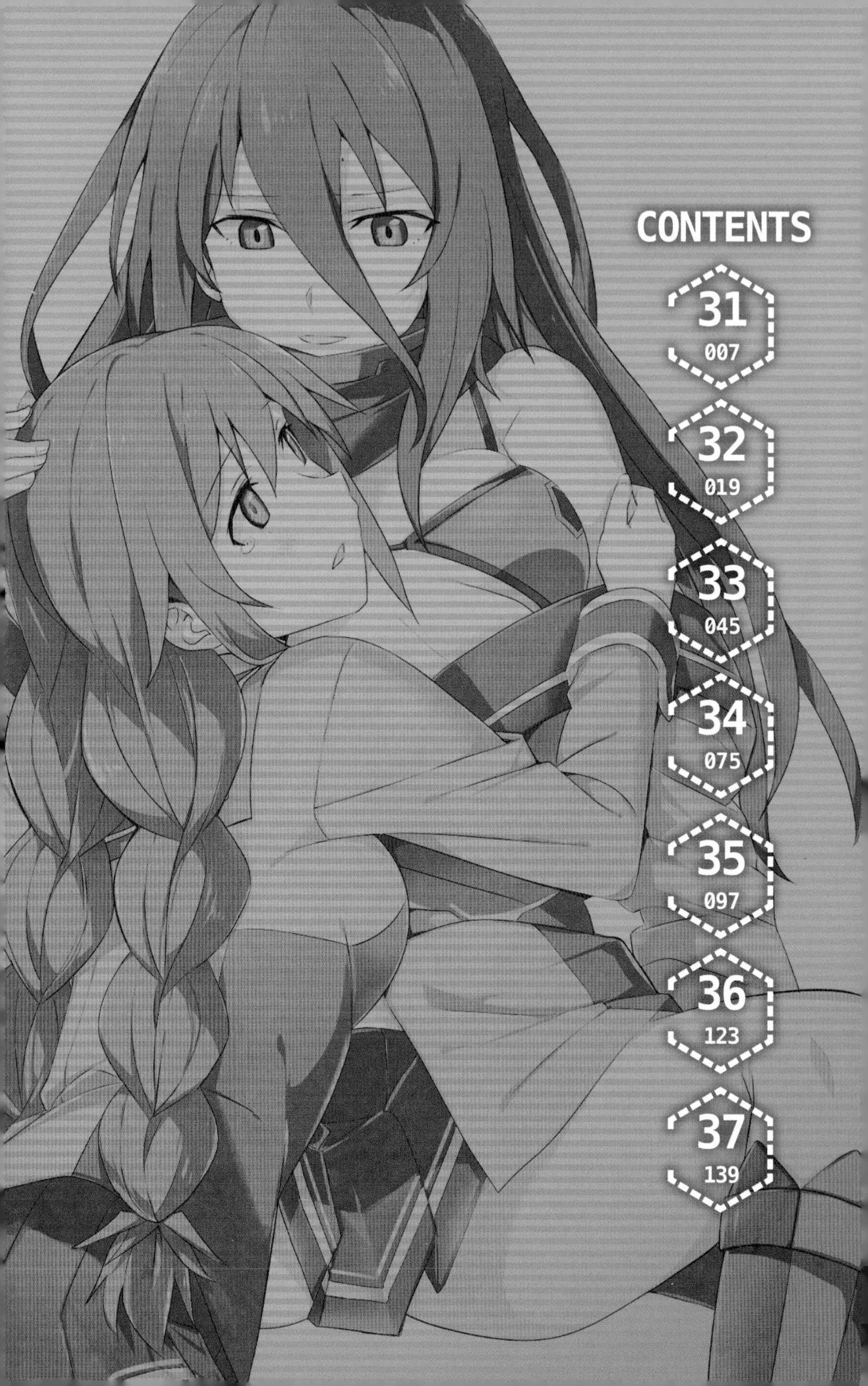

CONTENTS

ART: **Ningen**
ORIGINAL STORY: **Yuu Miyazaki**
CHARACTER DESIGN: **okiura**

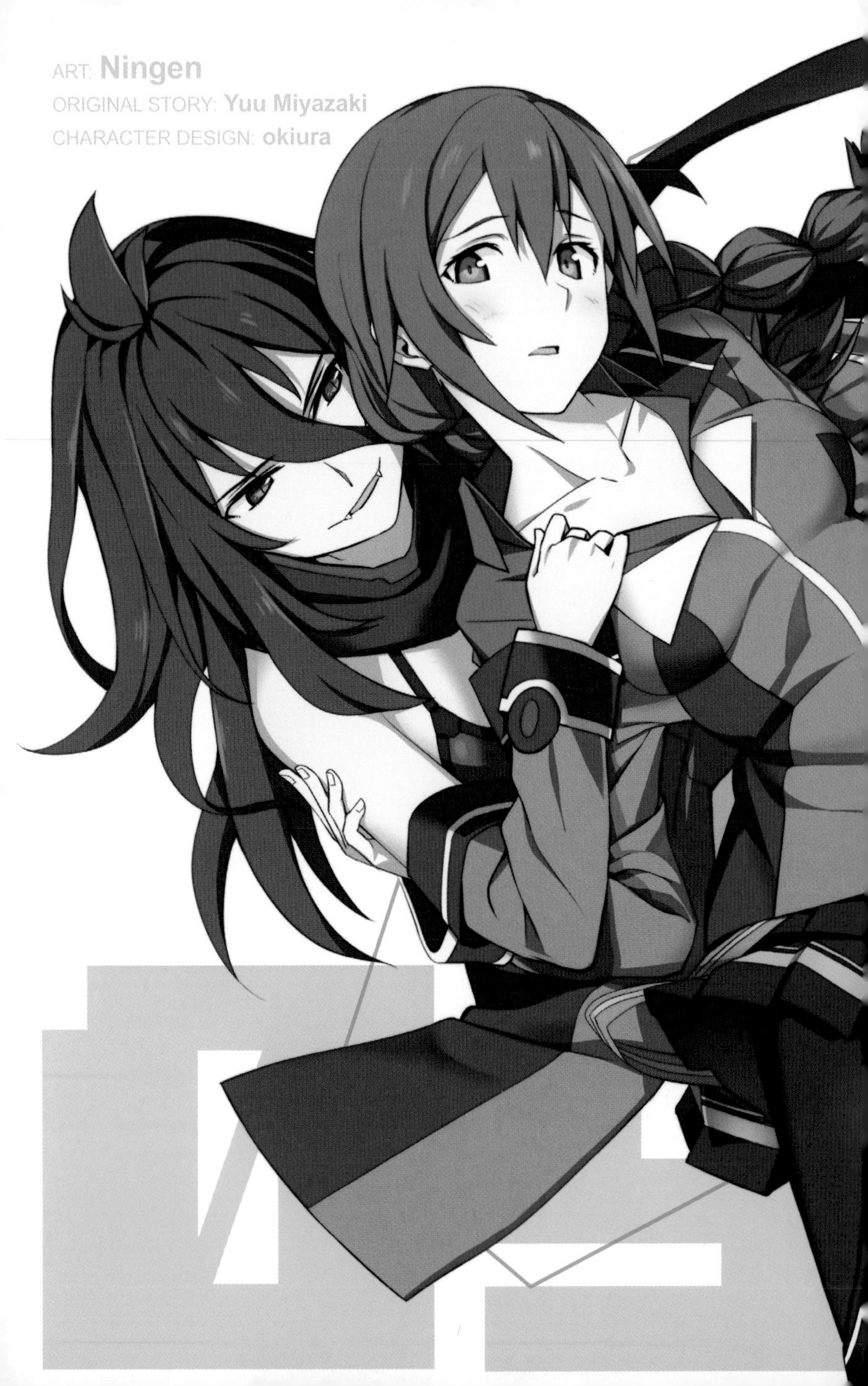

THE ASTERISK WAR

05

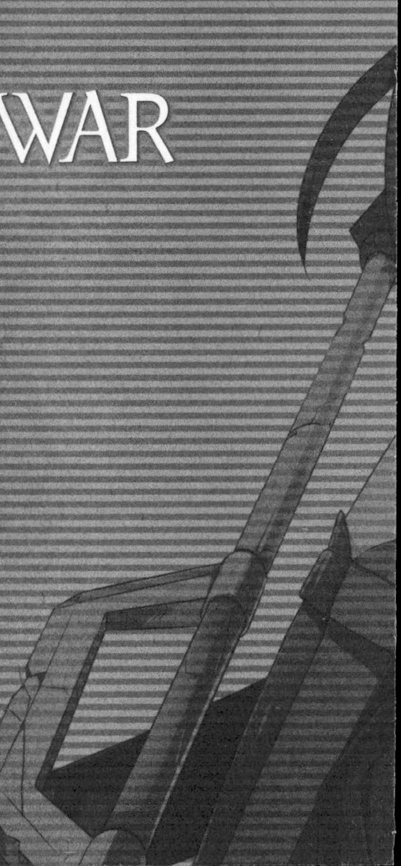

ART: **Ningen**
ORIGINAL STORY: **Yuu Miyazaki**
CHARACTER DESIGN: **okiura**

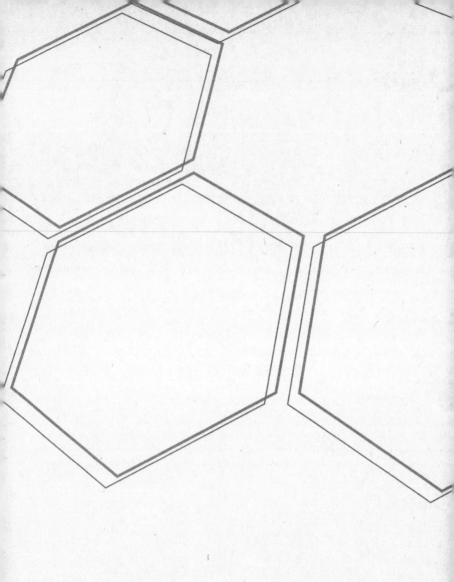

THE
ASTERISK WAR

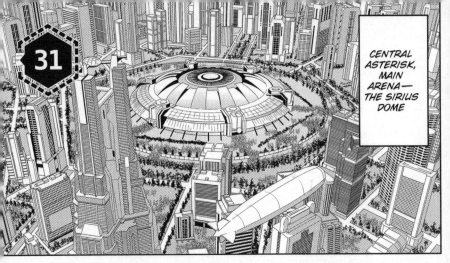

31

CENTRAL
ASTERISK,
MAIN
ARENA—
THE SIRIUS
DOME

YAAAY!

CHAIRMAN
OF THE
FESTA
EXECUTIVE
COMMITTEE,
MADIATH
MESA

RAAAAAH!

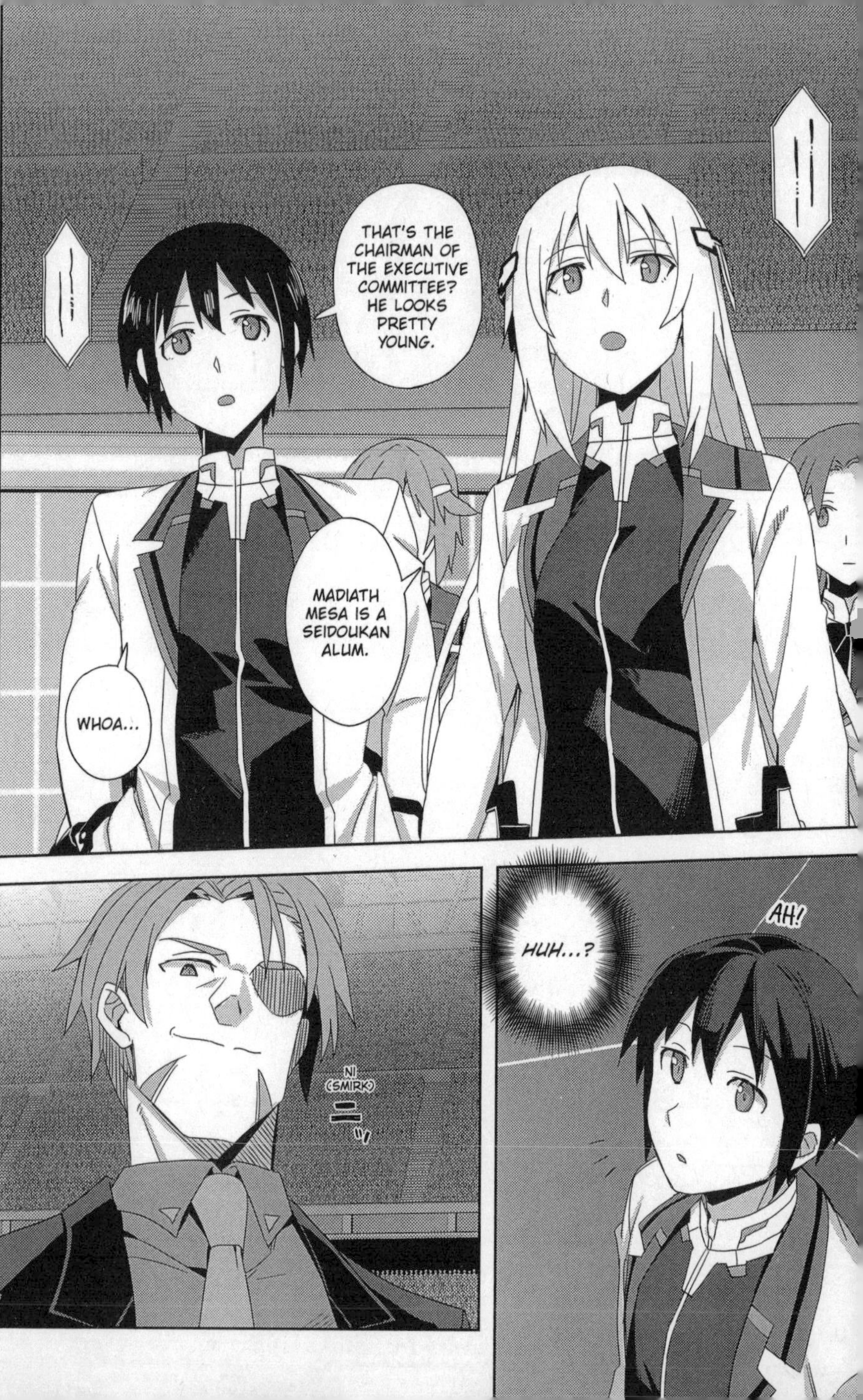
THAT'S THE CHAIRMAN OF THE EXECUTIVE COMMITTEE? HE LOOKS PRETTY YOUNG.
MADIATH MESA IS A SEIDOUKAN ALUM.
WHOA...
AH!
HUH...?
NI (SMIRK)

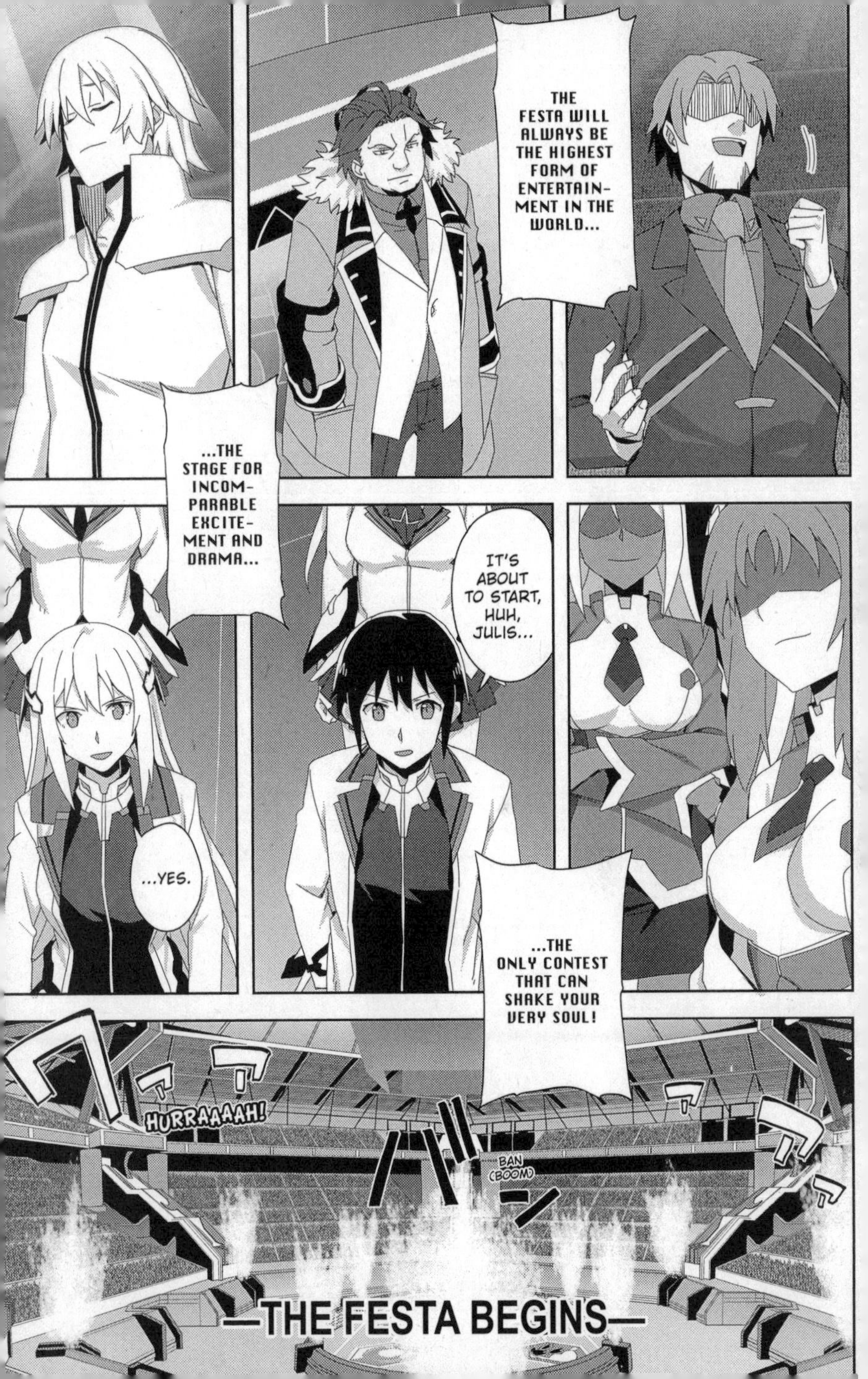
THE FESTA WILL ALWAYS BE THE HIGHEST FORM OF ENTERTAIN-MENT IN THE WORLD...
...THE STAGE FOR INCOM-PARABLE EXCITE-MENT AND DRAMA...
IT'S ABOUT TO START, HUH, JULIS...
...YES.
...THE ONLY CONTEST THAT CAN SHAKE YOUR VERY SOUL!
HURRAAAAH!
BAN (BOOM)
—THE FESTA BEGINS—

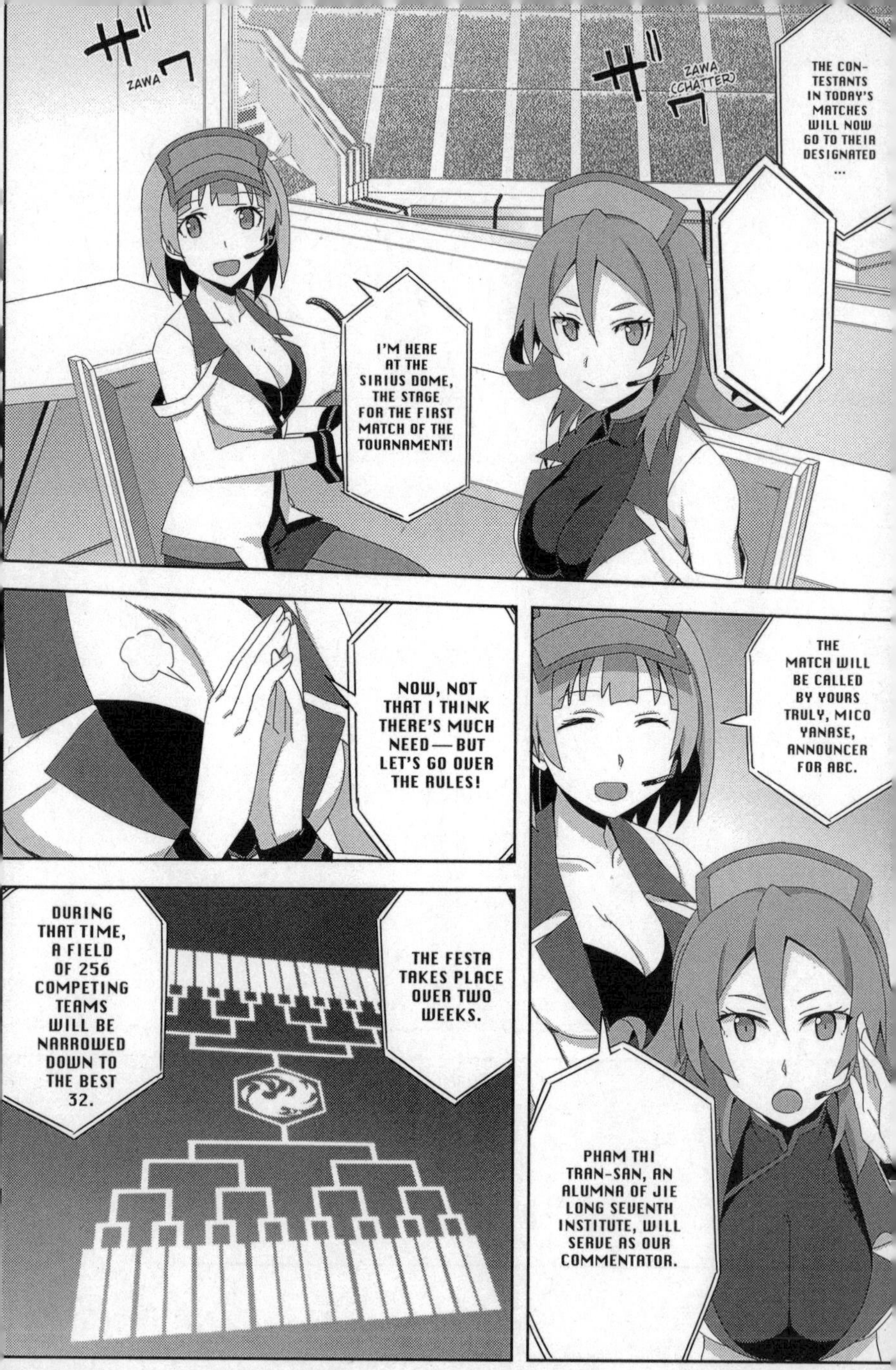
THE CONTESTANTS IN TODAY'S MATCHES WILL NOW GO TO THEIR DESIGNATED ...
ZAWA (CHATTER)
I'M HERE AT THE SIRIUS DOME, THE STAGE FOR THE FIRST MATCH OF THE TOURNAMENT!
ZAWA
THE MATCH WILL BE CALLED BY YOURS TRULY, MICO YANASE, ANNOUNCER FOR ABC.
PHAM THI TRAN-SAN, AN ALUMNA OF JIE LONG SEVENTH INSTITUTE, WILL SERVE AS OUR COMMENTATOR.
NOW, NOT THAT I THINK THERE'S MUCH NEED—BUT LET'S GO OVER THE RULES!
THE FESTA TAKES PLACE OVER TWO WEEKS.
DURING THAT TIME, A FIELD OF 256 COMPETING TEAMS WILL BE NARROWED DOWN TO THE BEST 32.

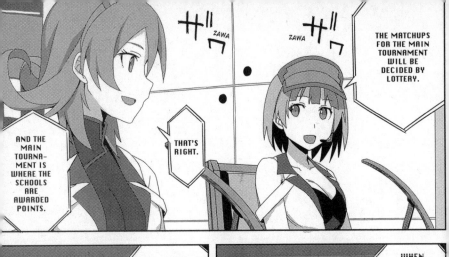

ZAWA
ZAWA
THE MATCHUPS FOR THE MAIN TOURNAMENT WILL BE DECIDED BY LOTTERY.
THAT'S RIGHT.
AND THE MAIN TOURNAMENT IS WHERE THE SCHOOLS ARE AWARDED POINTS.
BADGE BROKEN
WHEN BOTH MEMBERS OF A TEAM LOSE EITHER THEIR SCHOOL CRESTS ...
... OR...
UNCONSCIOUS
...THEIR CONSCIOUSNESS, OR IF THEY FORFEIT, THE MATCH IS DECIDED.
THE SCHOOL CREST SYSTEM WILL ANNOUNCE THE OUTCOME.
RAAAAH!
THE RULINGS ON THE PROGRESS OF THE MATCH ARE COMPLETELY AUTOMATED—
NO NEED FOR REFEREES!
SO, LET'S TAKE A LOOK AT THE PRELIMINARIES!

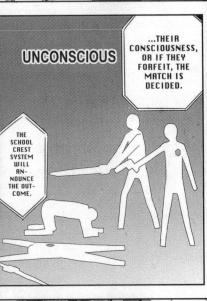

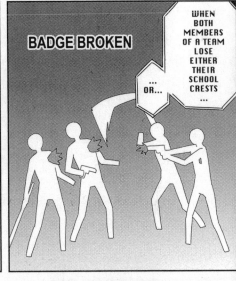

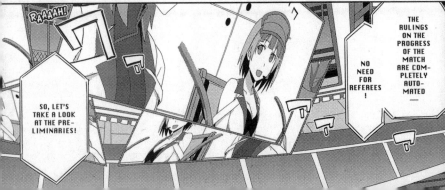

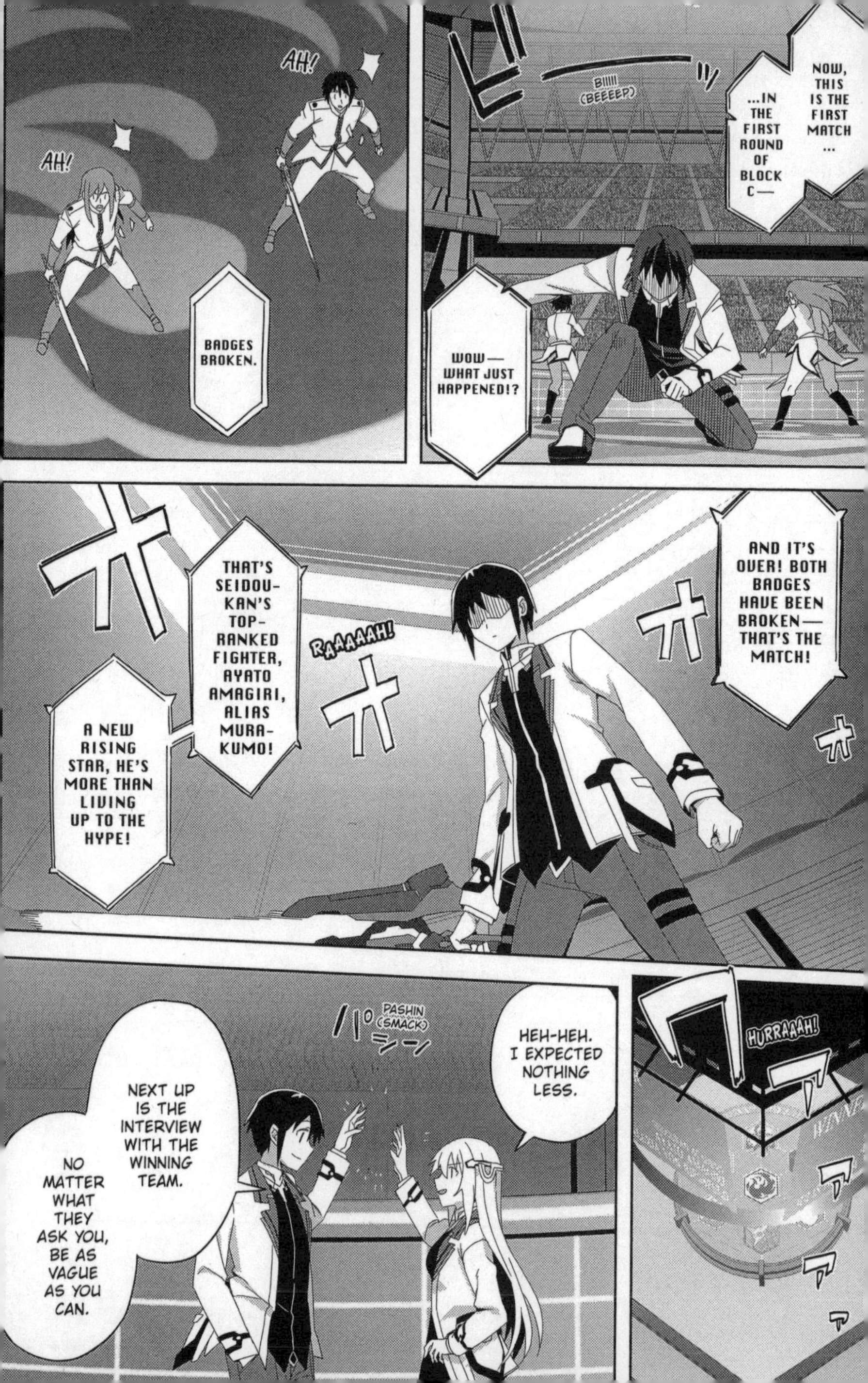
BIIIII (BEEEEP)
NOW, THIS IS THE FIRST MATCH...
...IN THE FIRST ROUND OF BLOCK C—
WOW— WHAT JUST HAPPENED!?
AH!
AH!
BADGES BROKEN.
AND IT'S OVER! BOTH BADGES HAVE BEEN BROKEN— THAT'S THE MATCH!
RAAAAAH!
THAT'S SEIDOUKAN'S TOP-RANKED FIGHTER, AYATO AMAGIRI, ALIAS MURAKUMO!
A NEW RISING STAR, HE'S MORE THAN LIVING UP TO THE HYPE!
HURRAAAH!
HEH-HEH. I EXPECTED NOTHING LESS.
PASHIN (SMACK)
NEXT UP IS THE INTERVIEW WITH THE WINNING TEAM.
NO MATTER WHAT THEY ASK YOU, BE AS VAGUE AS YOU CAN.

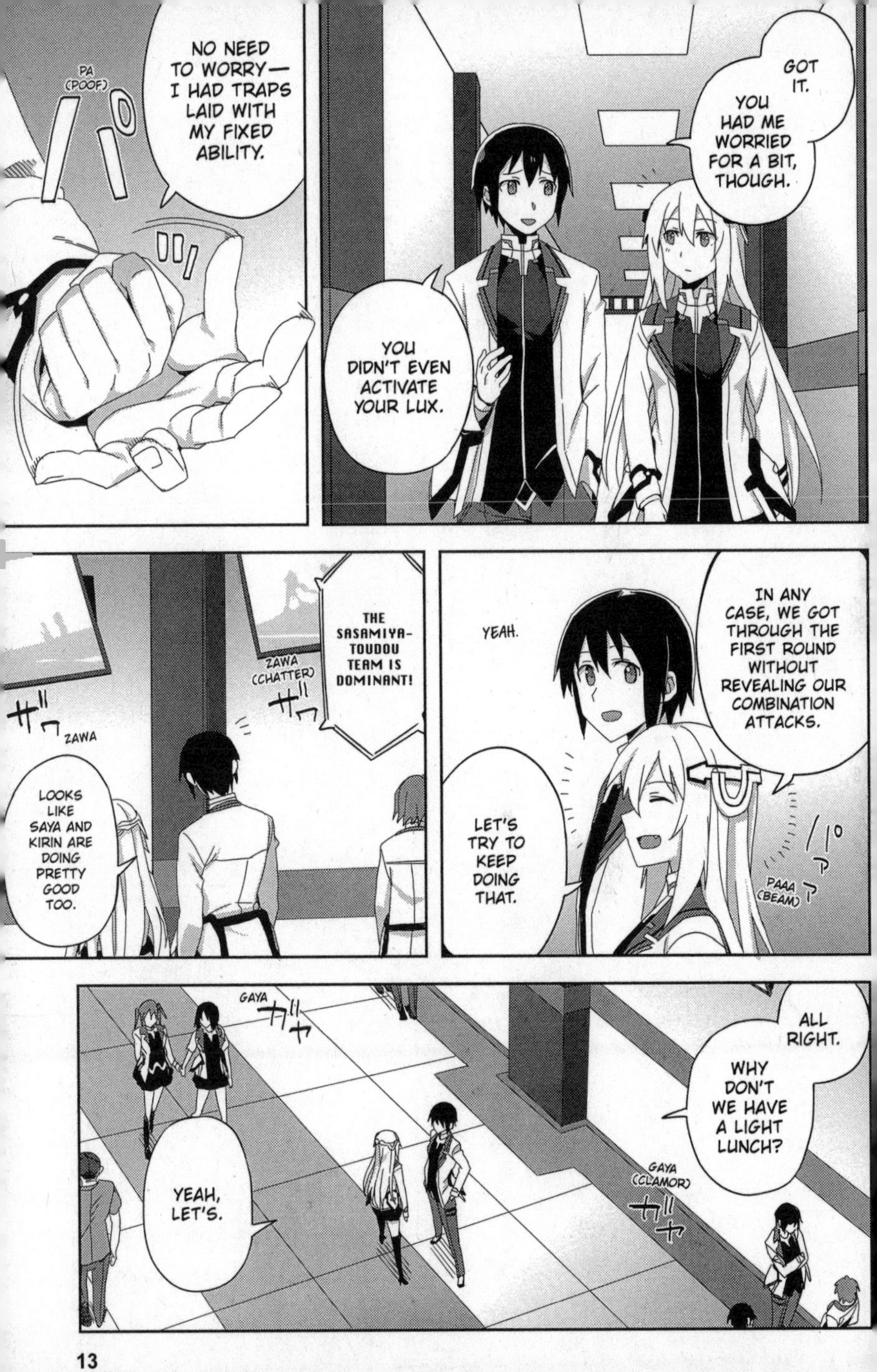
GOT IT.
YOU HAD ME WORRIED FOR A BIT, THOUGH.
YOU DIDN'T EVEN ACTIVATE YOUR LUX.
NO NEED TO WORRY— I HAD TRAPS LAID WITH MY FIXED ABILITY.
PA (POOF)
IN ANY CASE, WE GOT THROUGH THE FIRST ROUND WITHOUT REVEALING OUR COMBINATION ATTACKS.
YEAH.
PAAA (BEAM)
LET'S TRY TO KEEP DOING THAT.
THE SASAMIYA-TOUDOU TEAM IS DOMINANT!
ZAWA (CHATTER)
ZAWA
LOOKS LIKE SAYA AND KIRIN ARE DOING PRETTY GOOD TOO.
ALL RIGHT.
WHY DON'T WE HAVE A LIGHT LUNCH?
GAYA (CLAMOR)
GAYA
YEAH, LET'S.

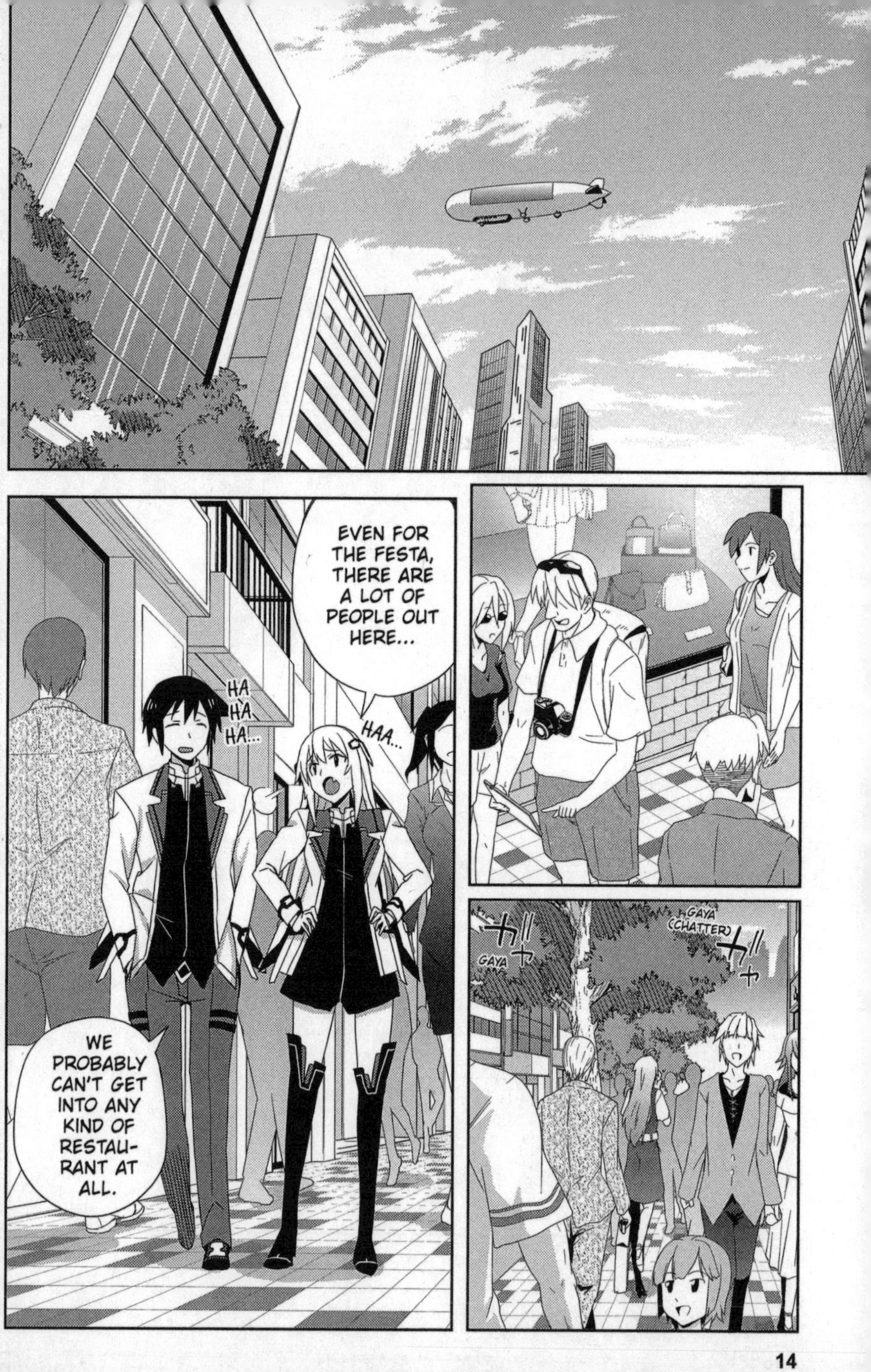
GAYA (CHATTER)
ガヤ
GAYA
ガヤ
EVEN FOR THE FESTA, THERE ARE A LOT OF PEOPLE OUT HERE...
HAA...
HA HA HA...
WE PROBABLY CAN'T GET INTO ANY KIND OF RESTAU-RANT AT ALL.

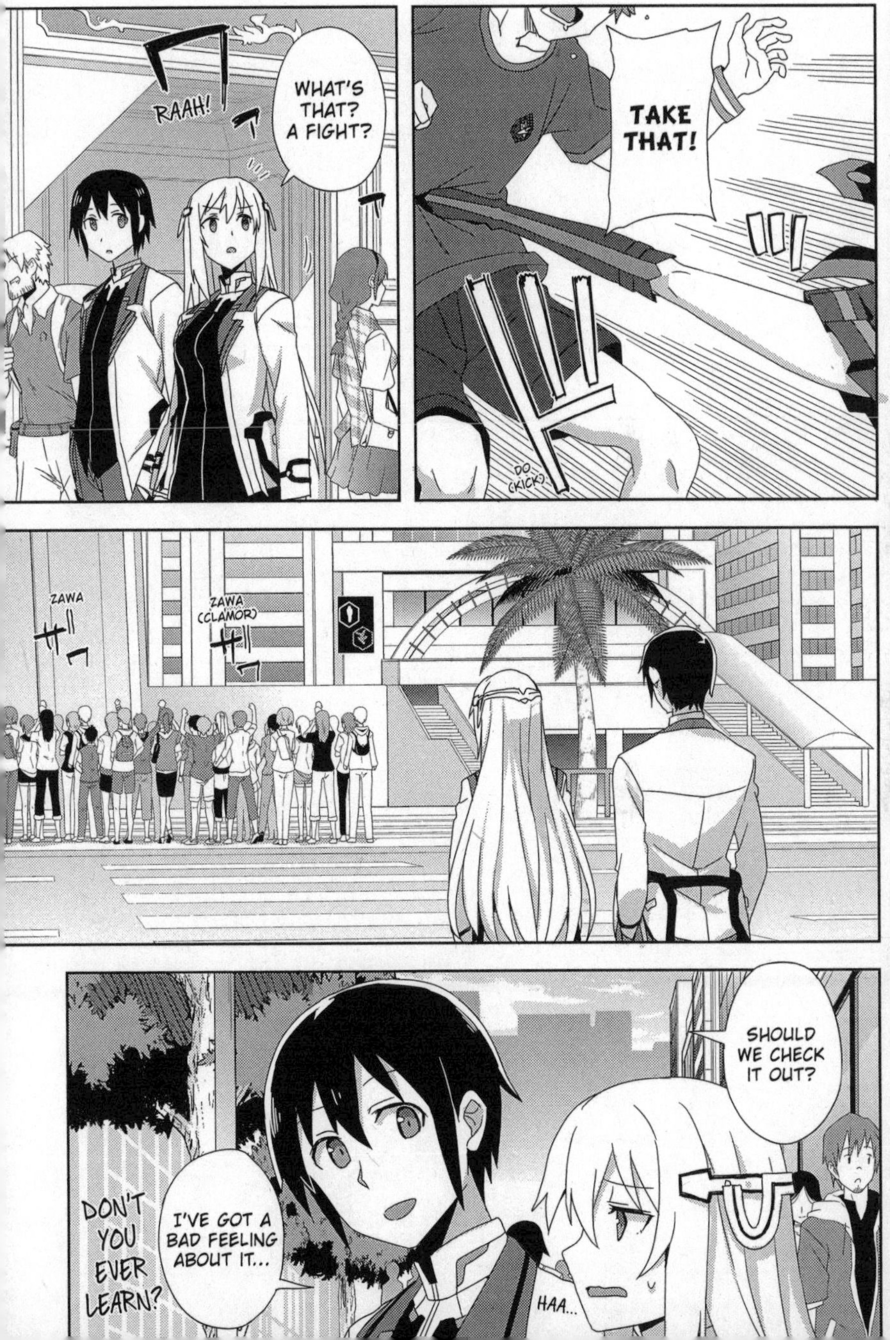
TAKE THAT!
DO (KICK)
RAAH!
WHAT'S THAT? A FIGHT?
ZAWA (CLAMOR)
ZAWA
SHOULD WE CHECK IT OUT?
HAA...
I'VE GOT A BAD FEELING ABOUT IT...
DON'T YOU EVER LEARN?

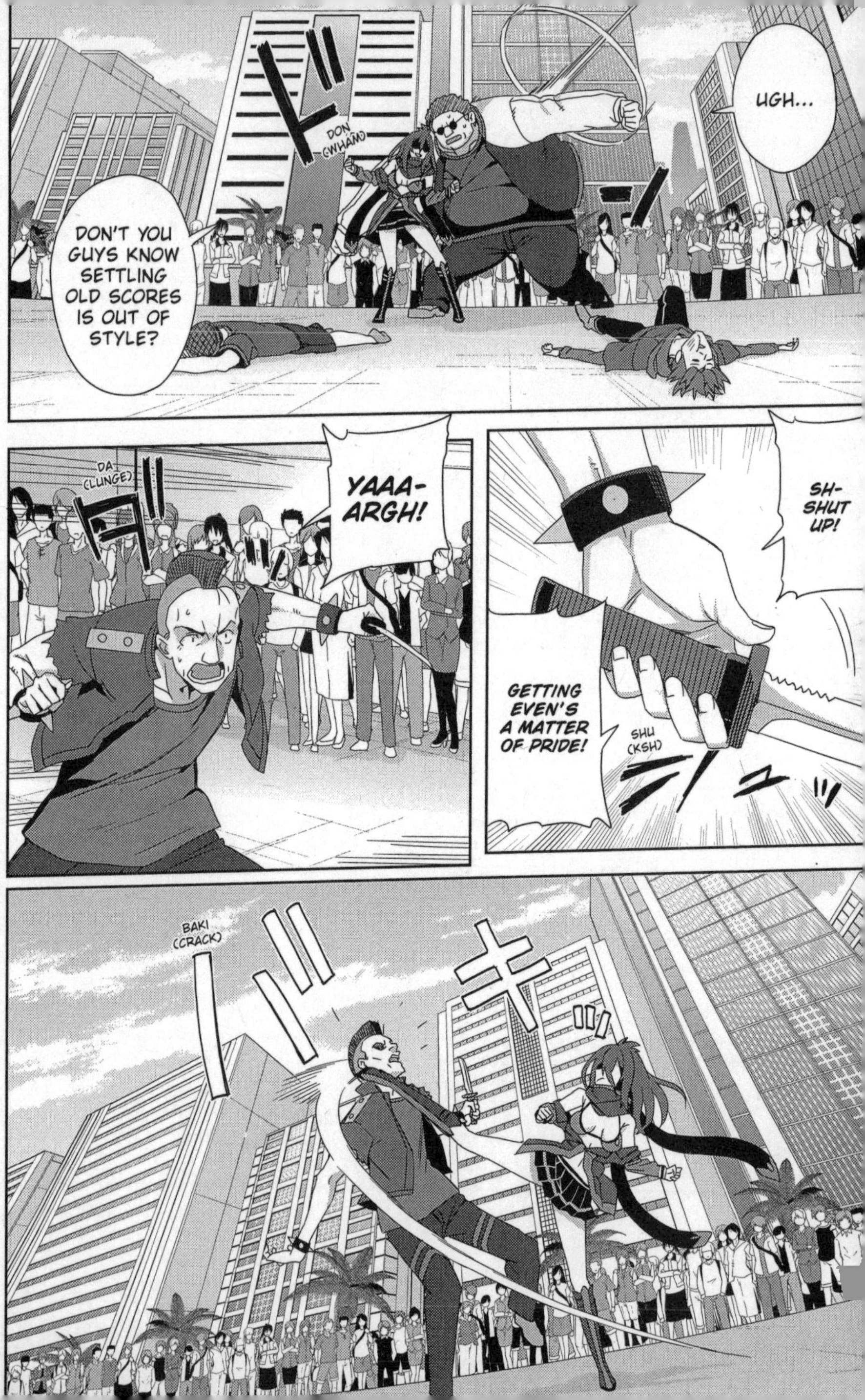
UGH...
DON (WHAM)
DON'T YOU GUYS KNOW SETTLING OLD SCORES IS OUT OF STYLE?
SH-SHUT UP!
GETTING EVEN'S A MATTER OF PRIDE!
SHU (KSH)
YAAA-ARGH!
DA (LUNGE)
BAKI (CRACK)

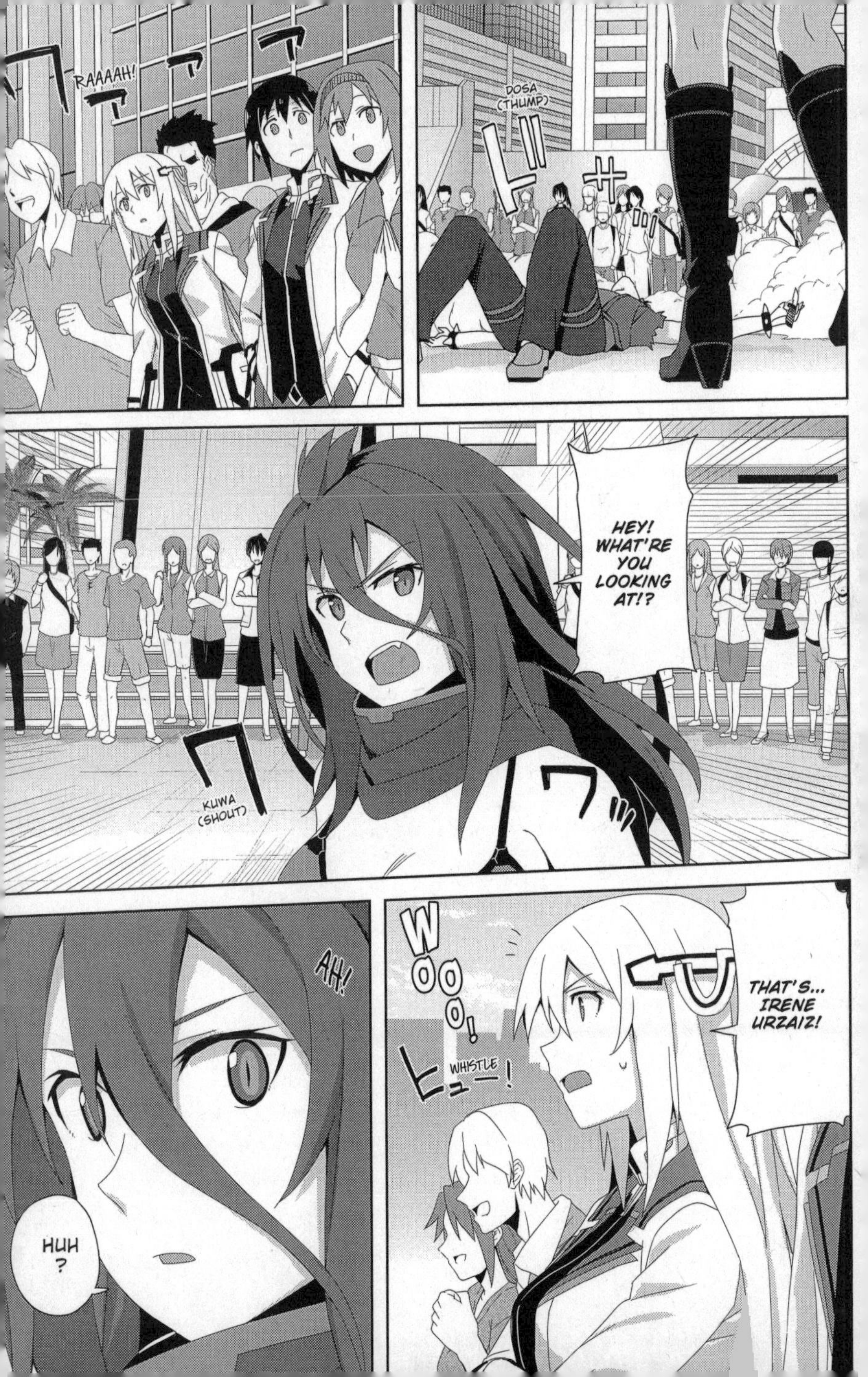
DOSA (THUMP)
RAAAAH!
HEY! WHAT'RE YOU LOOKING AT!?
KUWA (SHOUT)
THAT'S... IRENE URZAIZ!
WOOO!
WHISTLE!
AH!
HUH?

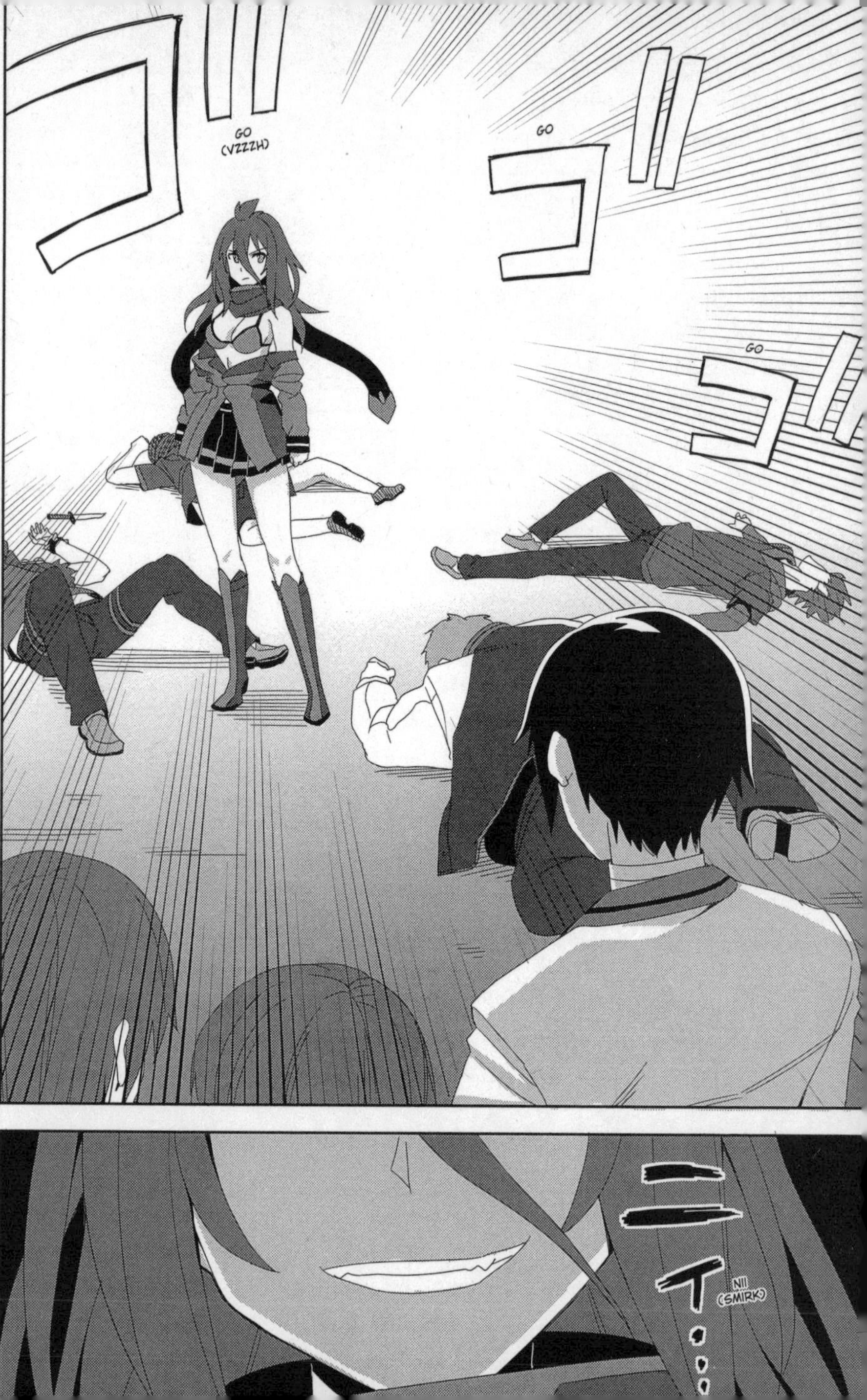
GO
GO (VZZZH)
GO
NII (SMIRK)

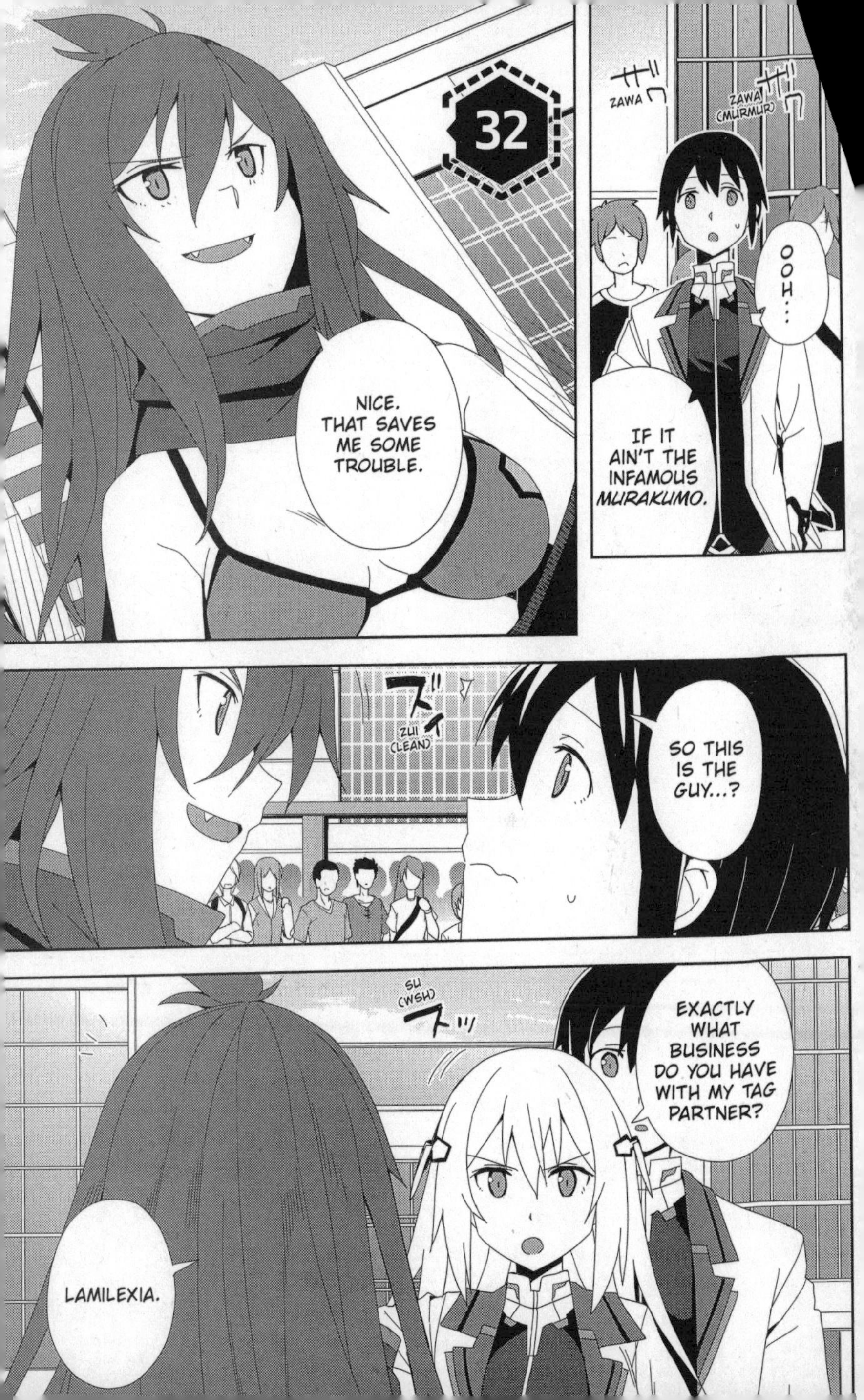
ZAWA
ZAWA (MURMUR)
OOH...
IF IT AIN'T THE INFAMOUS MURAKUMO.
32
NICE. THAT SAVES ME SOME TROUBLE.
SO THIS IS THE GUY...?
ZUI (LEAN)
SU (WSH)
EXACTLY WHAT BUSINESS DO YOU HAVE WITH MY TAG PARTNER?
LAMILEXIA.

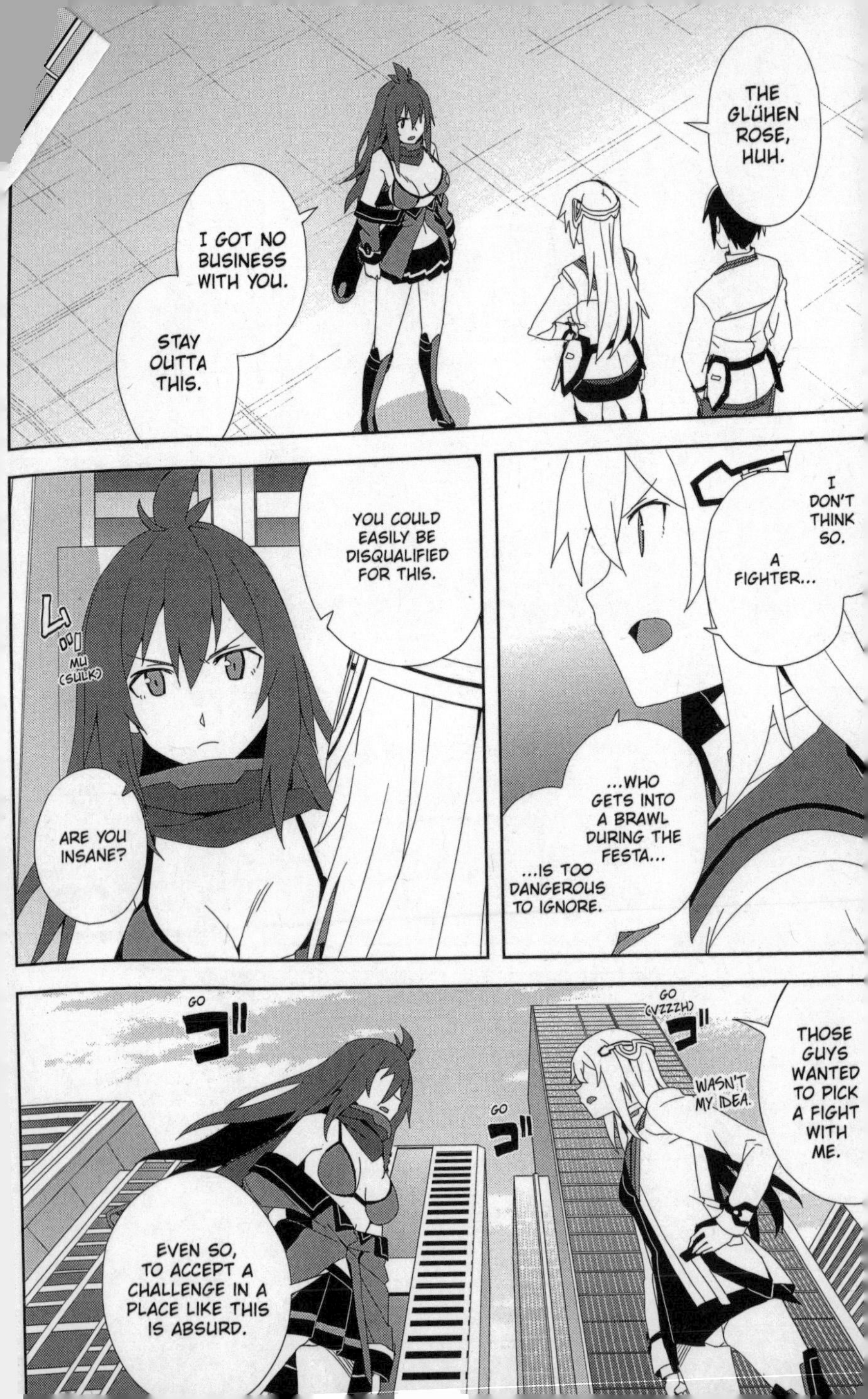
THE GLÜHEN ROSE, HUH.
I GOT NO BUSINESS WITH YOU.
STAY OUTTA THIS.
I DON'T THINK SO.
A FIGHTER...
...WHO GETS INTO A BRAWL DURING THE FESTA...
...IS TOO DANGEROUS TO IGNORE.
YOU COULD EASILY BE DISQUALIFIED FOR THIS.
ム
MU (SULK)
ARE YOU INSANE?
THOSE GUYS WANTED TO PICK A FIGHT WITH ME.
WASN'T MY IDEA.
ゴ
GO (VZZZH)
ゴ
GO
ゴ
GO
EVEN SO, TO ACCEPT A CHALLENGE IN A PLACE LIKE THIS IS ABSURD.

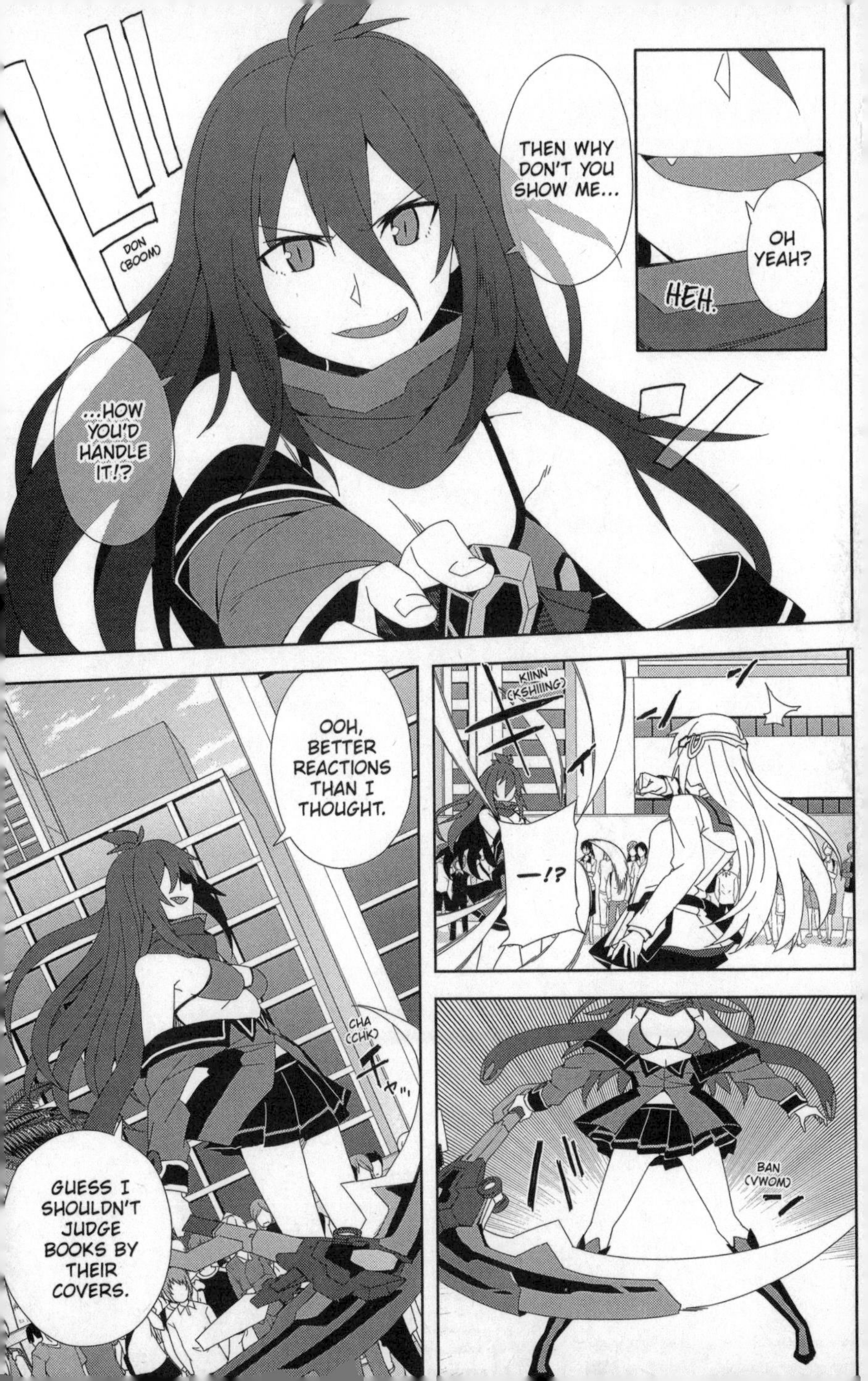

OH YEAH?
HEH.
THEN WHY DON'T YOU SHOW ME...
DON (BOOM)
...HOW YOU'D HANDLE IT!?
KIINN (KSHIIING)
—!?
BAN (VWOM)
OOH, BETTER REACTIONS THAN I THOUGHT.
CHA (CHK)
GUESS I SHOULDN'T JUDGE BOOKS BY THEIR COVERS.

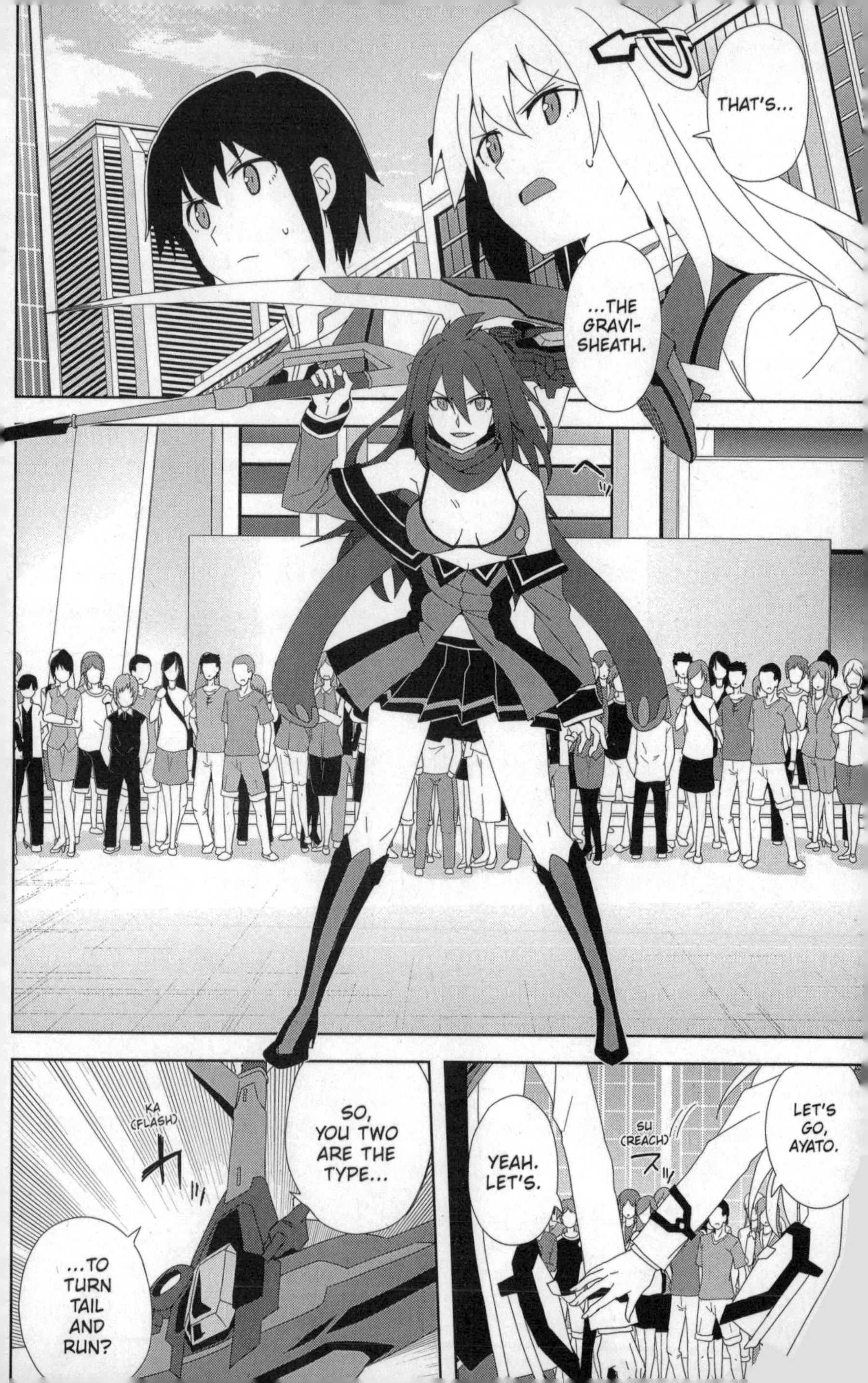
THAT'S...
...THE GRAVI-SHEATH.
LET'S GO, AYATO.
SU (REACH)
YEAH. LET'S.
SO, YOU TWO ARE THE TYPE...
KA (FLASH)
...TO TURN TAIL AND RUN?

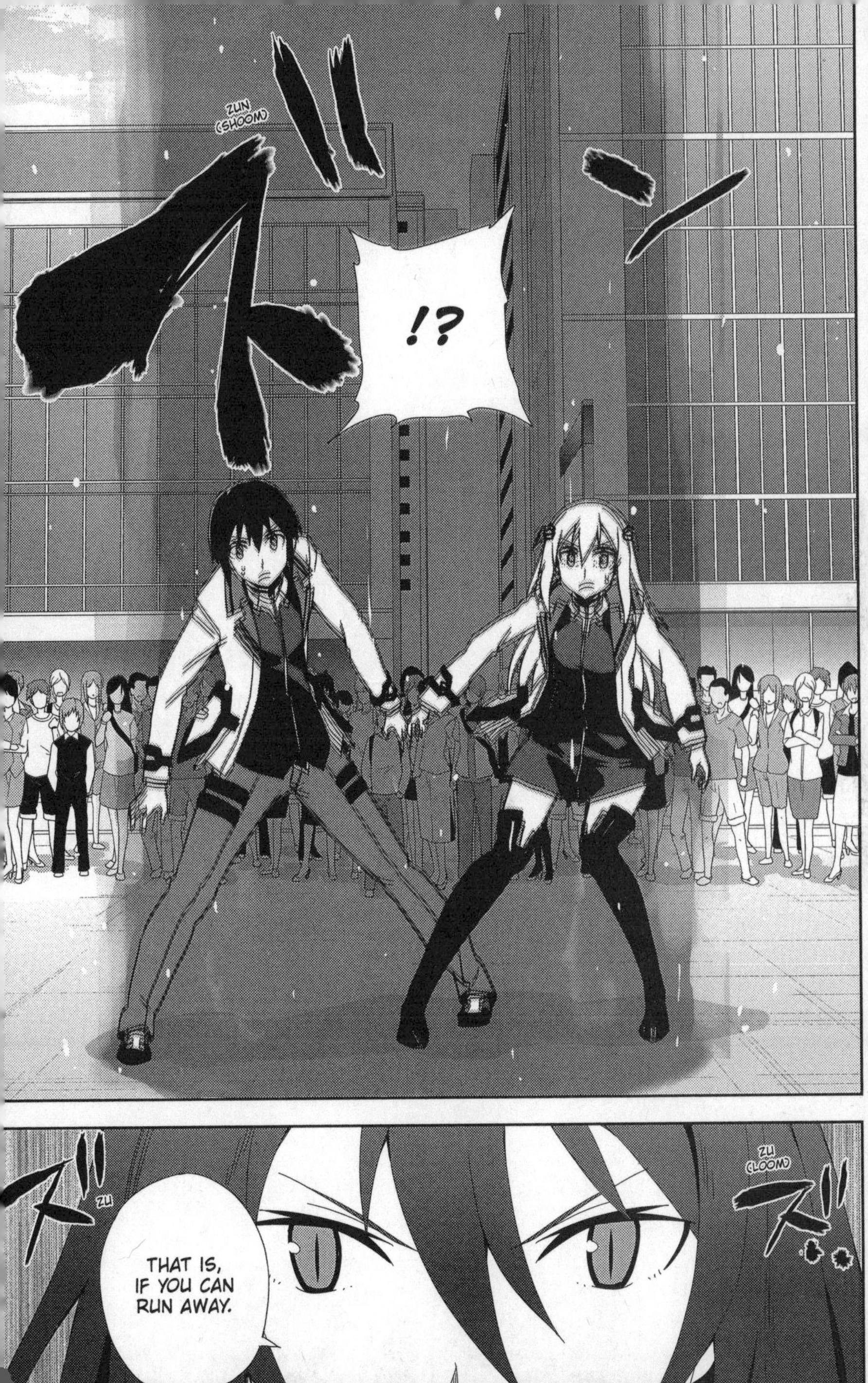
ZUN
(SHOOM)
!?
ZU
(LOOM)
ZU
THAT IS, IF YOU CAN RUN AWAY.

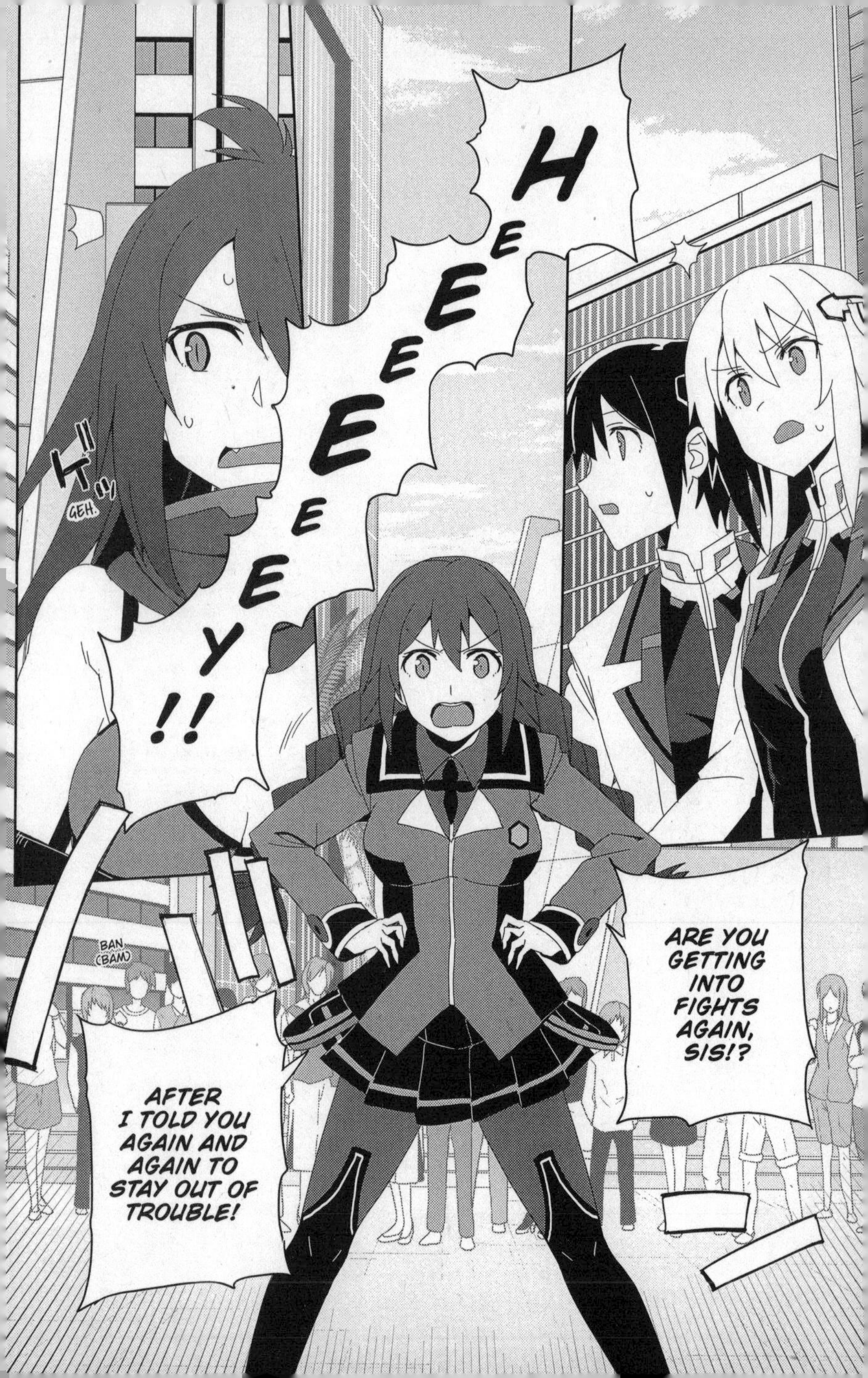
HEEEEEEY!!
GEH.
ARE YOU GETTING INTO FIGHTS AGAIN, SIS!?
BAN (BAM)
AFTER I TOLD YOU AGAIN AND AGAIN TO STAY OUT OF TROUBLE!

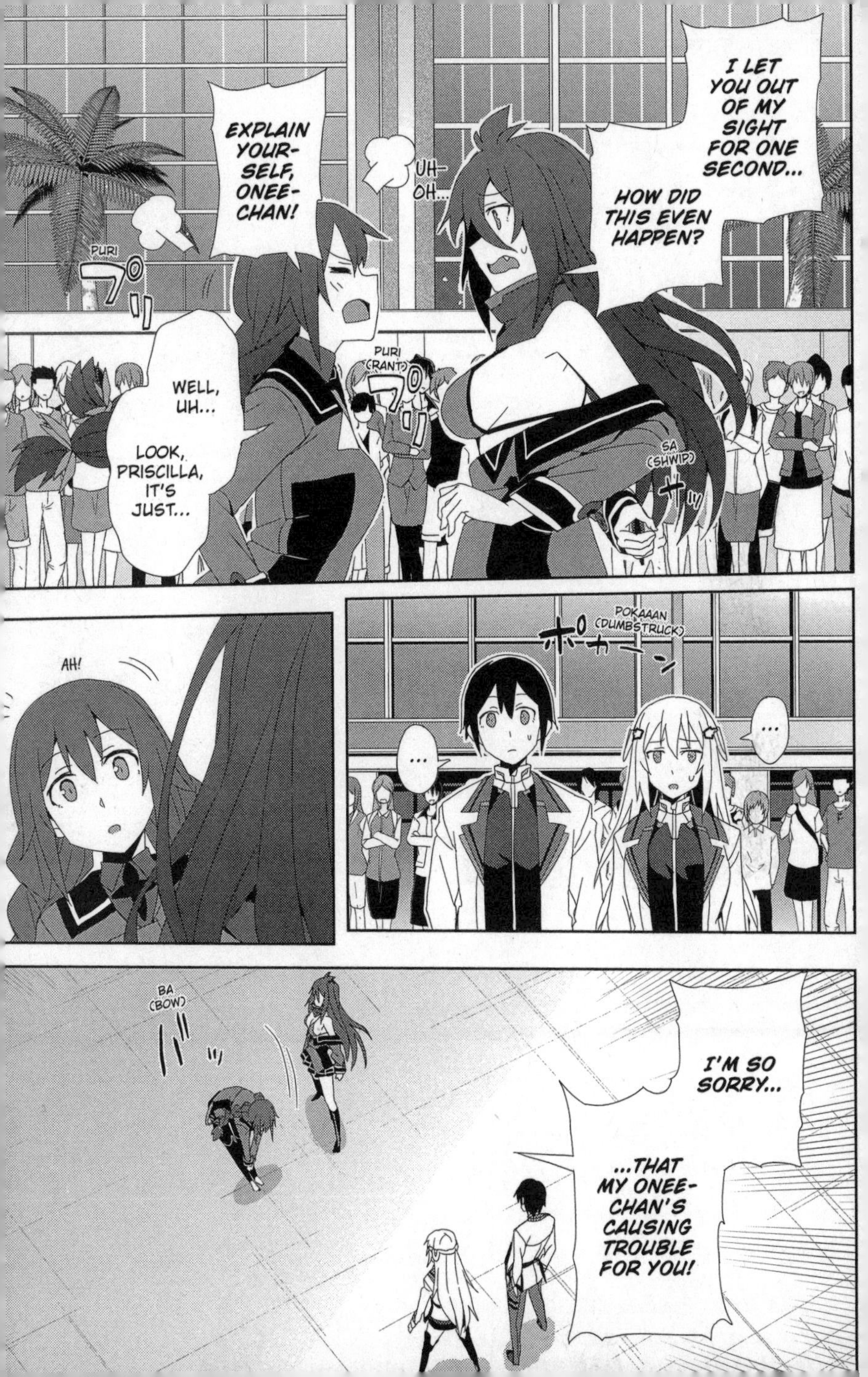
I LET YOU OUT OF MY SIGHT FOR ONE SECOND...
HOW DID THIS EVEN HAPPEN?
UH-OH...
EXPLAIN YOURSELF, ONEE-CHAN!
PURI
PURI (RANT)
SA (SHWIP)
WELL, UH...
LOOK, PRISCILLA, IT'S JUST...
POKAAAN (DUMBSTRUCK)
...
...
AH!
I'M SO SORRY...
...THAT MY ONEE-CHAN'S CAUSING TROUBLE FOR YOU!
BA (BOW)

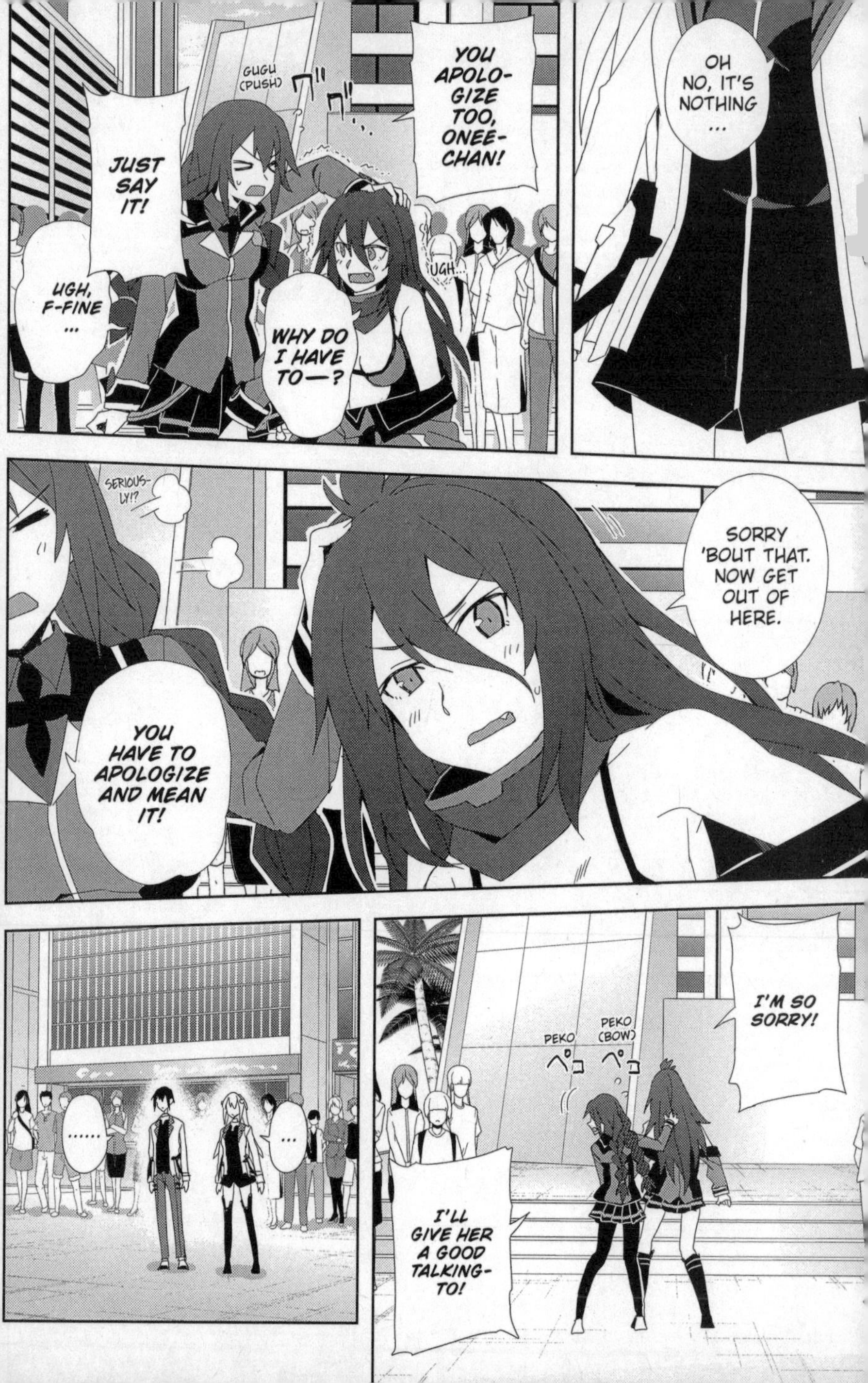
OH NO, IT'S NOTHING ...
YOU APOLOGIZE TOO, ONEE-CHAN!
GUGU (PUSH)
JUST SAY IT!
UGH...
WHY DO I HAVE TO—?
UGH, F-FINE ...
SORRY 'BOUT THAT. NOW GET OUT OF HERE.
SERIOUSLY!?
YOU HAVE TO APOLOGIZE AND MEAN IT!
I'M SO SORRY!
PEKO (BOW)
PEKO
I'LL GIVE HER A GOOD TALKING-TO!
...
......

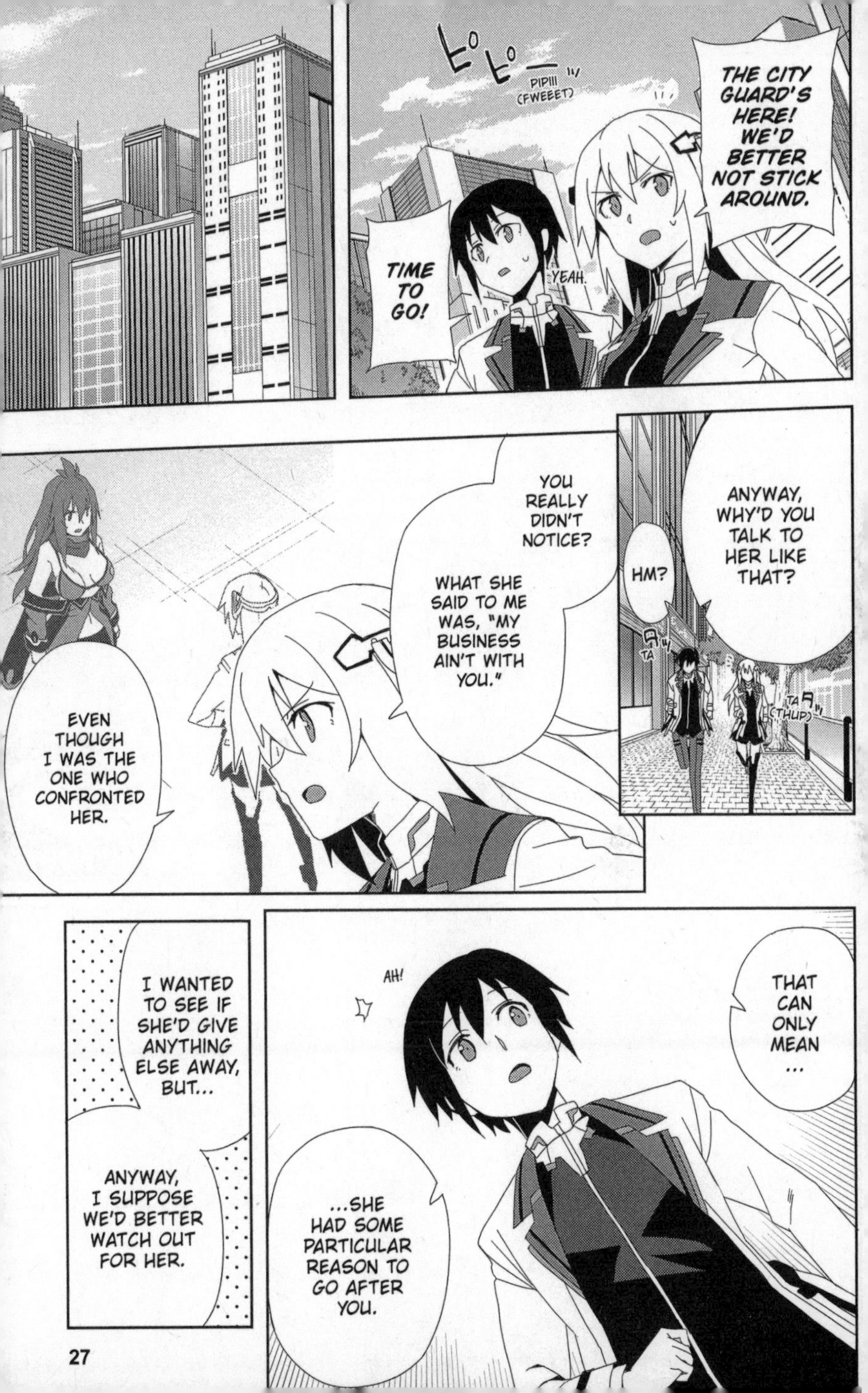
ピピー
PIPIII
(FWEEEET)
THE CITY GUARD'S HERE! WE'D BETTER NOT STICK AROUND.
YEAH.
TIME TO GO!
ANYWAY, WHY'D YOU TALK TO HER LIKE THAT?
HM?
タッ
TA
タッ
TA
(THUP)
YOU REALLY DIDN'T NOTICE?
WHAT SHE SAID TO ME WAS, "MY BUSINESS AIN'T WITH YOU."
EVEN THOUGH I WAS THE ONE WHO CONFRONTED HER.
THAT CAN ONLY MEAN ...
AH!
...SHE HAD SOME PARTICULAR REASON TO GO AFTER YOU.
I WANTED TO SEE IF SHE'D GIVE ANYTHING ELSE AWAY, BUT...
ANYWAY, I SUPPOSE WE'D BETTER WATCH OUT FOR HER.

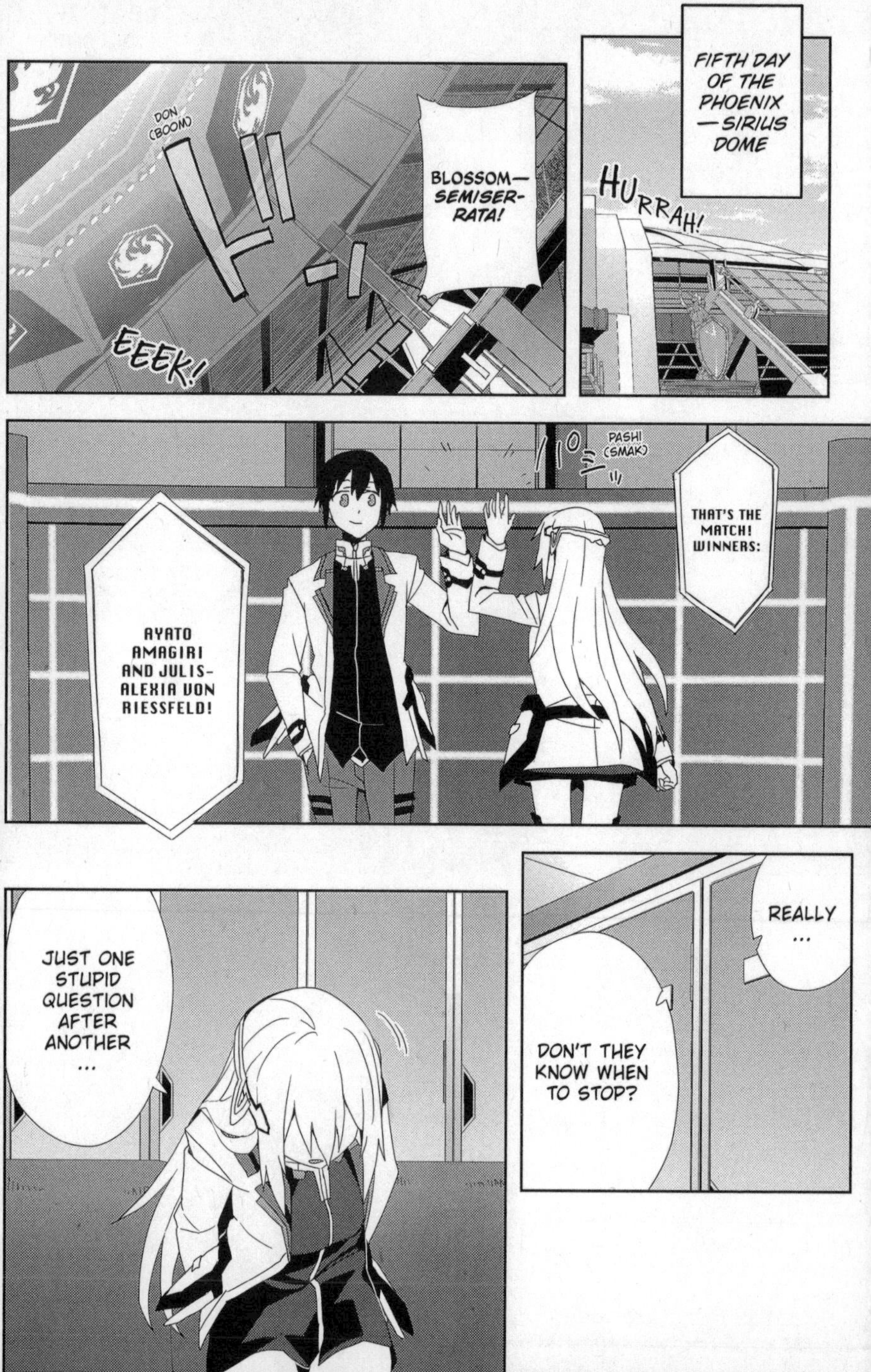
FIFTH DAY OF THE PHOENIX —SIRIUS DOME
HURRAH!
BLOSSOM— SEMISER- RATA!
DON (BOOM)
EEEK!
PASHI (SMAK)
THAT'S THE MATCH! WINNERS:
AYATO AMAGIRI AND JULIS- ALEXIA VON RIESSFELD!
REALLY ...
DON'T THEY KNOW WHEN TO STOP?
JUST ONE STUPID QUESTION AFTER ANOTHER ...

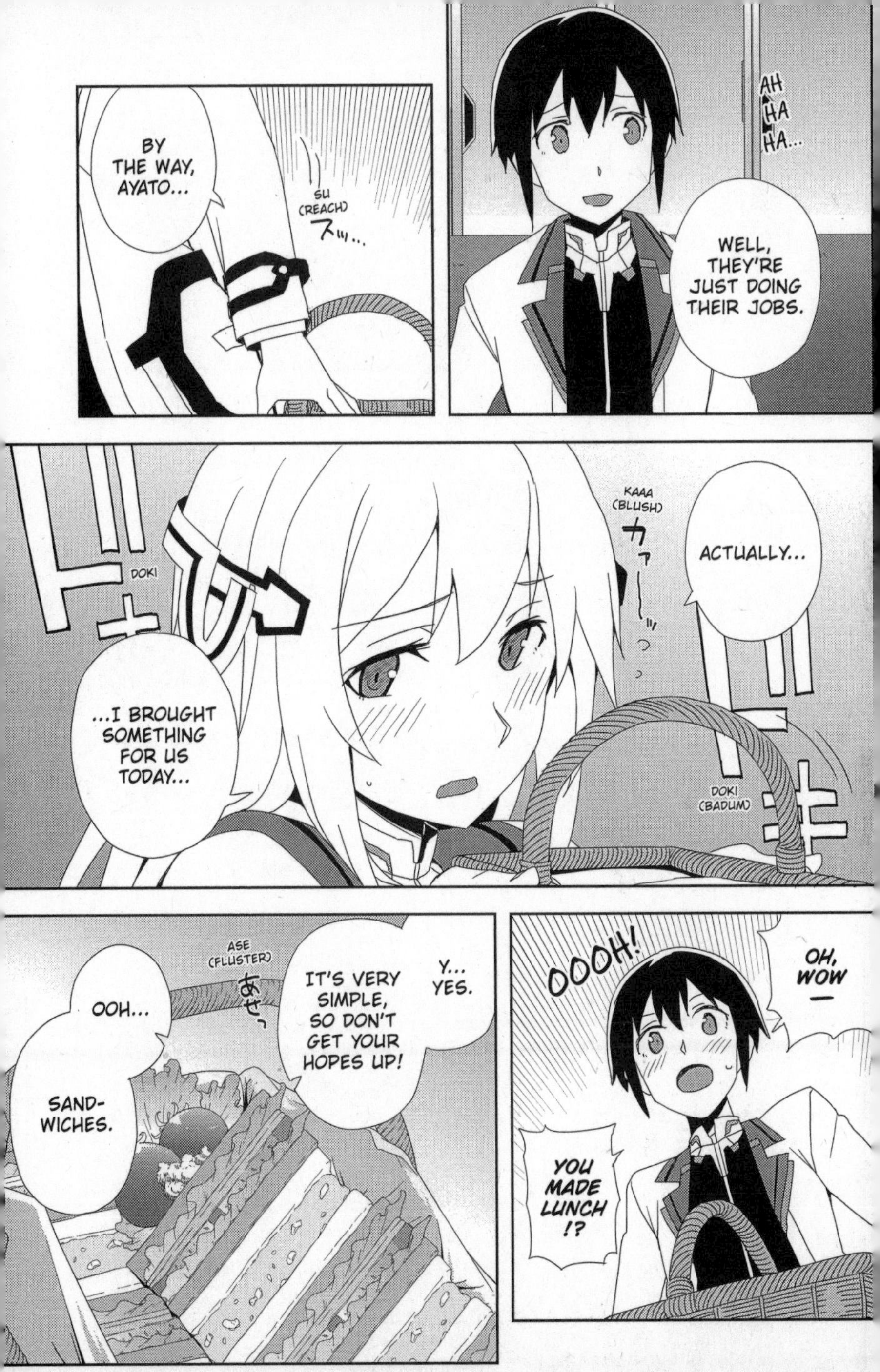
AH HA HA...
WELL, THEY'RE JUST DOING THEIR JOBS.
BY THE WAY, AYATO...
SU (REACH)
スッ...
ACTUALLY...
KAAA (BLUSH)
カァ～ッ
DOKI (BADUM)
...I BROUGHT SOMETHING FOR US TODAY...
DOKI
OH, WOW—
OOOH!
YOU MADE LUNCH!?
Y... YES.
IT'S VERY SIMPLE, SO DON'T GET YOUR HOPES UP!
ASE (FLUSTER)
あせっ
OOH...
SAND-WICHES.

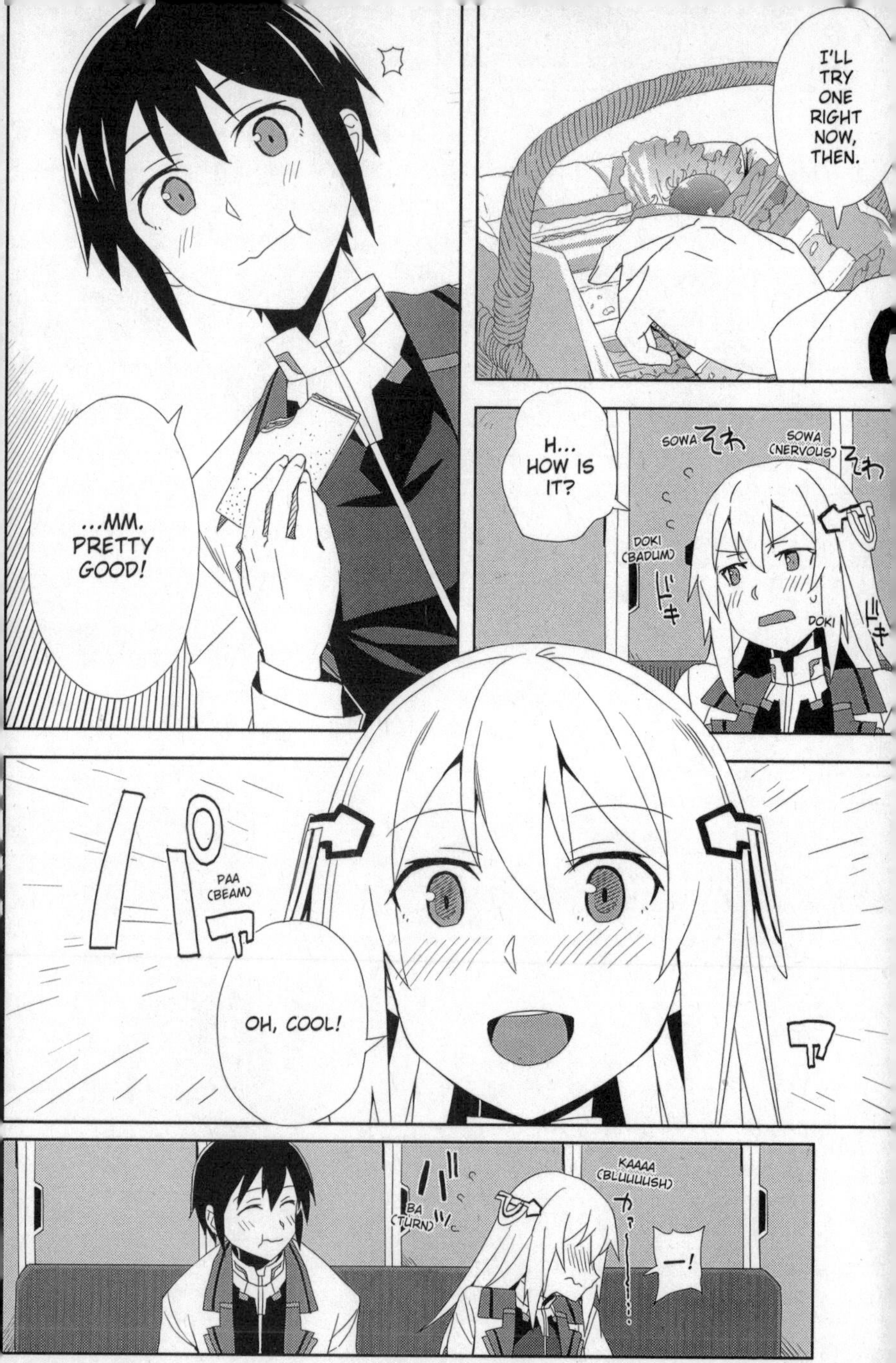
I'LL TRY ONE RIGHT NOW, THEN.
H... HOW IS IT?
SOWA
SOWA (NERVOUS)
DOKI (BADUM)
DOKI
...MM. PRETTY GOOD!
PAA (BEAM)
OH, COOL!
KAAAA (BLUUUUSH)
BA (TURN)
—!

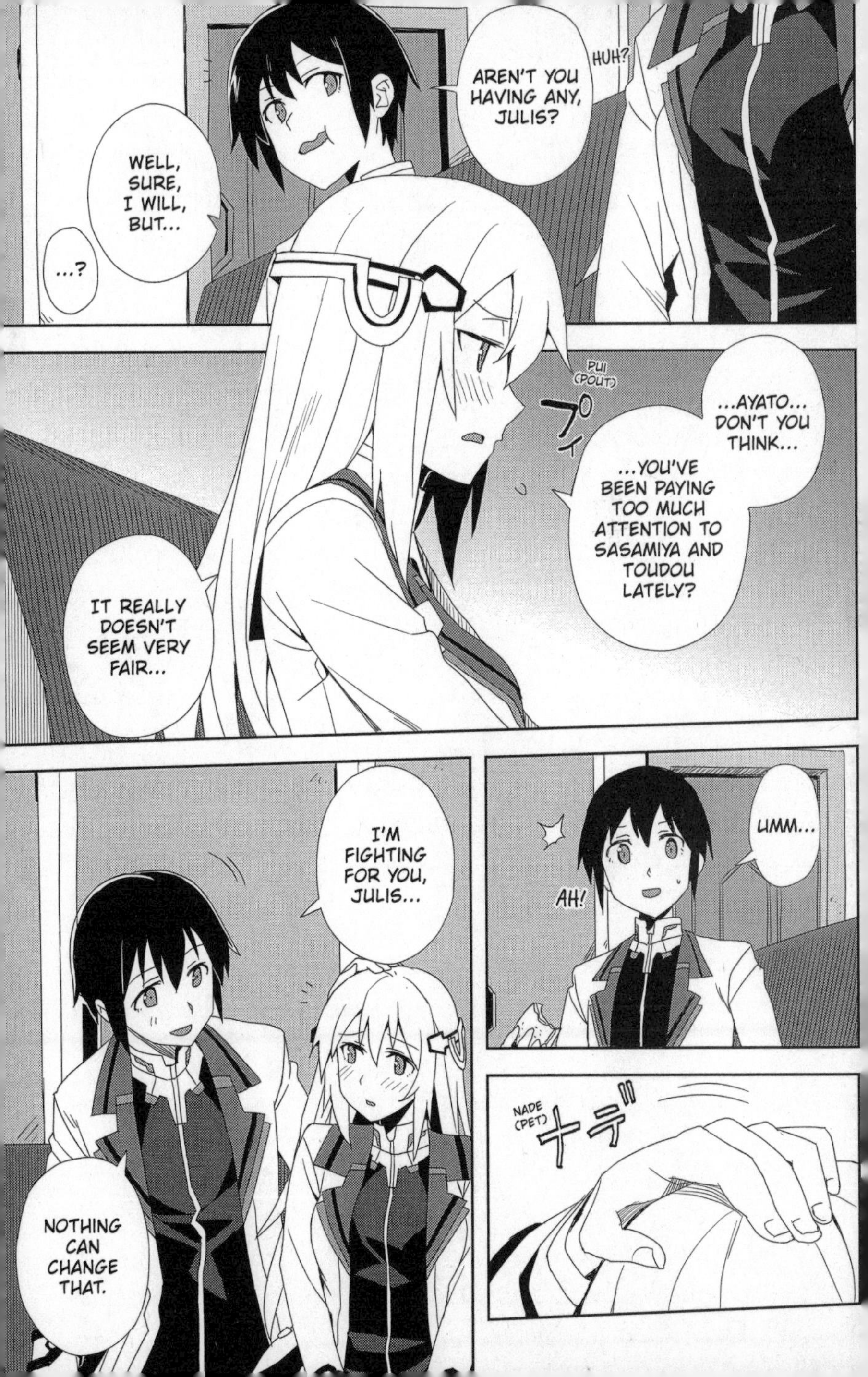
HUH?
AREN'T YOU HAVING ANY, JULIS?
WELL, SURE, I WILL, BUT...
...?
PUI (POUT)
プイ
...AYATO... DON'T YOU THINK...
...YOU'VE BEEN PAYING TOO MUCH ATTENTION TO SASAMIYA AND TOUDOU LATELY?
IT REALLY DOESN'T SEEM VERY FAIR...
UMM...
AH!
NADE (PET)
ナデ
I'M FIGHTING FOR YOU, JULIS...
NOTHING CAN CHANGE THAT.

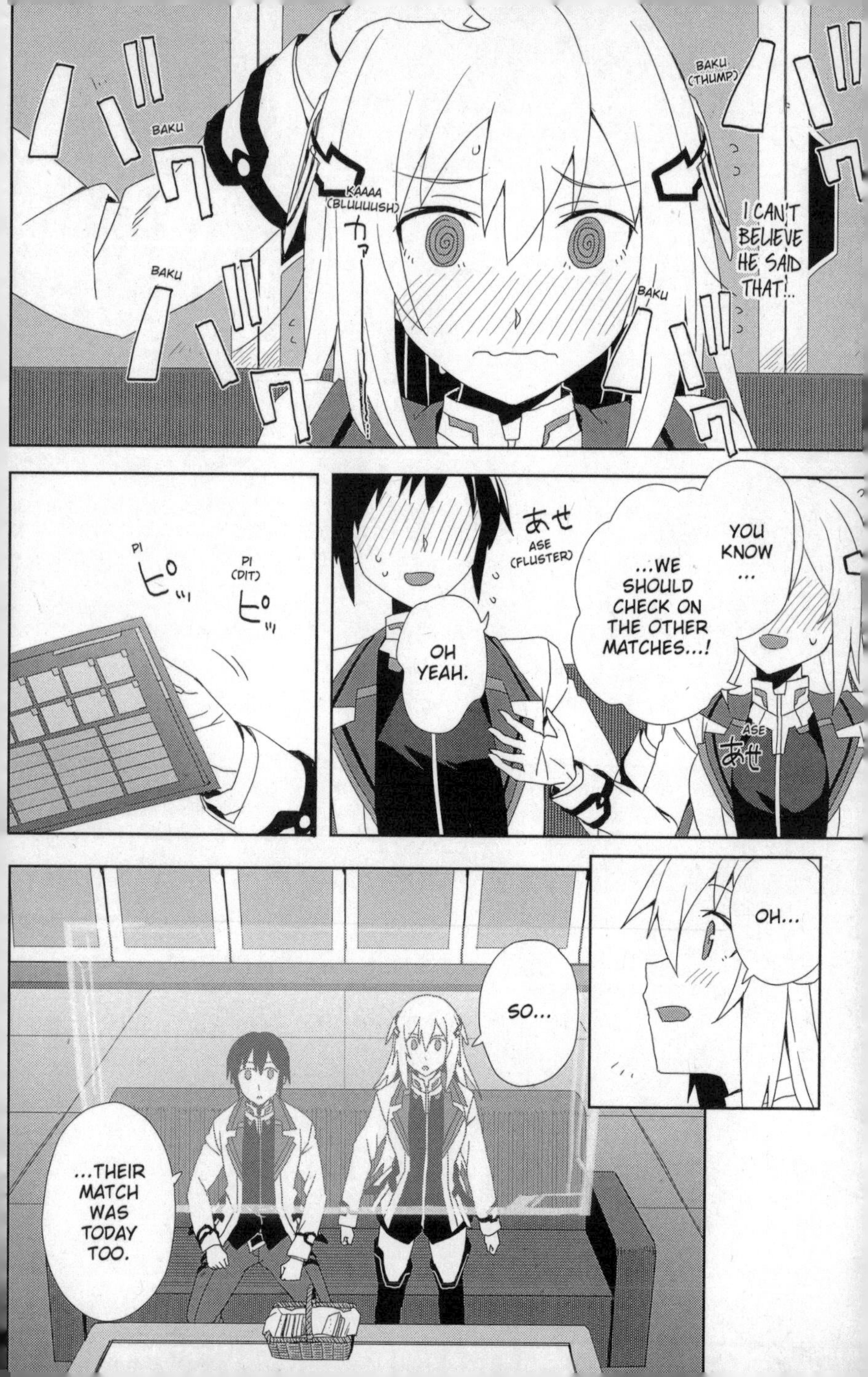
BAKU (THUMP)
I CAN'T BELIEVE HE SAID THAT!...
BAKU
KAAAA (BLUUUUSH)
カァ
BAKU
BAKU
YOU KNOW ...
...WE SHOULD CHECK ON THE OTHER MATCHES...!
ASE
あせ
あせ
ASE (FLUSTER)
OH YEAH.
PI (DIT)
ピッ
PI
ピッ
OH...
SO...
...THEIR MATCH WAS TODAY TOO.

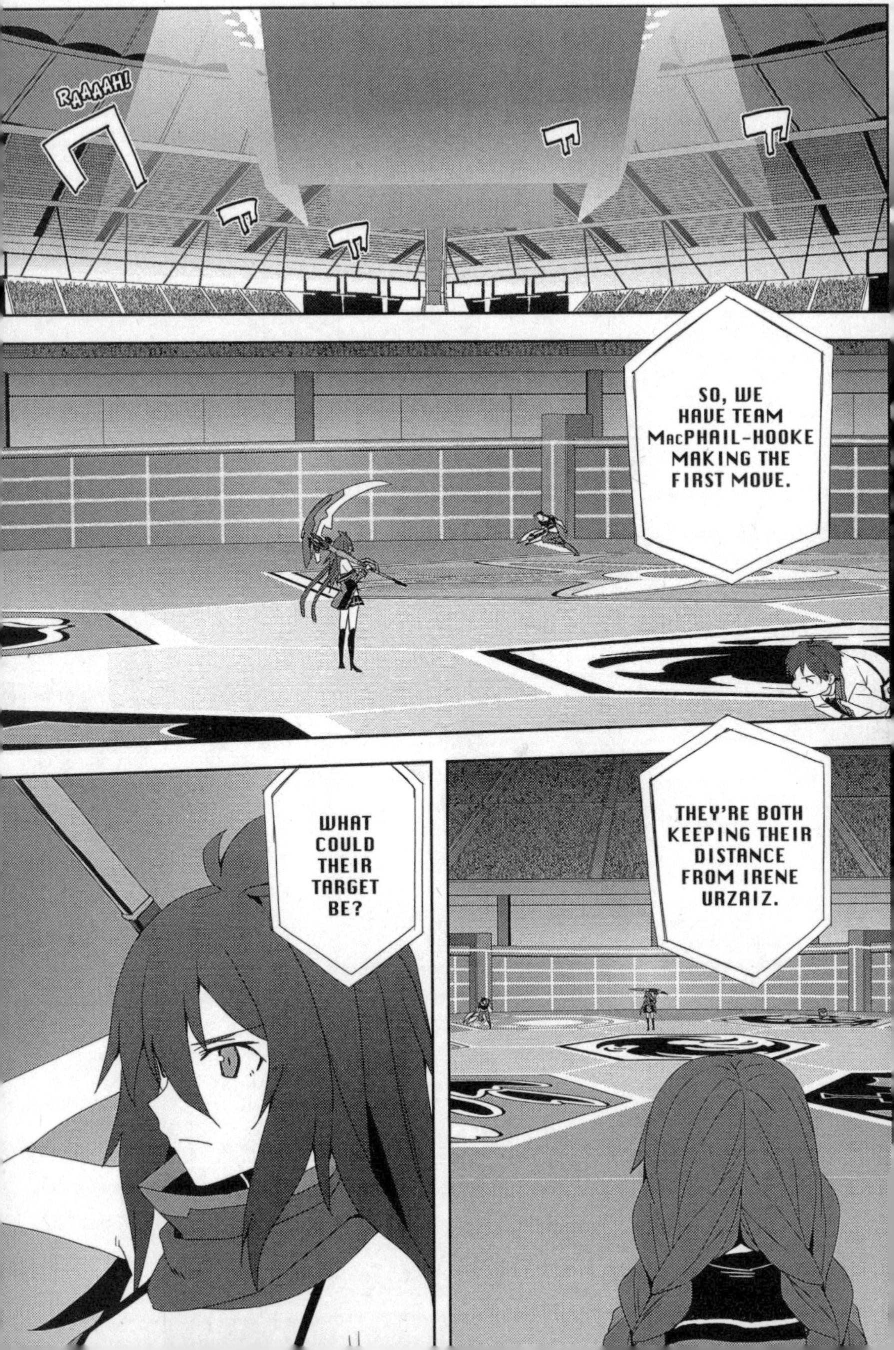
RAAAAH!
SO, WE HAVE TEAM MacPHAIL-HOOKE MAKING THE FIRST MOVE.
THEY'RE BOTH KEEPING THEIR DISTANCE FROM IRENE URZAIZ.
WHAT COULD THEIR TARGET BE?

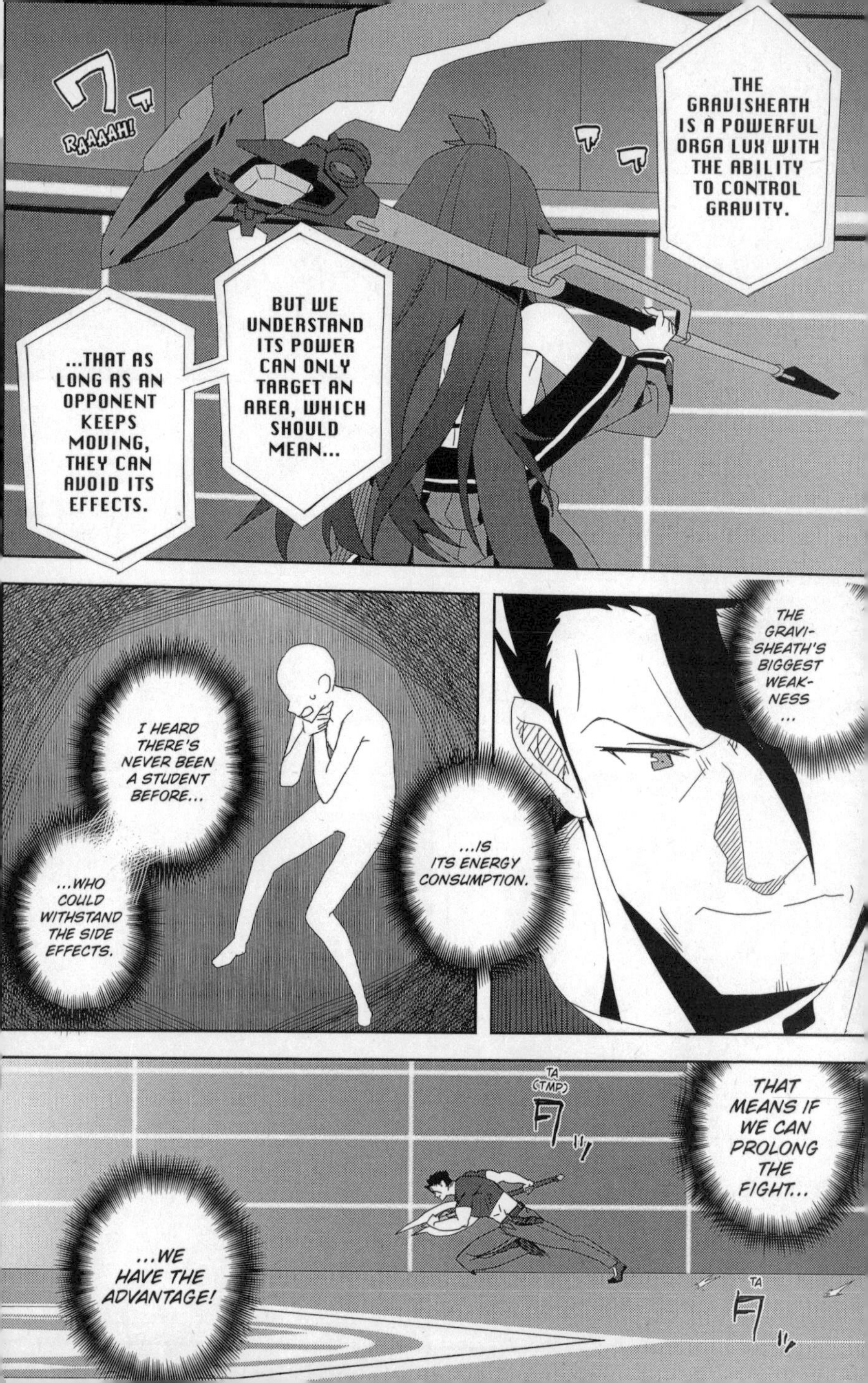
THE GRAVISHEATH IS A POWERFUL ORGA LUX WITH THE ABILITY TO CONTROL GRAVITY.
RAAAAH!
BUT WE UNDERSTAND ITS POWER CAN ONLY TARGET AN AREA, WHICH SHOULD MEAN...
...THAT AS LONG AS AN OPPONENT KEEPS MOVING, THEY CAN AVOID ITS EFFECTS.
THE GRAVI-SHEATH'S BIGGEST WEAK-NESS...
...IS ITS ENERGY CONSUMPTION.
I HEARD THERE'S NEVER BEEN A STUDENT BEFORE...
...WHO COULD WITHSTAND THE SIDE EFFECTS.
THAT MEANS IF WE CAN PROLONG THE FIGHT...
TA (TMP)
...WE HAVE THE ADVANTAGE!
TA

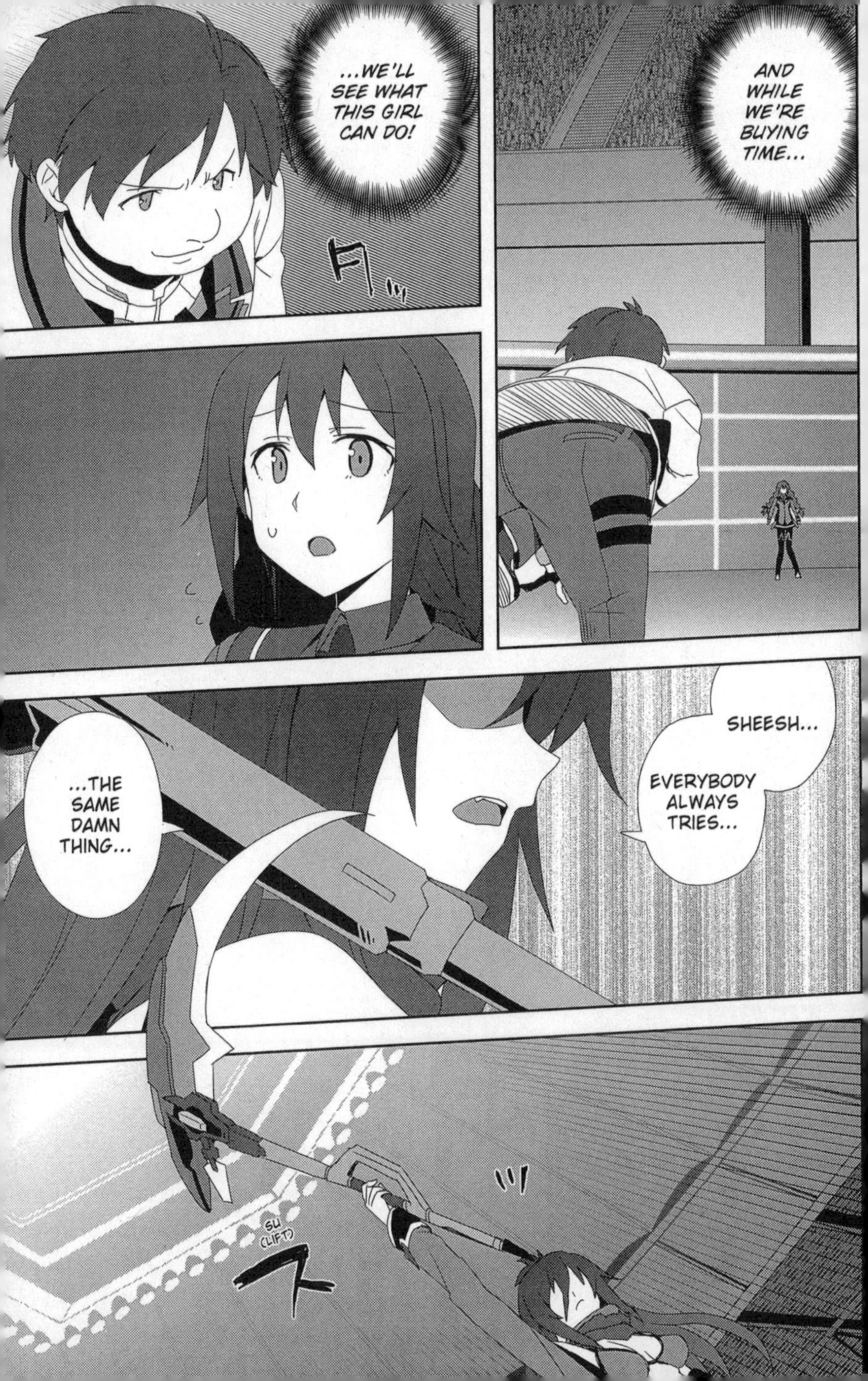
AND WHILE WE'RE BUYING TIME...
...WE'LL SEE WHAT THIS GIRL CAN DO!
SHEESH...
EVERYBODY ALWAYS TRIES...
...THE SAME DAMN THING...
SU (LIFT)

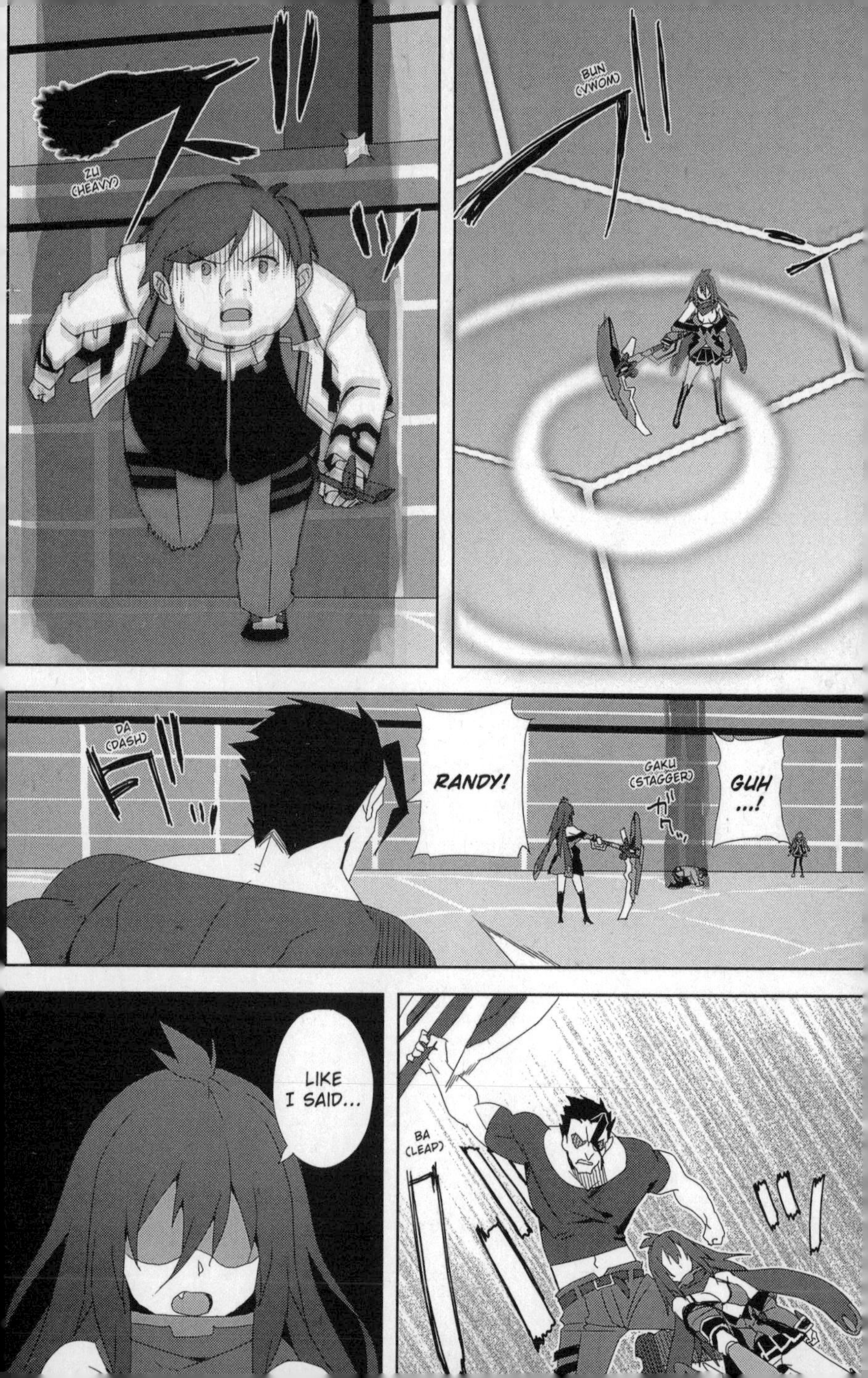
BUN (VWOM)
ZU (HEAVY)
GUH ...!
GAKU (STAGGER)
RANDY!
DA (DASH)
BA (LEAP)
LIKE I SAID...

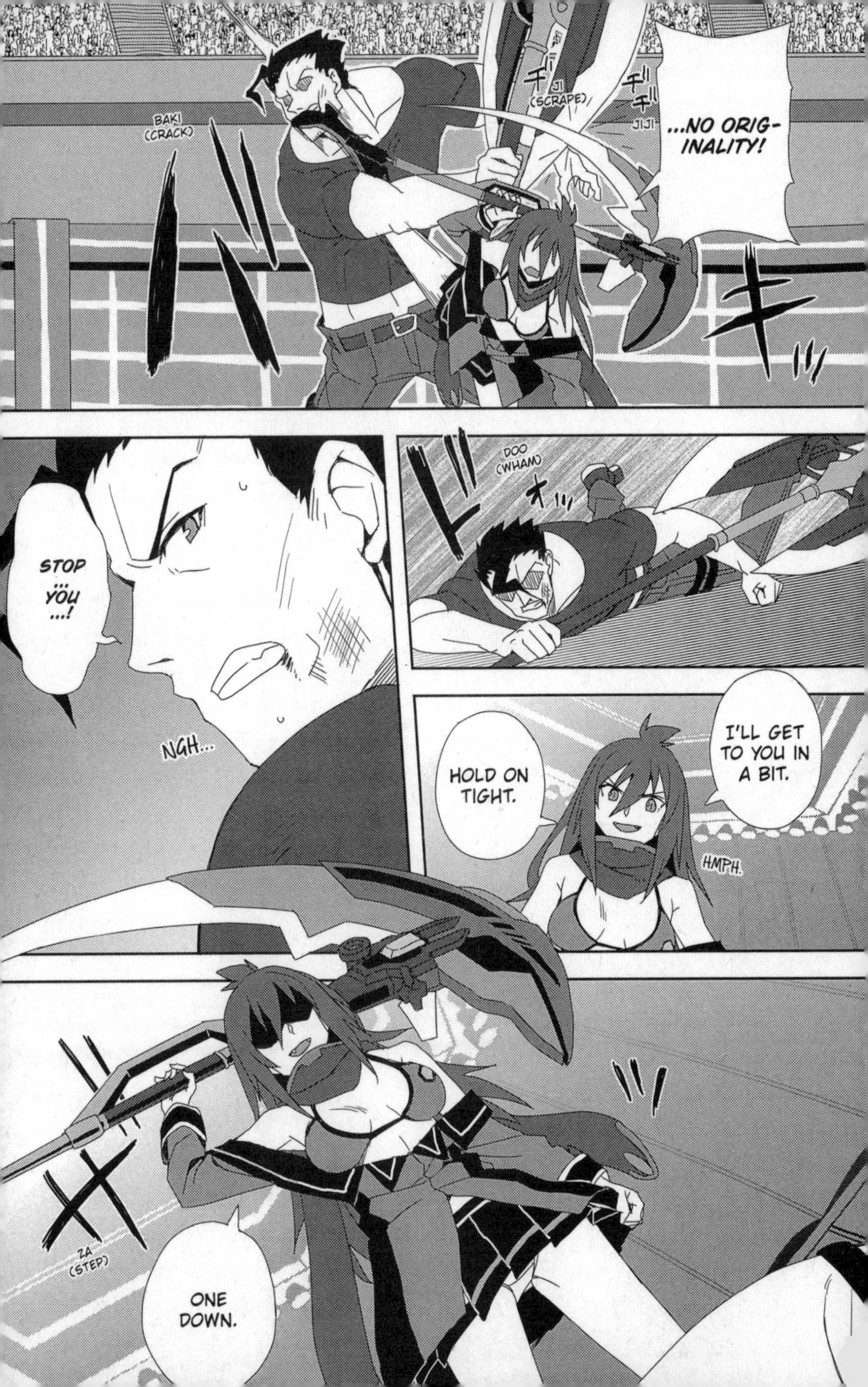
...NO ORIG-
INALITY!
JI
(SCRAPE)
JIJI
BAKI
(CRACK)
DOO
(WHAM)
I'LL GET TO YOU IN A BIT.
HOLD ON TIGHT.
HMPH.
STOP ... YOU ...!
NGH...
ZA
(STEP)
ONE DOWN.

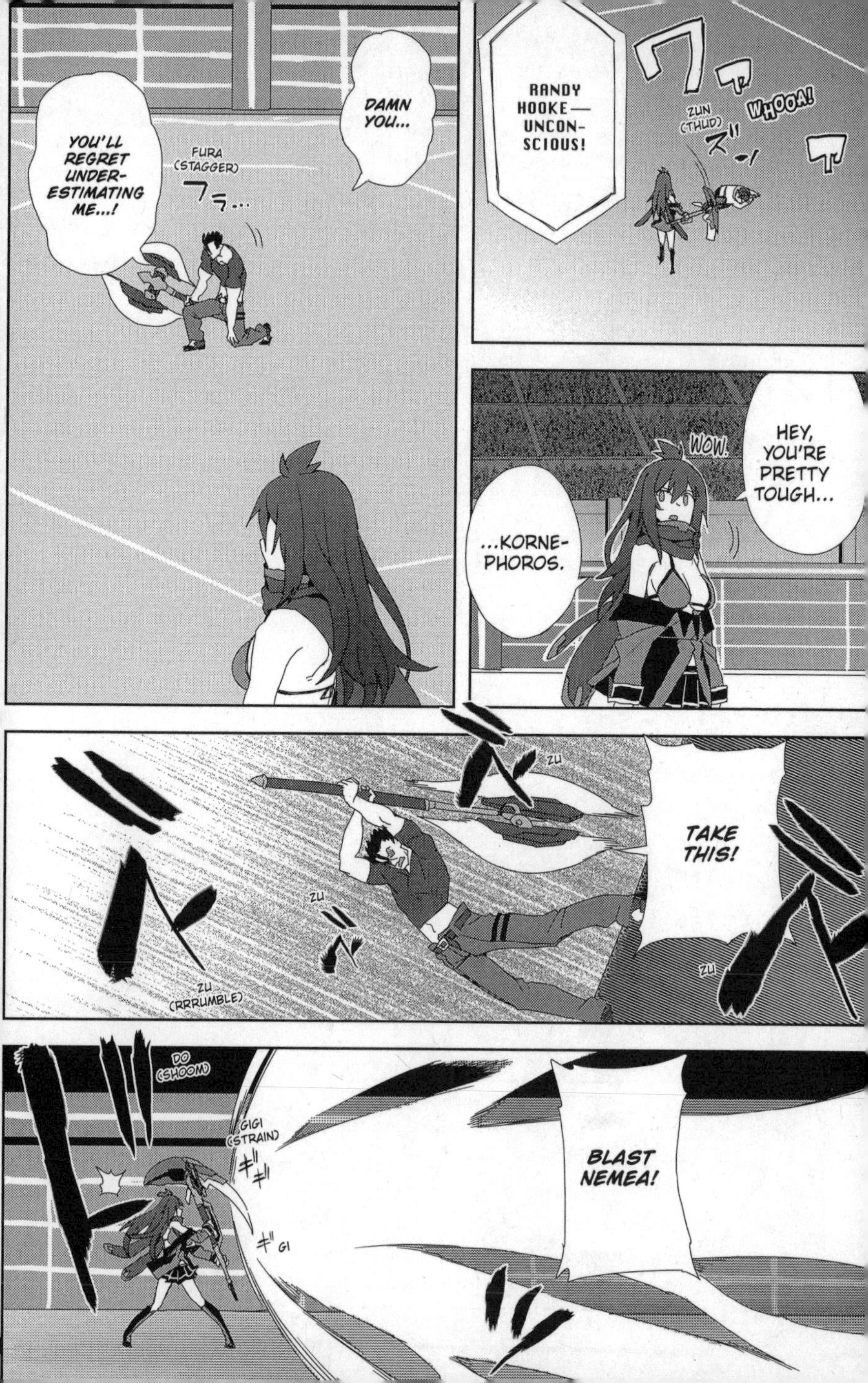
WHOOA!
ZUN (THUD)
RANDY HOOKE—UNCONSCIOUS!
HEY, YOU'RE PRETTY TOUGH...
WOW.
...KORNE-PHOROS.
DAMN YOU...
FURA (STAGGER)
YOU'LL REGRET UNDER-ESTIMATING ME...!
ZU
TAKE THIS!
ZU
ZU
ZU (RRRUMBLE)
BLAST NEMEA!
GIGI (STRAIN)
GI
DO (SHOOM)

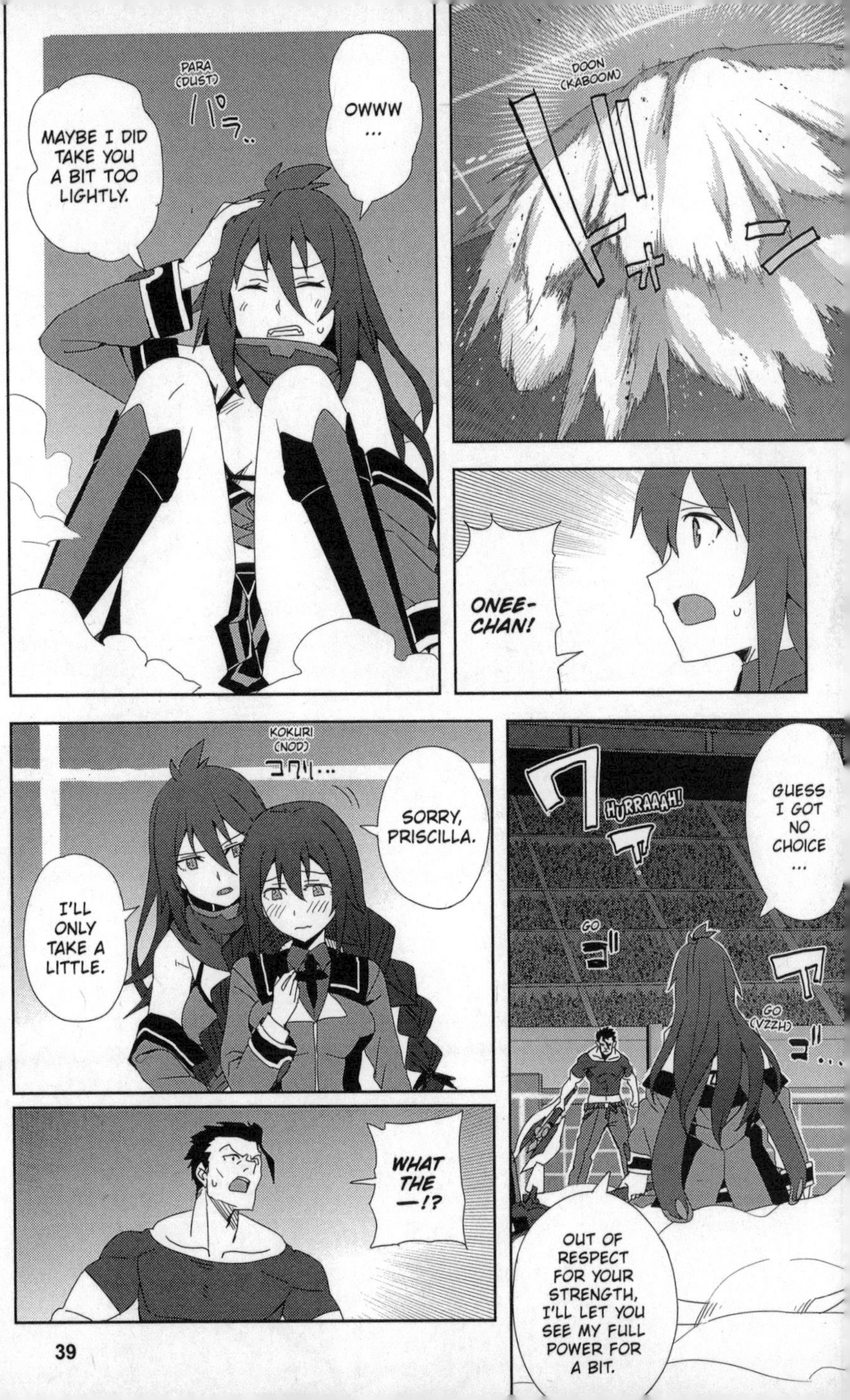
DOON (KABOOM)
ONEE-CHAN!
OWWW ...
PARA (DUST)
MAYBE I DID TAKE YOU A BIT TOO LIGHTLY.
GUESS I GOT NO CHOICE ...
HURRAAAH!
GO
GO (VZZH)
OUT OF RESPECT FOR YOUR STRENGTH, I'LL LET YOU SEE MY FULL POWER FOR A BIT.
KOKURI (NOD)
SORRY, PRISCILLA.
I'LL ONLY TAKE A LITTLE.
WHAT THE —!?

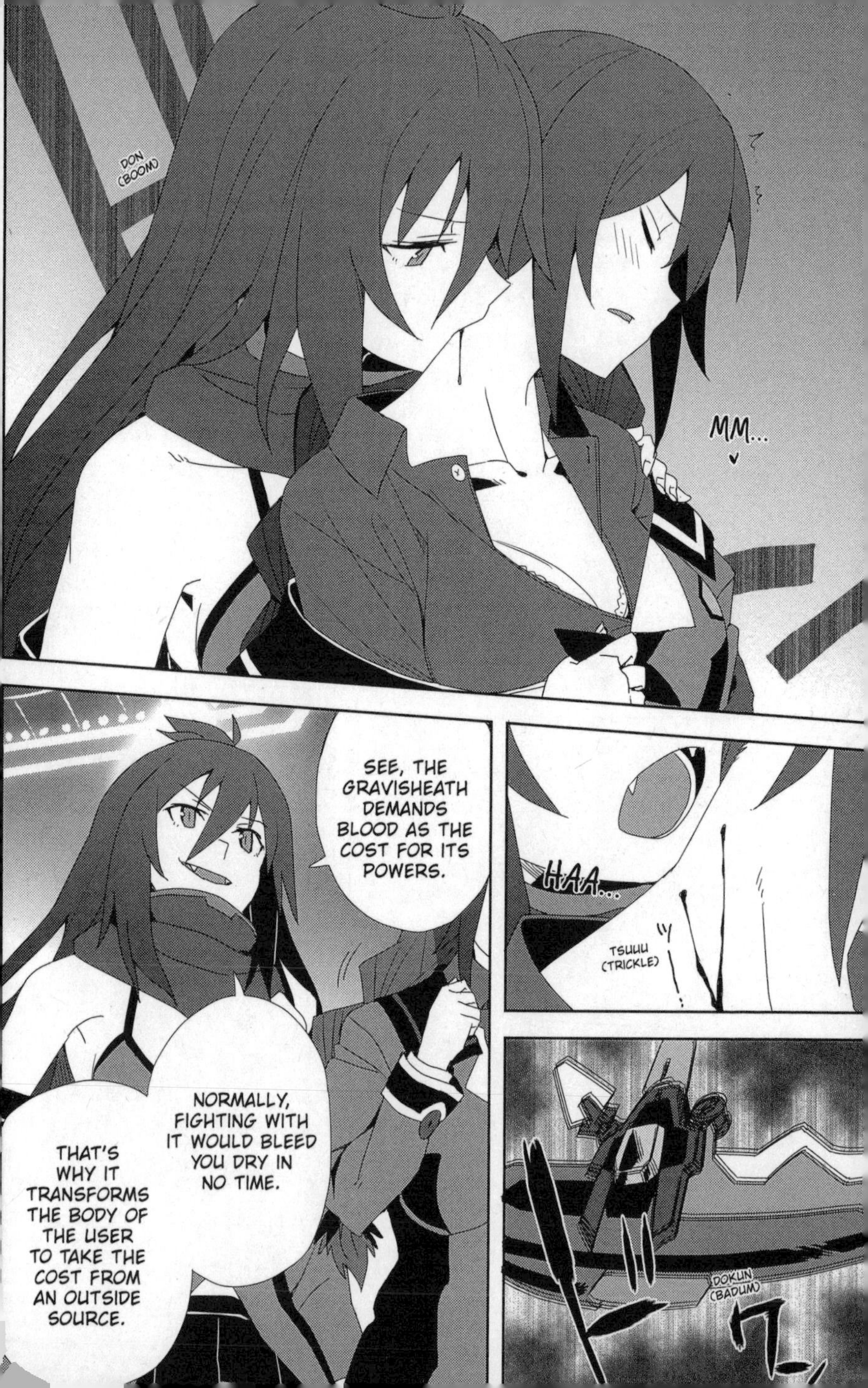
MM... ♥
DON (BOOM)
HAA...
TSUUU (TRICKLE)
DOKUN (BADUM)
SEE, THE GRAVISHEATH DEMANDS BLOOD AS THE COST FOR ITS POWERS.
NORMALLY, FIGHTING WITH IT WOULD BLEED YOU DRY IN NO TIME.
THAT'S WHY IT TRANSFORMS THE BODY OF THE USER TO TAKE THE COST FROM AN OUTSIDE SOURCE.

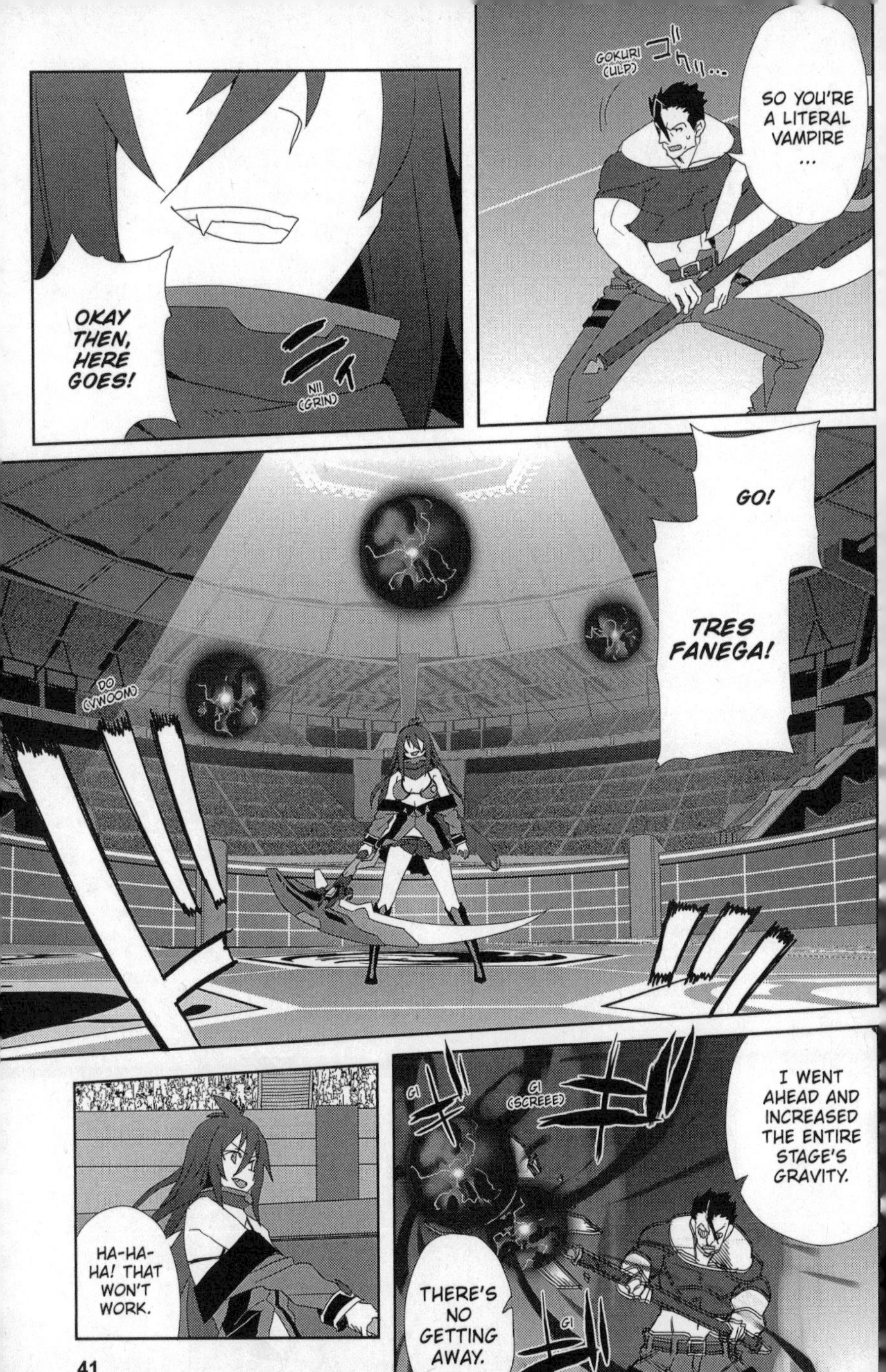
GOKURI (ULP)
SO YOU'RE A LITERAL VAMPIRE ...
OKAY THEN, HERE GOES!
NII (GRIN)
GO!
TRES FANEGA!
DO (VWOOM)
I WENT AHEAD AND INCREASED THE ENTIRE STAGE'S GRAVITY.
GI
GI (SCREEE)
THERE'S NO GETTING AWAY.
GI
HA-HA-HA! THAT WON'T WORK.

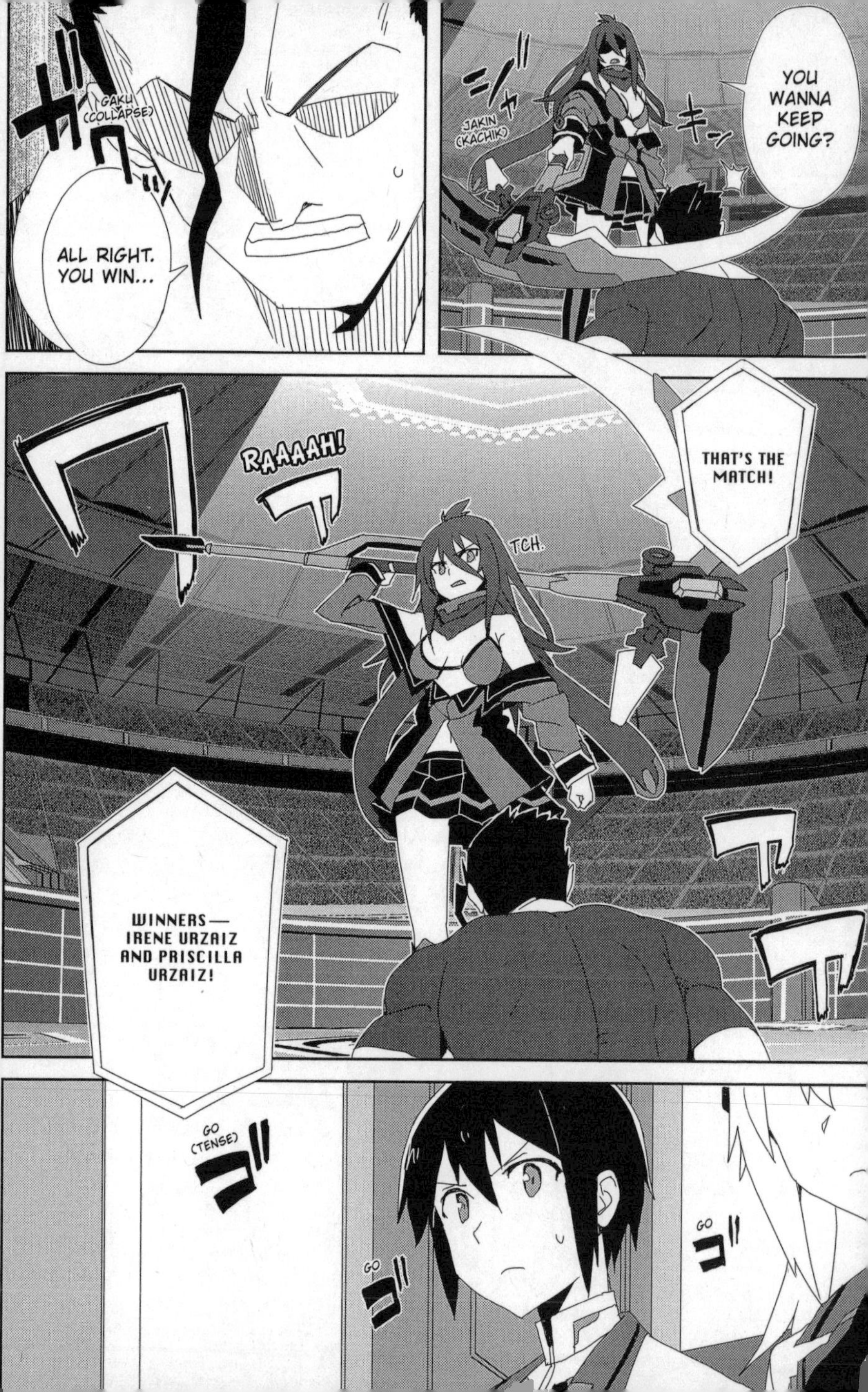
YOU WANNA KEEP GOING?
JAKIN (KACHIK)
GAKU (COLLAPSE)
ALL RIGHT. YOU WIN...
THAT'S THE MATCH!
RAAAAH!
TCH.
WINNERS— IRENE URZAIZ AND PRISCILLA URZAIZ!
GO (TENSE)
GO
GO

THE ASTERISK WAR

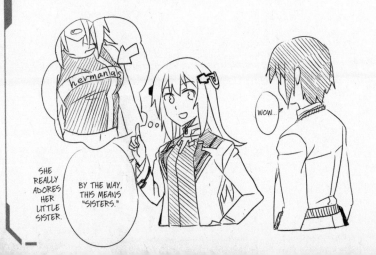

WOW...
hermanas
BY THE WAY, THIS MEANS "SISTERS."
SHE REALLY ADORES HER LITTLE SISTER.

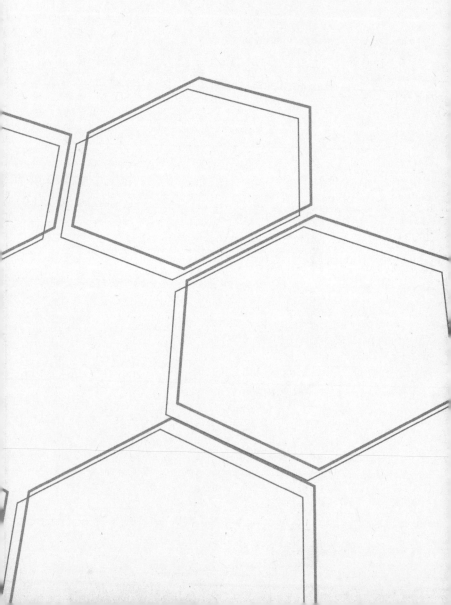

THE
ASTERISK WAR

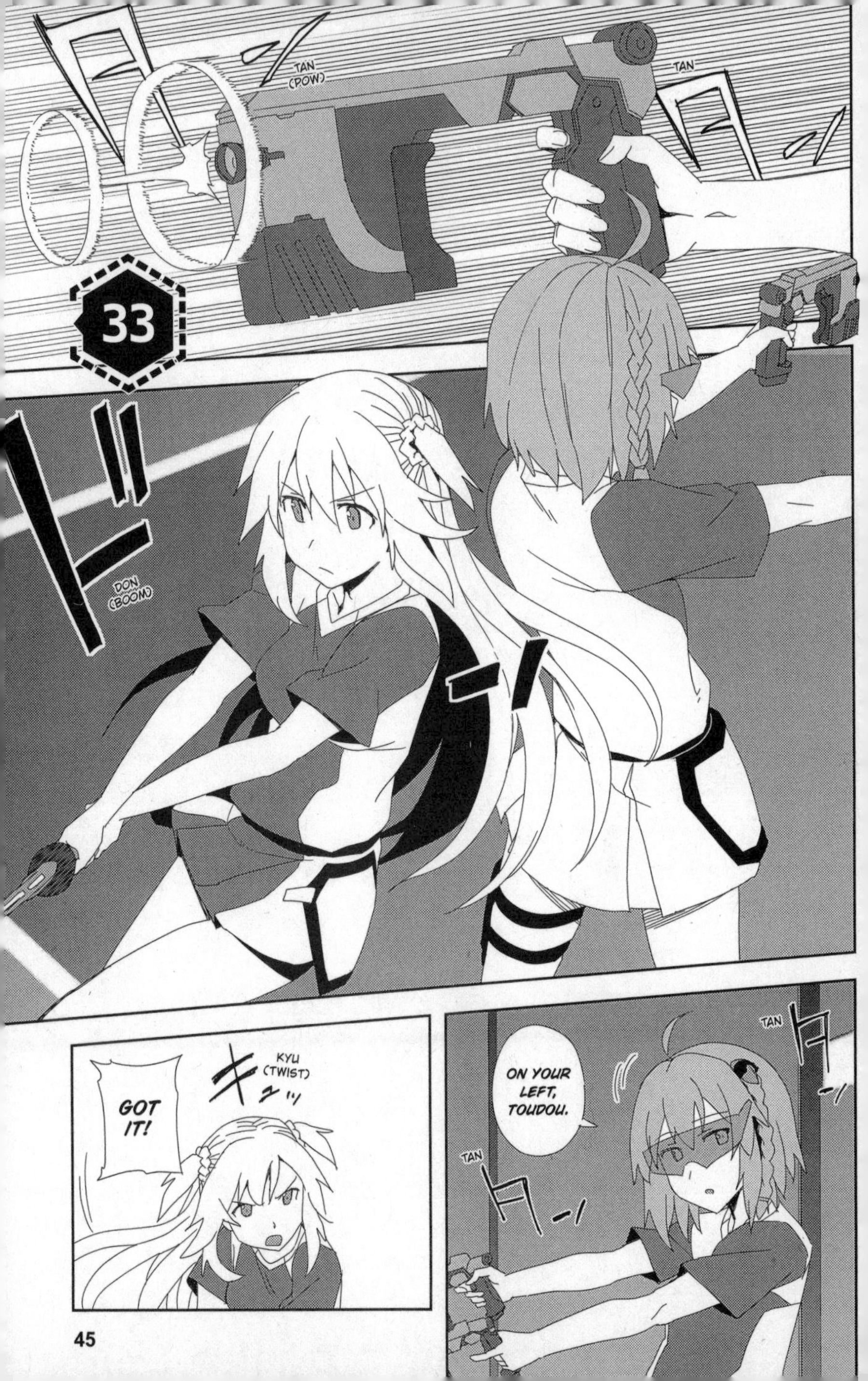
TAN
TAN (POW)
33
DON (BOOM)
ON YOUR LEFT, TOUDOU.
TAN
TAN
KYU (TWIST)
GOT IT!

GUGUGU
(STRAIN)

SASA-MIYA-SENPAI!!

ZUA
(ZOOM)

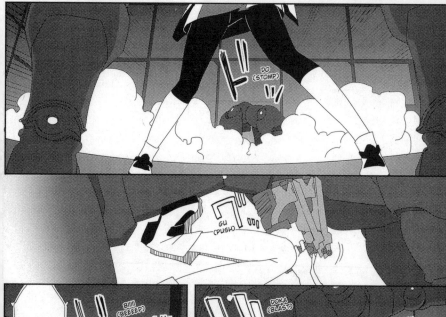

DO
(STOMP)

GU
(PUSH)

SIMU-LATION ENDED.

Bшшш
(BEEEEP)

SAYA & KIRIN   37

AYATO & JULIS   151

DOKA
(BLAST)

DON
(BANG)

EEK!

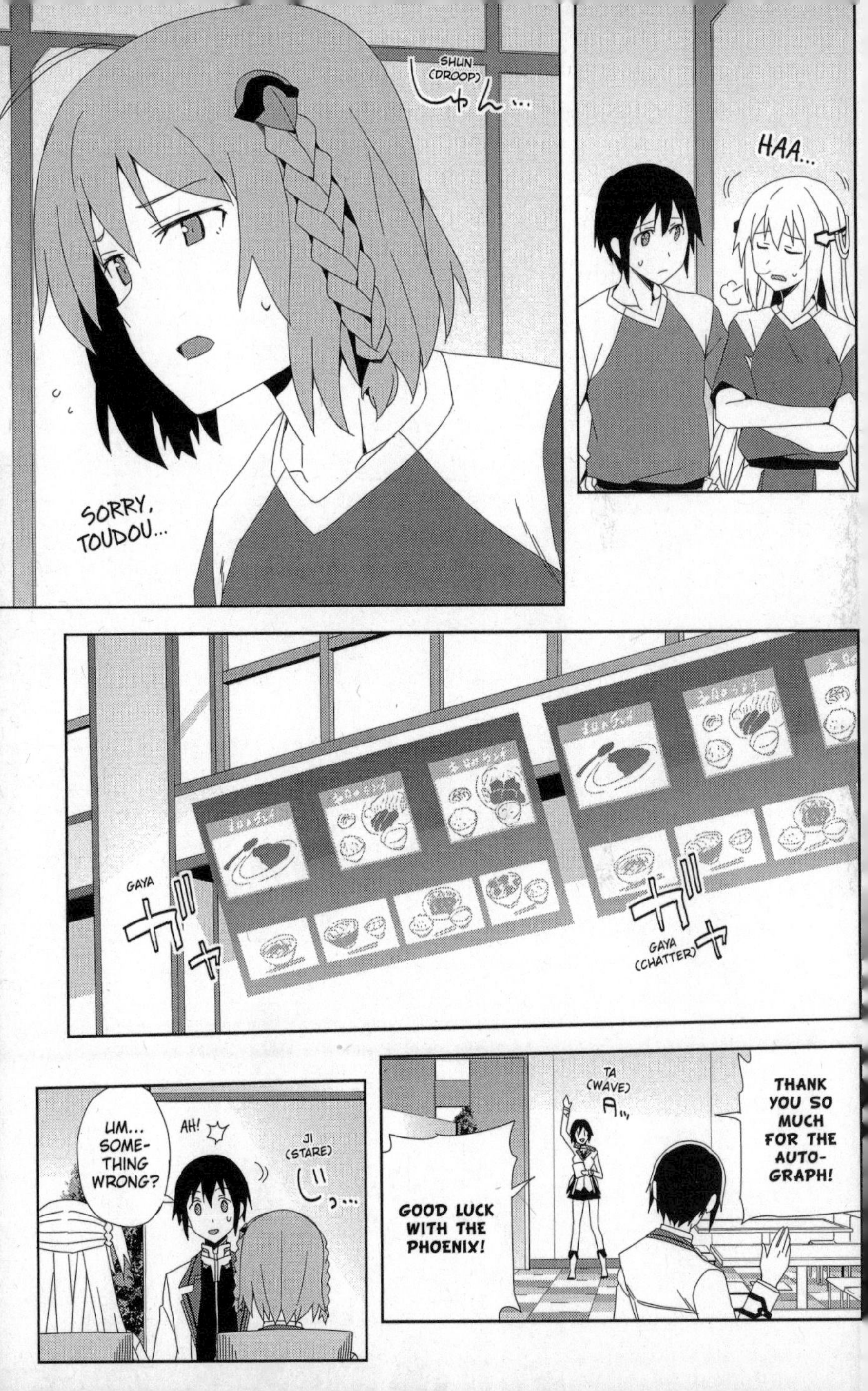
HAA...
SHUN (DROOP)
しゅん...
SORRY, TOUDOU...
GAYA (CHATTER)
ガヤ
GAYA
ガヤ
THANK YOU SO MUCH FOR THE AUTO-GRAPH!
TA (WAVE)
GOOD LUCK WITH THE PHOENIX!
JI (STARE)
じっ...
AH!
UM... SOME-THING WRONG?

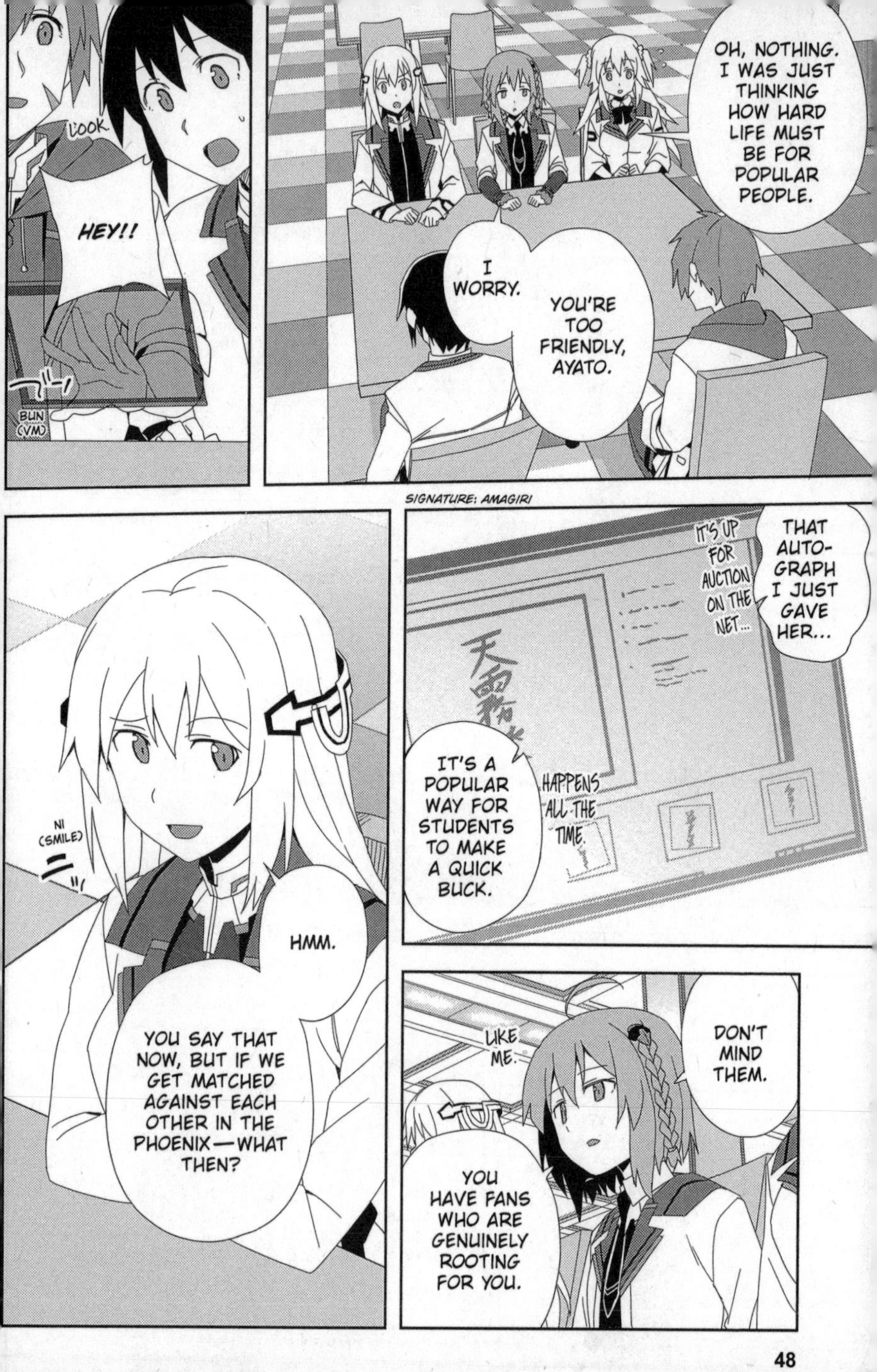
OH, NOTHING. I WAS JUST THINKING HOW HARD LIFE MUST BE FOR POPULAR PEOPLE.
I WORRY.
YOU'RE TOO FRIENDLY, AYATO.
LOOK.
HEY!!
BUN (VM)
SIGNATURE: AMAGIRI
THAT AUTO-GRAPH I JUST GAVE HER...
IT'S UP FOR AUCTION ON THE NET...
IT'S A POPULAR WAY FOR STUDENTS TO MAKE A QUICK BUCK.
HAPPENS ALL THE TIME.
DON'T MIND THEM.
LIKE ME.
YOU HAVE FANS WHO ARE GENUINELY ROOTING FOR YOU.
NI (SMILE)
HMM.
YOU SAY THAT NOW, BUT IF WE GET MATCHED AGAINST EACH OTHER IN THE PHOENIX—WHAT THEN?

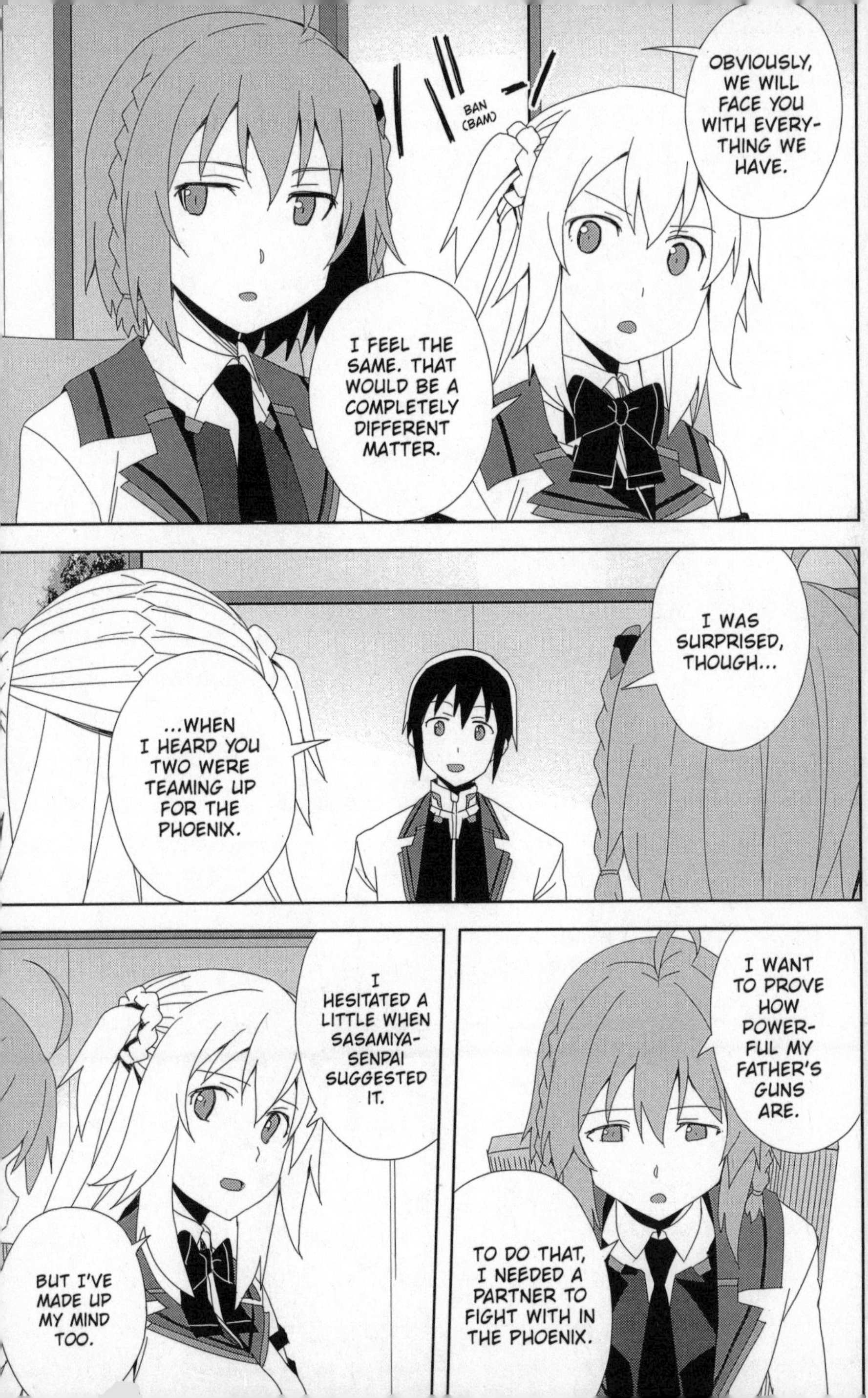
OBVIOUSLY, WE WILL FACE YOU WITH EVERY-THING WE HAVE.
BAN (BAM)
I FEEL THE SAME. THAT WOULD BE A COMPLETELY DIFFERENT MATTER.
I WAS SURPRISED, THOUGH...
...WHEN I HEARD YOU TWO WERE TEAMING UP FOR THE PHOENIX.
I WANT TO PROVE HOW POWER-FUL MY FATHER'S GUNS ARE.
TO DO THAT, I NEEDED A PARTNER TO FIGHT WITH IN THE PHOENIX.
I HESITATED A LITTLE WHEN SASAMIYA-SENPAI SUGGESTED IT.
BUT I'VE MADE UP MY MIND TOO.

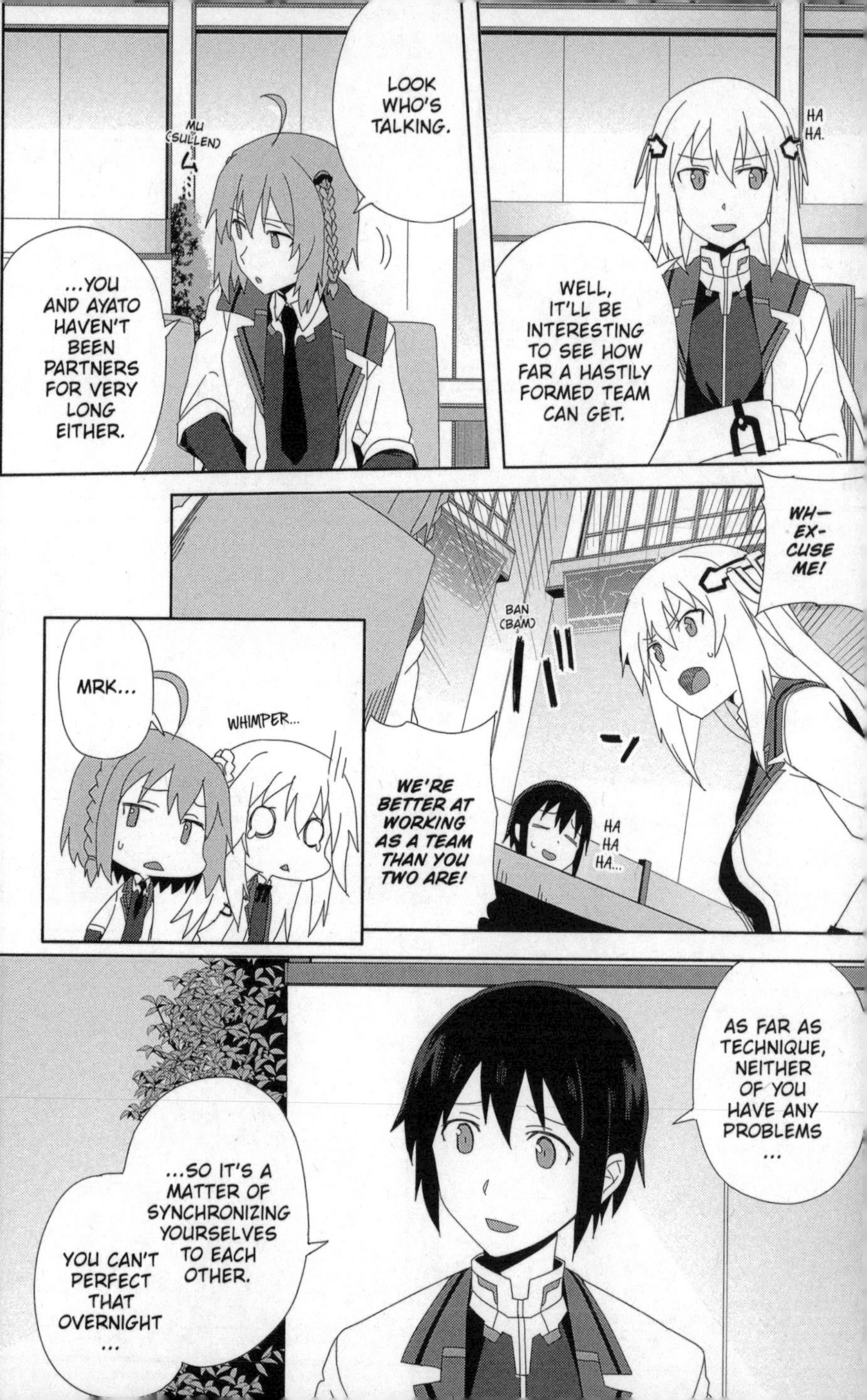
HA HA.
WELL, IT'LL BE INTERESTING TO SEE HOW FAR A HASTILY FORMED TEAM CAN GET.
LOOK WHO'S TALKING.
MU (SULLEN)
...YOU AND AYATO HAVEN'T BEEN PARTNERS FOR VERY LONG EITHER.
WH— EX-CUSE ME!
BAN (BAM)
WE'RE BETTER AT WORKING AS A TEAM THAN YOU TWO ARE!
HA HA HA...
MRK...
WHIMPER...
AS FAR AS TECHNIQUE, NEITHER OF YOU HAVE ANY PROBLEMS ...
...SO IT'S A MATTER OF SYNCHRONIZING YOURSELVES TO EACH OTHER.
YOU CAN'T PERFECT THAT OVERNIGHT ...

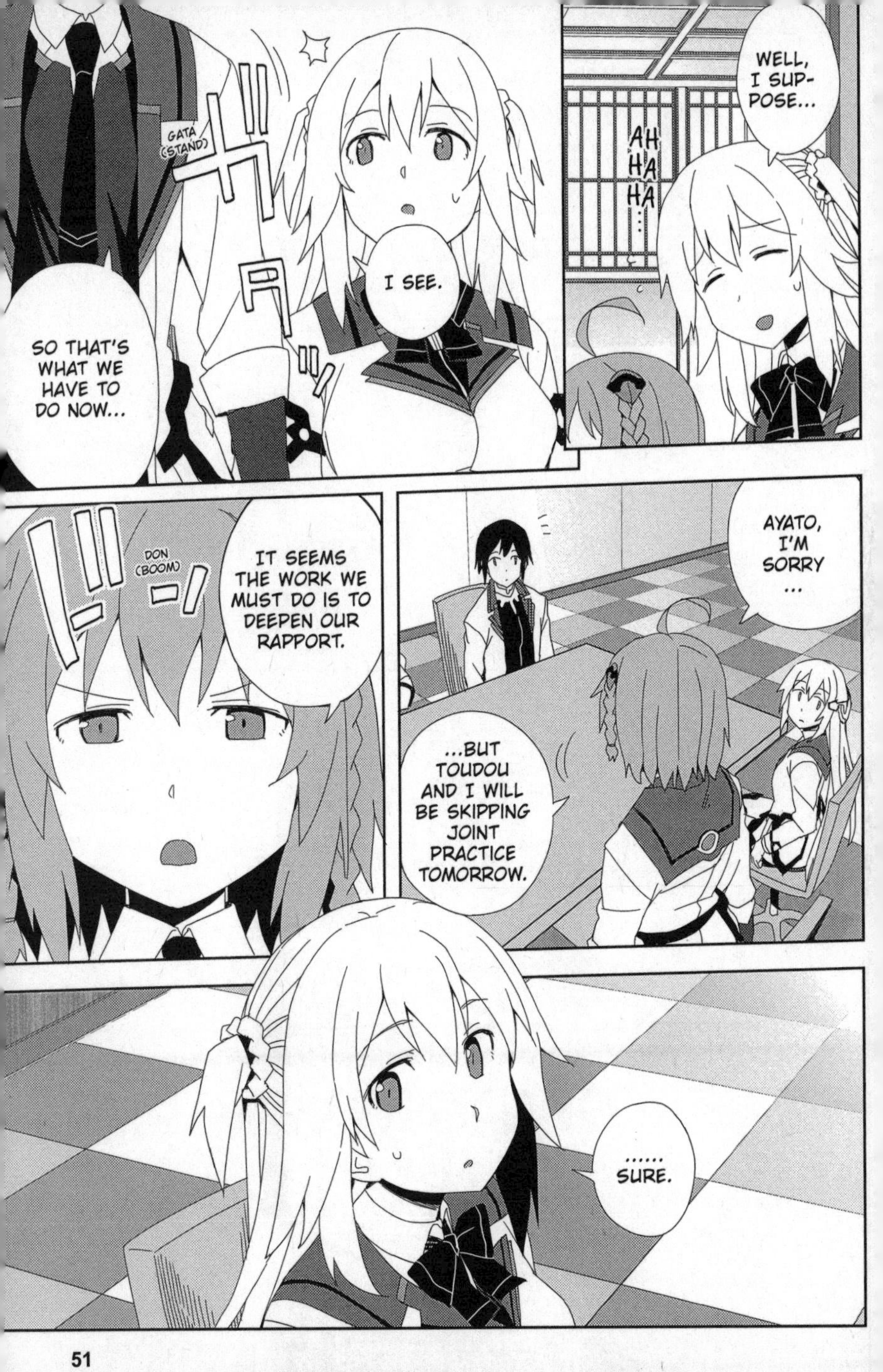
WELL, I SUPPOSE...
AH HA HA...
GATA (STAND)
I SEE.
SO THAT'S WHAT WE HAVE TO DO NOW...
AYATO, I'M SORRY...
...BUT TOUDOU AND I WILL BE SKIPPING JOINT PRACTICE TOMORROW.
IT SEEMS THE WORK WE MUST DO IS TO DEEPEN OUR RAPPORT.
DON (BOOM)
......SURE.

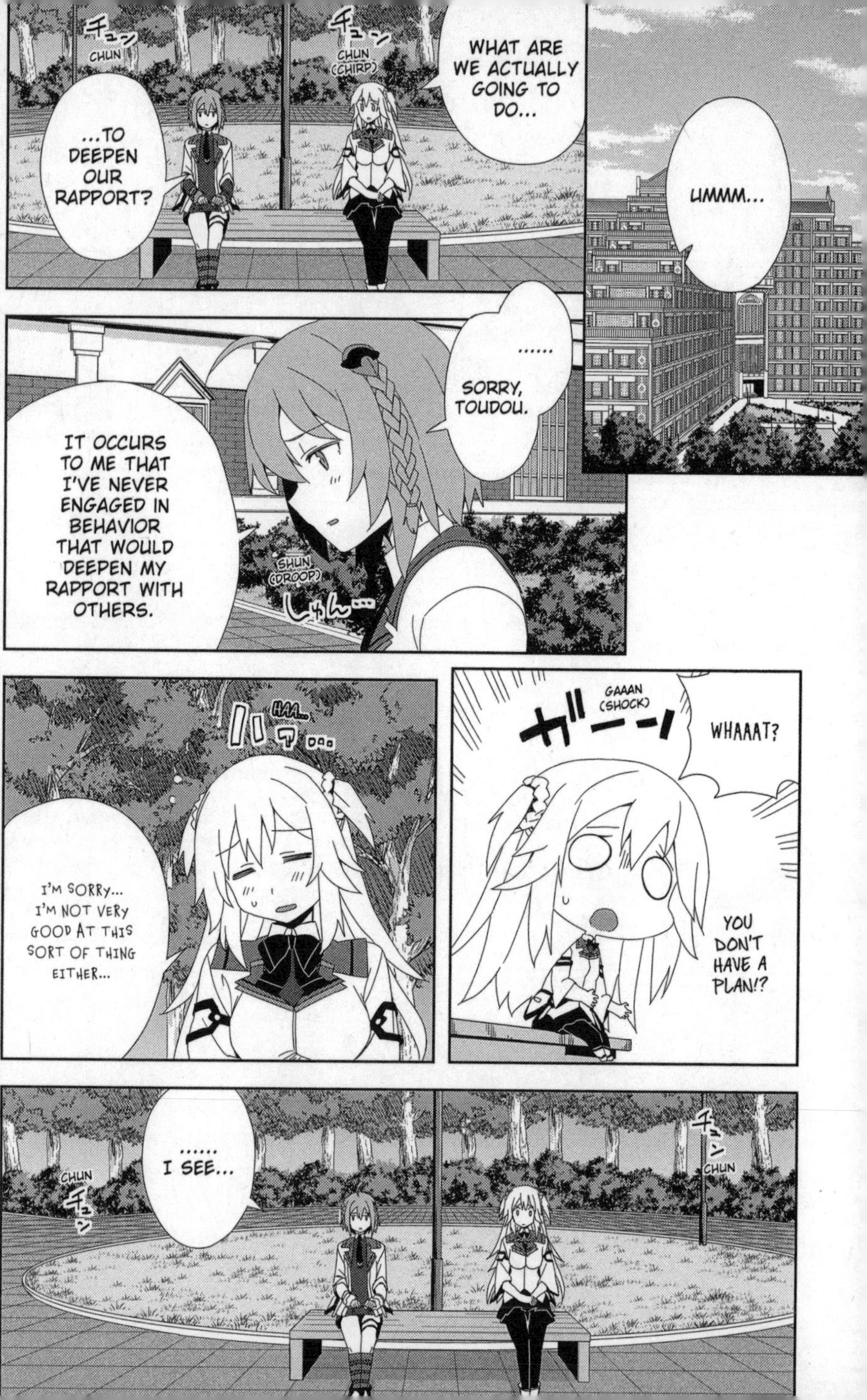
UMMM...
チュン
CHUN
(CHIRP)
WHAT ARE WE ACTUALLY GOING TO DO...
チュン
CHUN
...TO DEEPEN OUR RAPPORT?
......
SORRY, TOUDOU.
IT OCCURS TO ME THAT I'VE NEVER ENGAGED IN BEHAVIOR THAT WOULD DEEPEN MY RAPPORT WITH OTHERS.
SHUN
(DROOP)
しゅん…
GAAAN
(SHOCK)
ガーン
WHAAAT?
YOU DON'T HAVE A PLAN!?
HAA...
ハァ…
I'M SORRY... I'M NOT VERY GOOD AT THIS SORT OF THING EITHER...
チュン
CHUN
......
I SEE...
CHUN
チュン

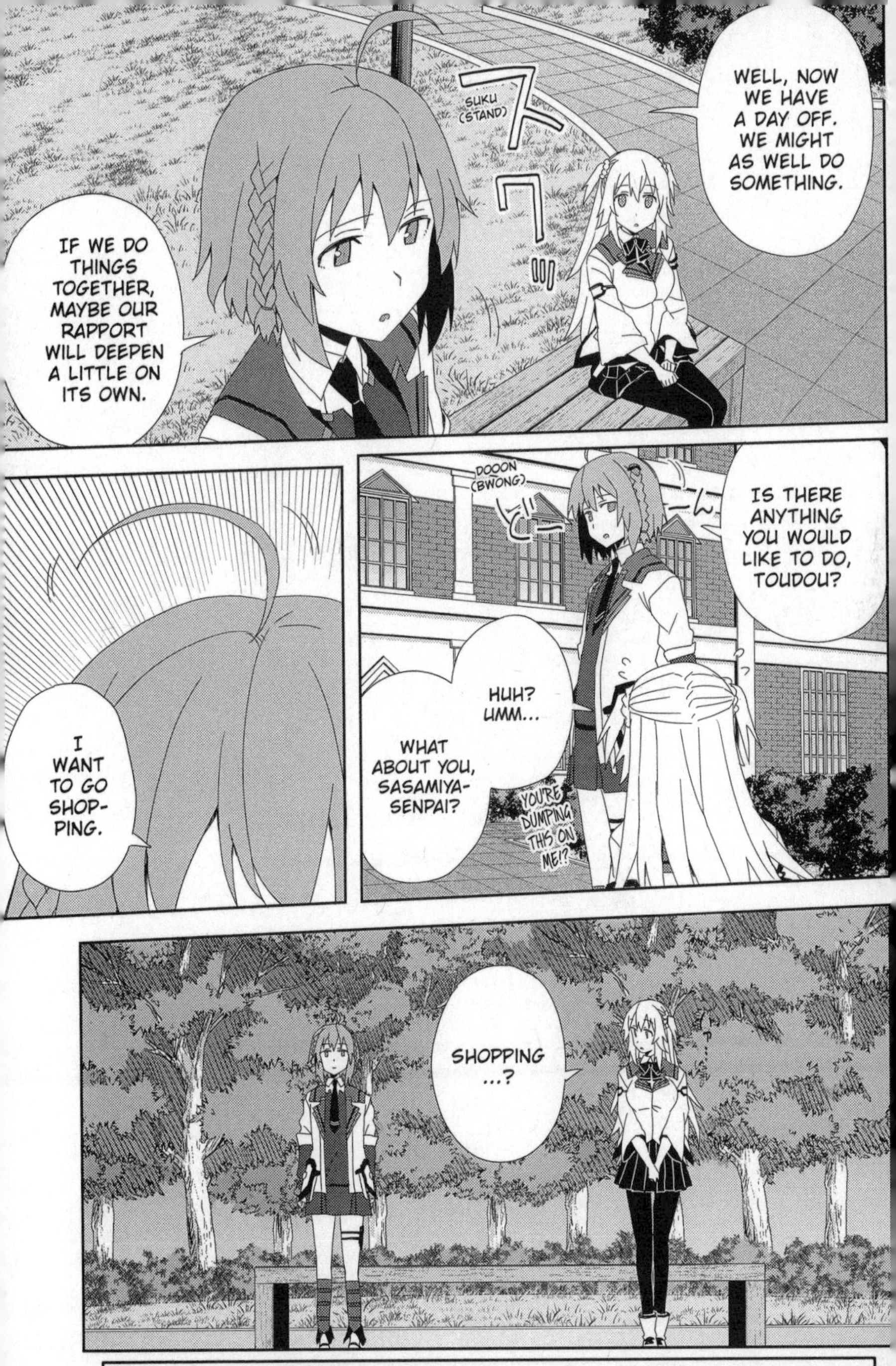
WELL, NOW WE HAVE A DAY OFF. WE MIGHT AS WELL DO SOMETHING.
SUKU (STAND)
IF WE DO THINGS TOGETHER, MAYBE OUR RAPPORT WILL DEEPEN A LITTLE ON ITS OWN.
IS THERE ANYTHING YOU WOULD LIKE TO DO, TOUDOU?
DOOON (BWONG)
HUH? UMM...
WHAT ABOUT YOU, SASAMIYA-SENPAI?
YOU'RE DUMPING THIS ON ME!?
I WANT TO GO SHOP-PING.
SHOPPING ...?

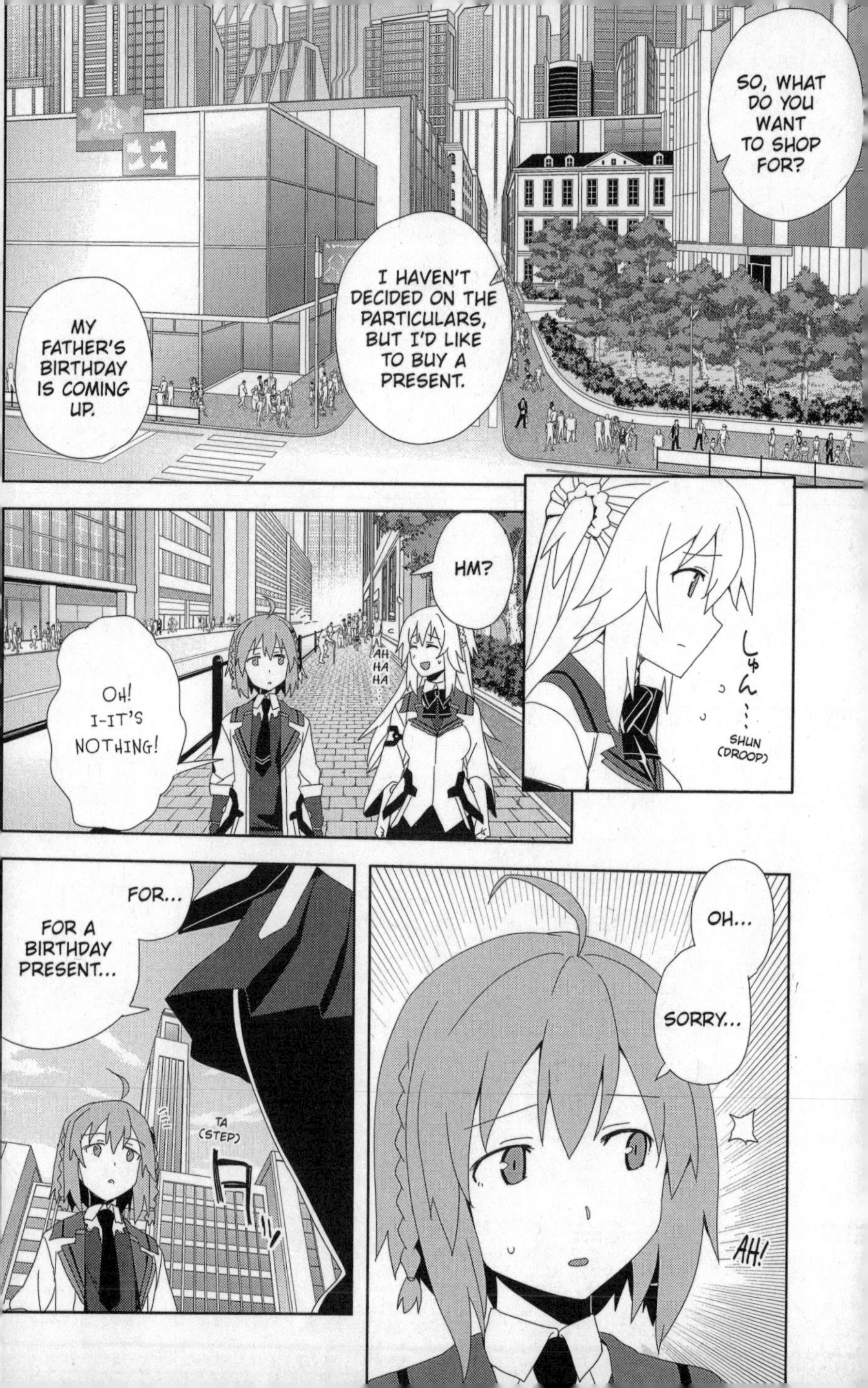
SO, WHAT DO YOU WANT TO SHOP FOR?
I HAVEN'T DECIDED ON THE PARTICULARS, BUT I'D LIKE TO BUY A PRESENT.
MY FATHER'S BIRTHDAY IS COMING UP.
しゅん…
SHUN (DROOP)
HM?
AH HA HA
OH! I-IT'S NOTHING!
OH...
SORRY...
AH!
FOR...
FOR A BIRTHDAY PRESENT...
TA (STEP)

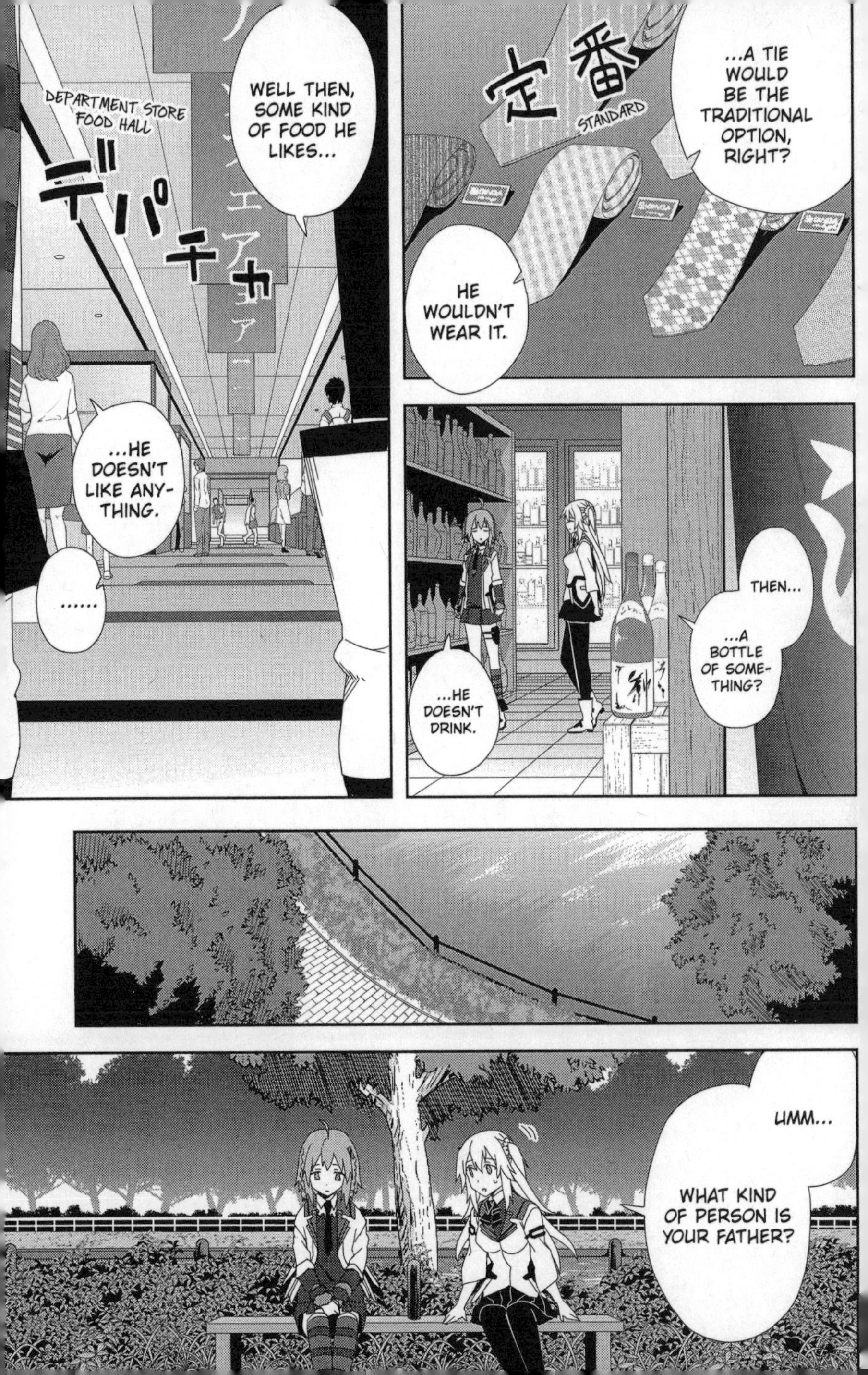
定番
STANDARD
...A TIE WOULD BE THE TRADITIONAL OPTION, RIGHT?
HE WOULDN'T WEAR IT.
THEN...
...A BOTTLE OF SOME-THING?
...HE DOESN'T DRINK.
WELL THEN, SOME KIND OF FOOD HE LIKES...
DEPARTMENT STORE FOOD HALL
デパチカ
...HE DOESN'T LIKE ANY-THING.
......
UMM...
WHAT KIND OF PERSON IS YOUR FATHER?

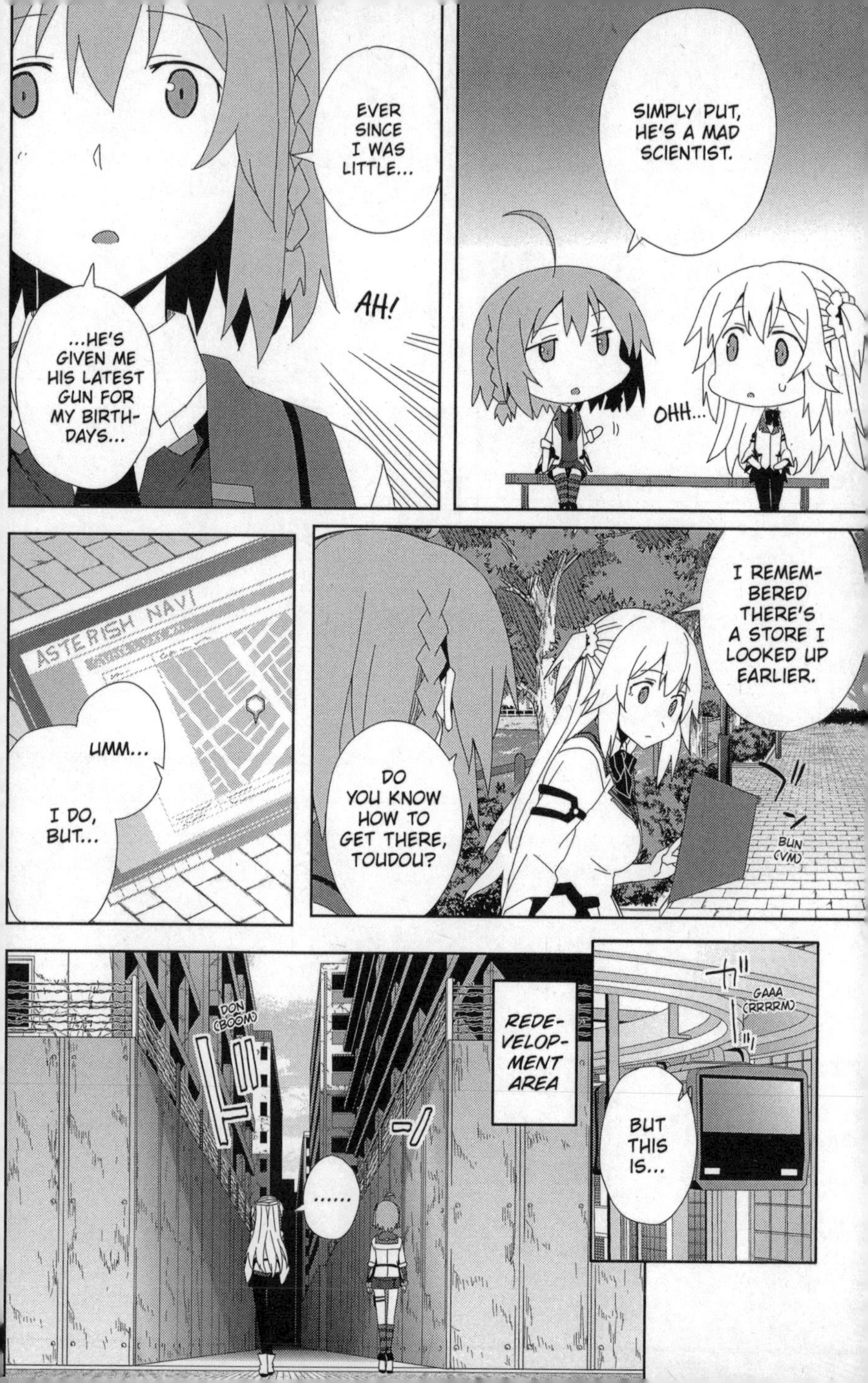
SIMPLY PUT, HE'S A MAD SCIENTIST.
OHH...
EVER SINCE I WAS LITTLE...
...HE'S GIVEN ME HIS LATEST GUN FOR MY BIRTH-DAYS...
AH!
I REMEM-BERED THERE'S A STORE I LOOKED UP EARLIER.
BUN (VM)
DO YOU KNOW HOW TO GET THERE, TOUDOU?
ASTERISH NAVI
UMM...
I DO, BUT...
GAAA (RRRRM)
BUT THIS IS...
REDE-VELOP-MENT AREA
DON (BOOM)
....

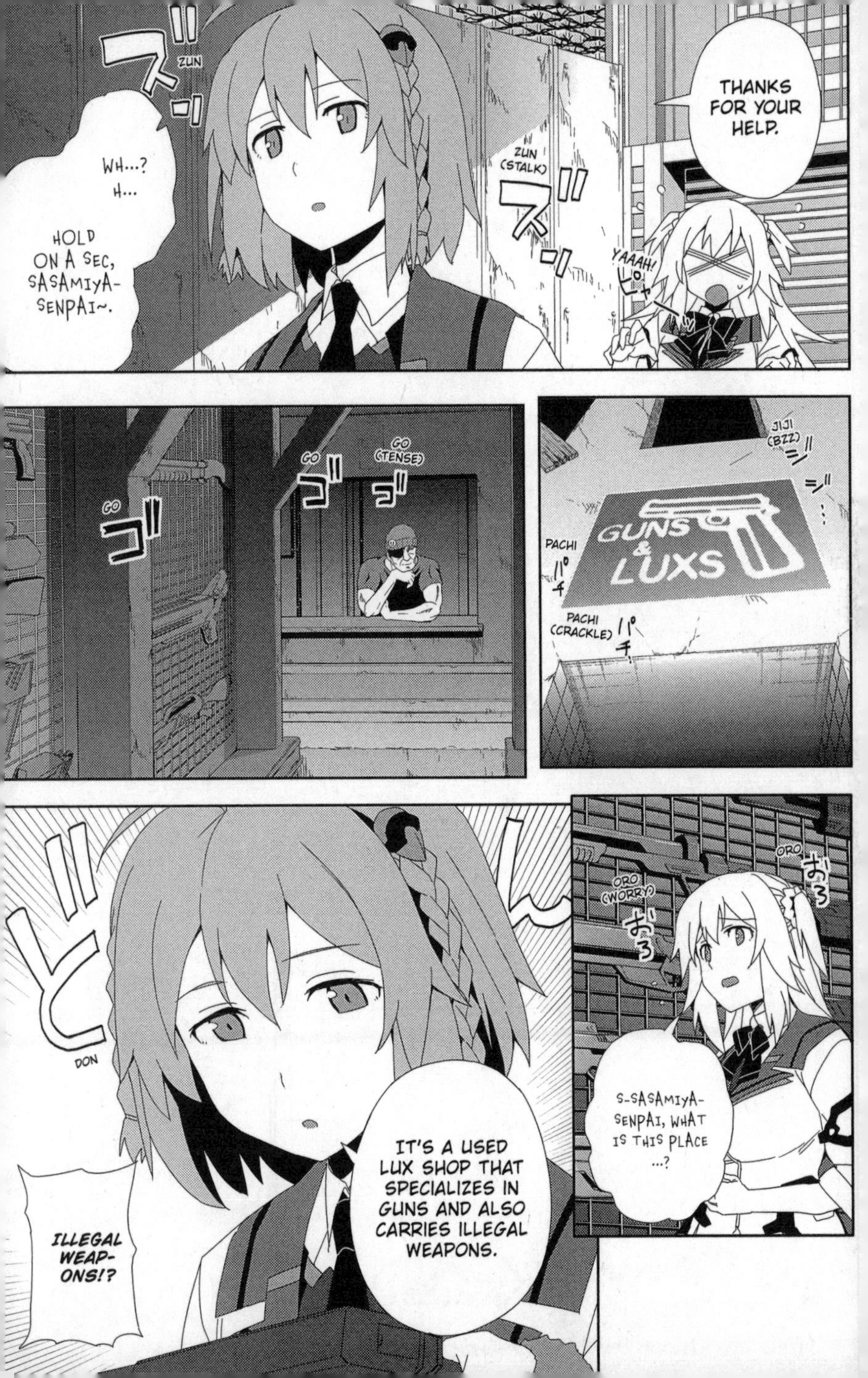
THANKS FOR YOUR HELP.
ZUN (STALK)
YAAAH!
ZUN
WH...? H...
HOLD ON A SEC, SASAMIYA-SENPAI~.
JIJI (BZZ)
GUNS & LUXS
PACHI
PACHI (CRACKLE)
GO (TENSE)
GO
GO
ORO
ORO (WORRY)
S-SASAMIYA-SENPAI, WHAT IS THIS PLACE ...?
DON
IT'S A USED LUX SHOP THAT SPECIALIZES IN GUNS AND ALSO CARRIES ILLEGAL WEAPONS.
ILLEGAL WEAP-ONS!?

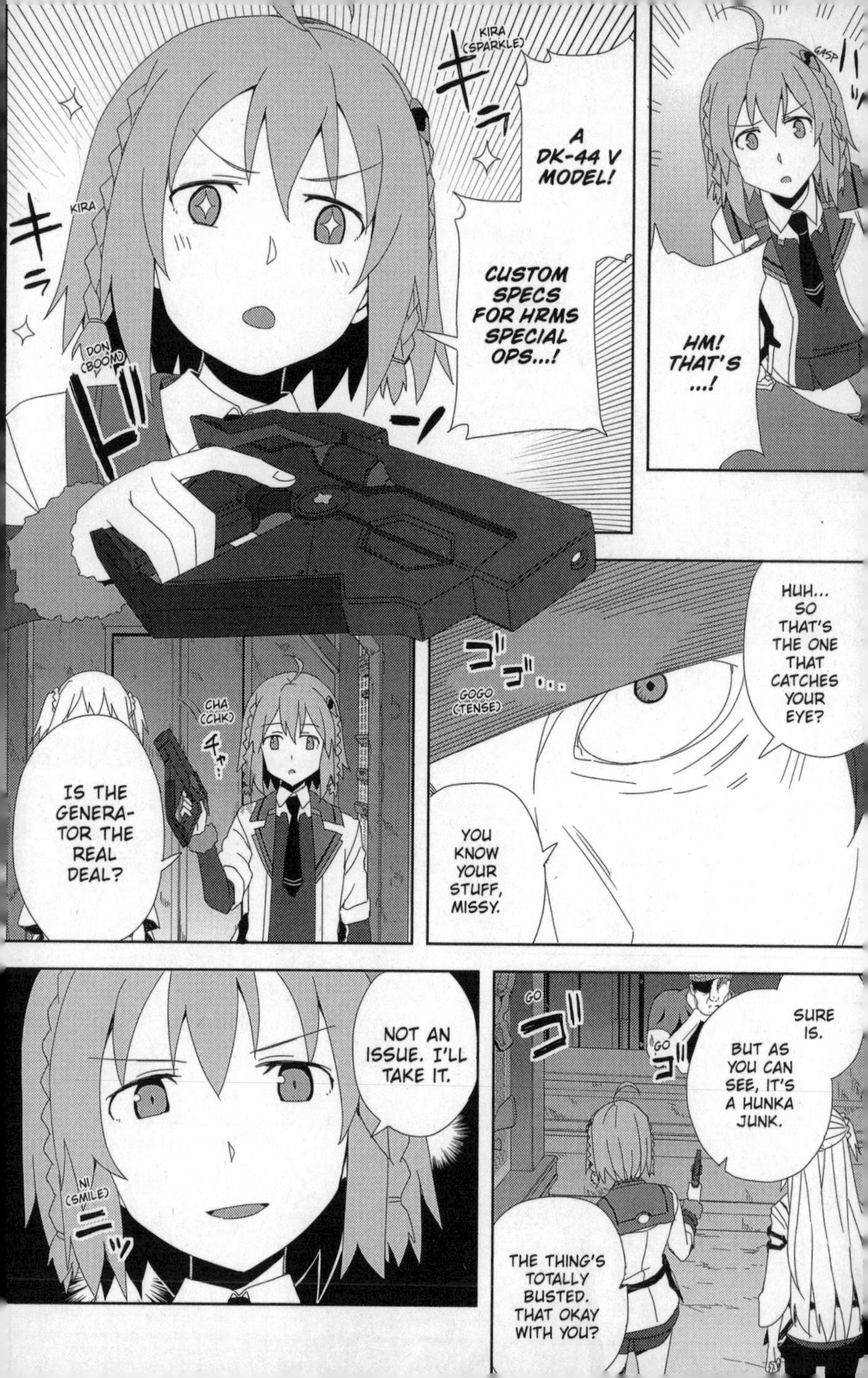
GASP
HM! THAT'S ...!
KIRA (SPARKLE)
キラ
A DK-44 V MODEL!
CUSTOM SPECS FOR HRMS SPECIAL OPS...!
KIRA
キラ
DON (BOOM)
ドン
HUH... SO THAT'S THE ONE THAT CATCHES YOUR EYE?
ゴゴ...
GOGO (TENSE)
YOU KNOW YOUR STUFF, MISSY.
CHA (CHK)
チャ..
IS THE GENERA-TOR THE REAL DEAL?
GO
ゴ
GO
ゴ
SURE IS.
BUT AS YOU CAN SEE, IT'S A HUNKA JUNK.
THE THING'S TOTALLY BUSTED. THAT OKAY WITH YOU?
NOT AN ISSUE. I'LL TAKE IT.
NI (SMILE)
ニッ

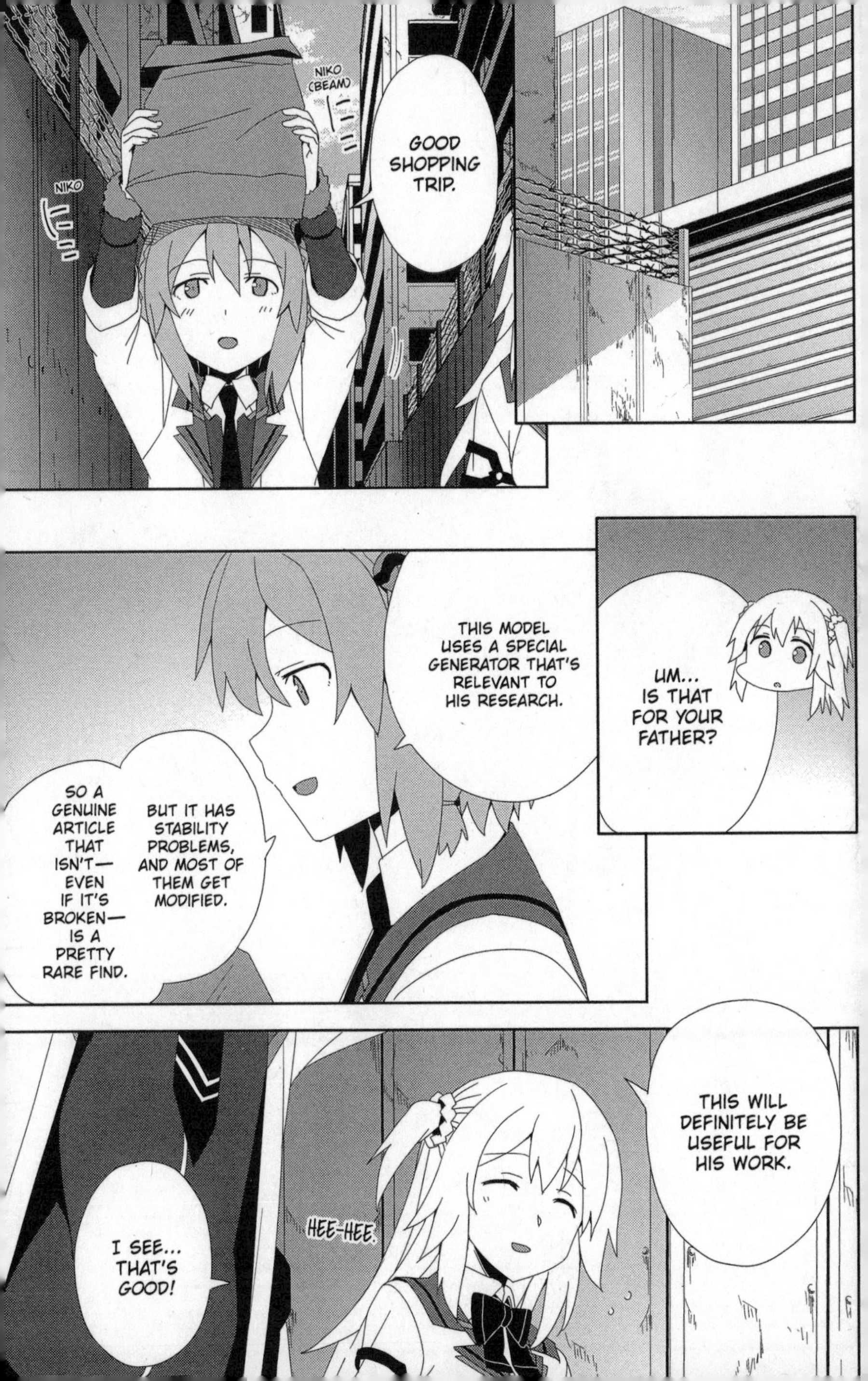
GOOD SHOPPING TRIP.
NIKO (BEAM)
NIKO
UM... IS THAT FOR YOUR FATHER?
THIS MODEL USES A SPECIAL GENERATOR THAT'S RELEVANT TO HIS RESEARCH.
BUT IT HAS STABILITY PROBLEMS, AND MOST OF THEM GET MODIFIED.
SO A GENUINE ARTICLE THAT ISN'T—EVEN IF IT'S BROKEN—IS A PRETTY RARE FIND.
THIS WILL DEFINITELY BE USEFUL FOR HIS WORK.
HEE-HEE.
I SEE... THAT'S GOOD!

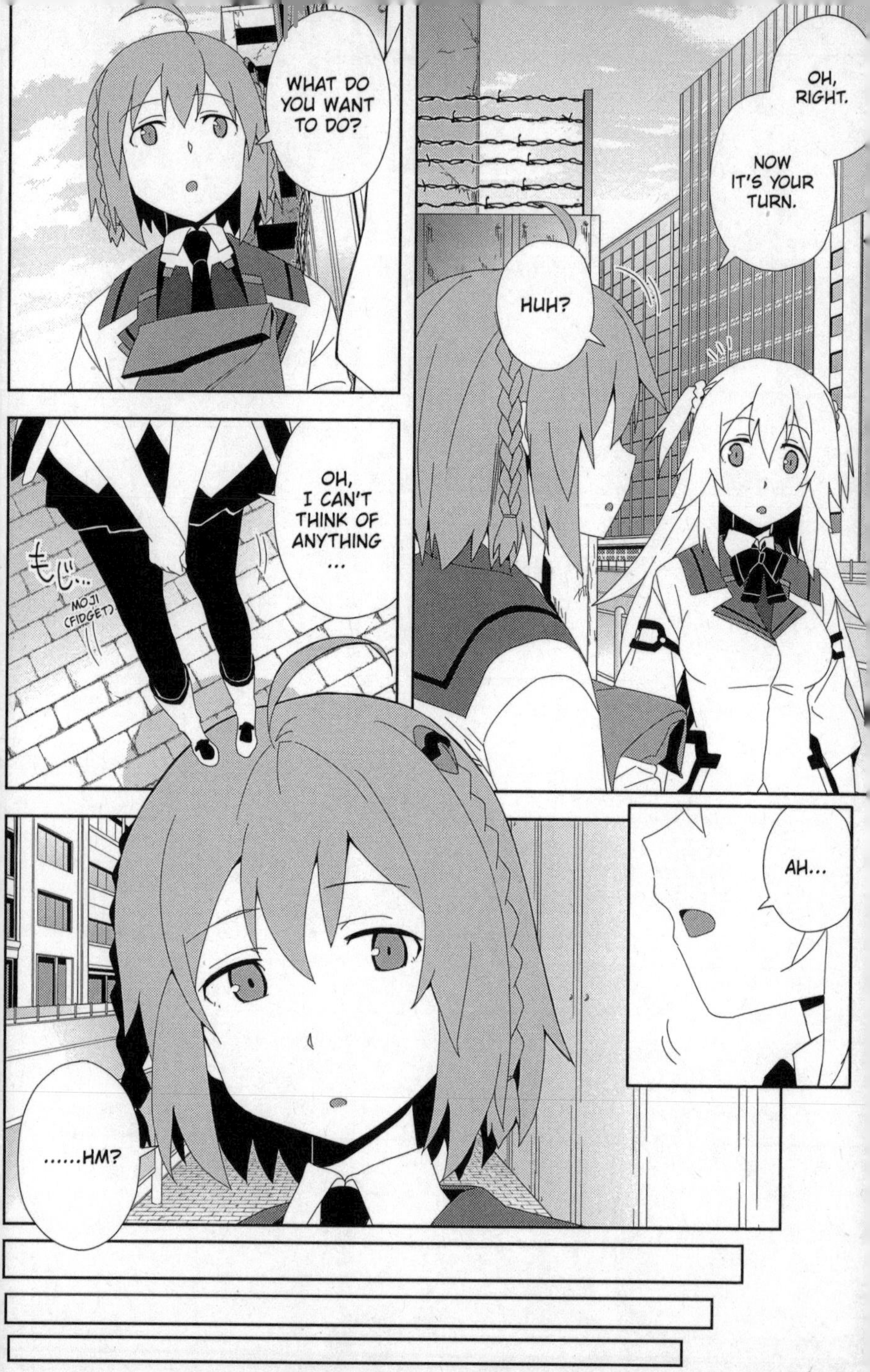
OH, RIGHT.
NOW IT'S YOUR TURN.
HUH?
WHAT DO YOU WANT TO DO?
OH, I CAN'T THINK OF ANYTHING...
もじ…
MOJI (FIDGET)
AH...
......HM?

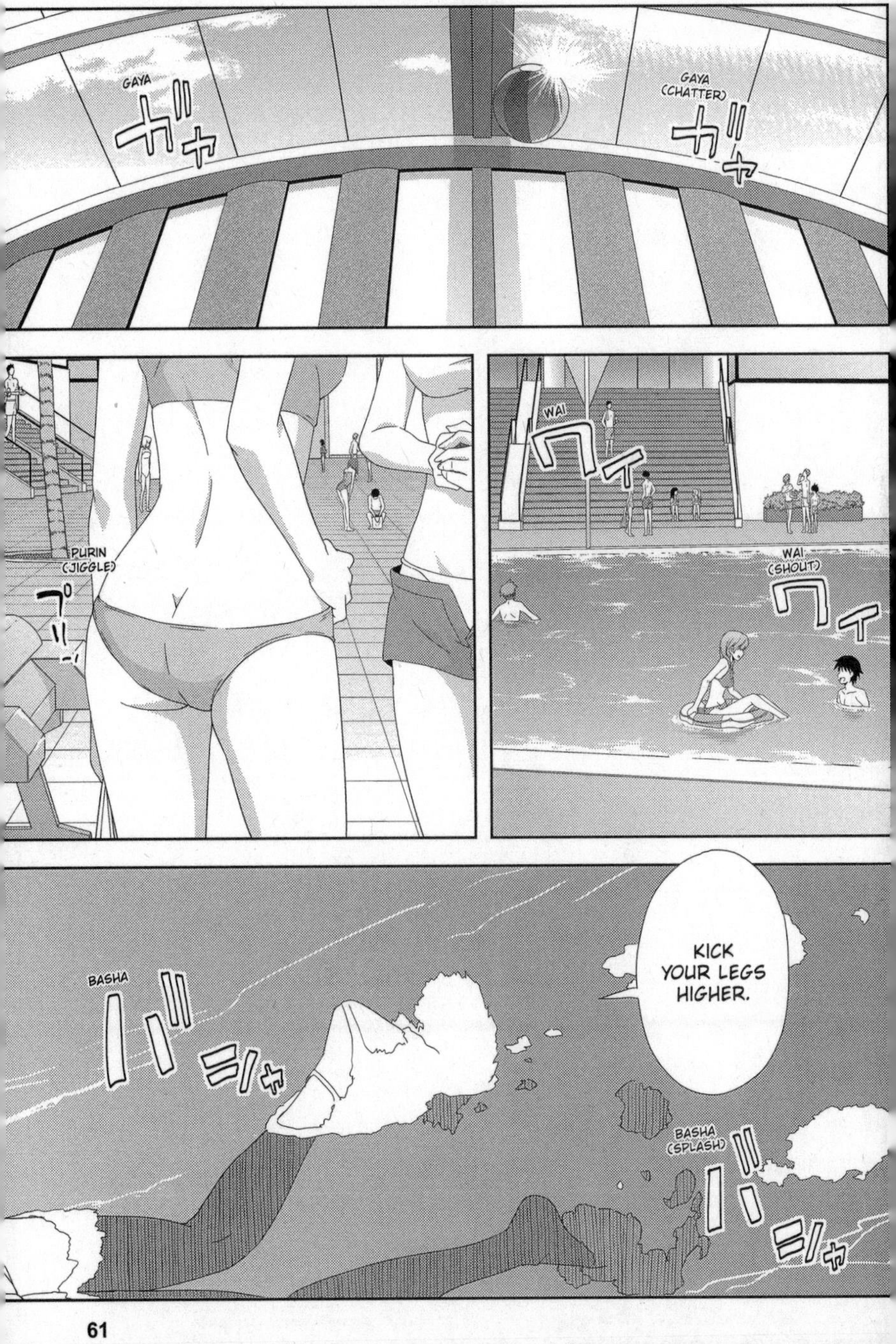
GAYA (CHATTER)
GAYA
WAI
WAI (SHOUT)
PURIN (JIGGLE)
KICK YOUR LEGS HIGHER.
BASHA (SPLASH)
BASHA

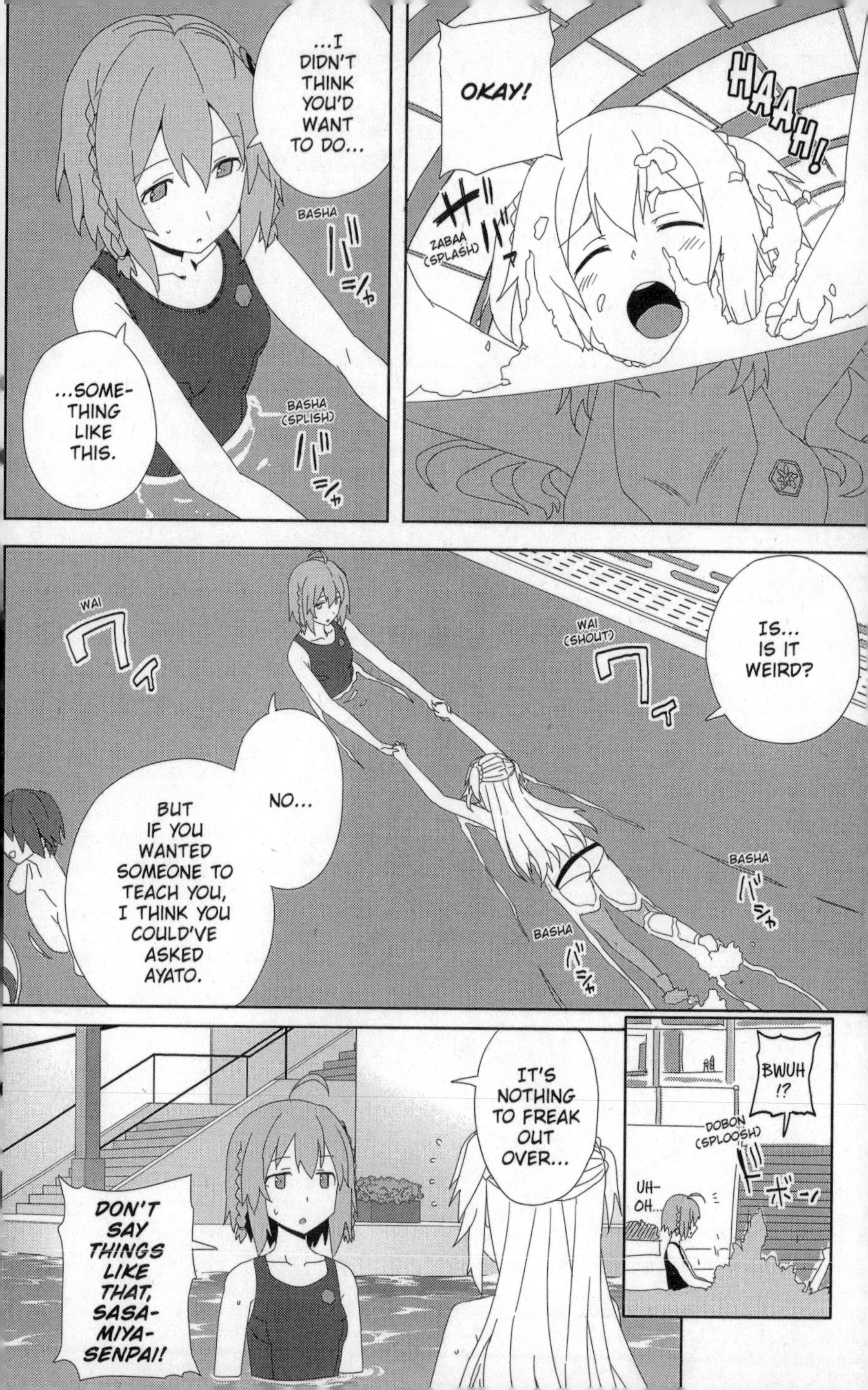
OKAY!
HAAAH!
ZABAA (SPLASH)
...I DIDN'T THINK YOU'D WANT TO DO...
BASHA
...SOME-THING LIKE THIS.
BASHA (SPLISH)
IS... IS IT WEIRD?
WAI (SHOUT)
WAI
NO...
BUT IF YOU WANTED SOMEONE TO TEACH YOU, I THINK YOU COULD'VE ASKED AYATO.
BASHA
BASHA
BWUH !?
DOBON (SPLOOSH)
UH-OH...
IT'S NOTHING TO FREAK OUT OVER...
DON'T SAY THINGS LIKE THAT, SASA-MIYA-SENPAI!

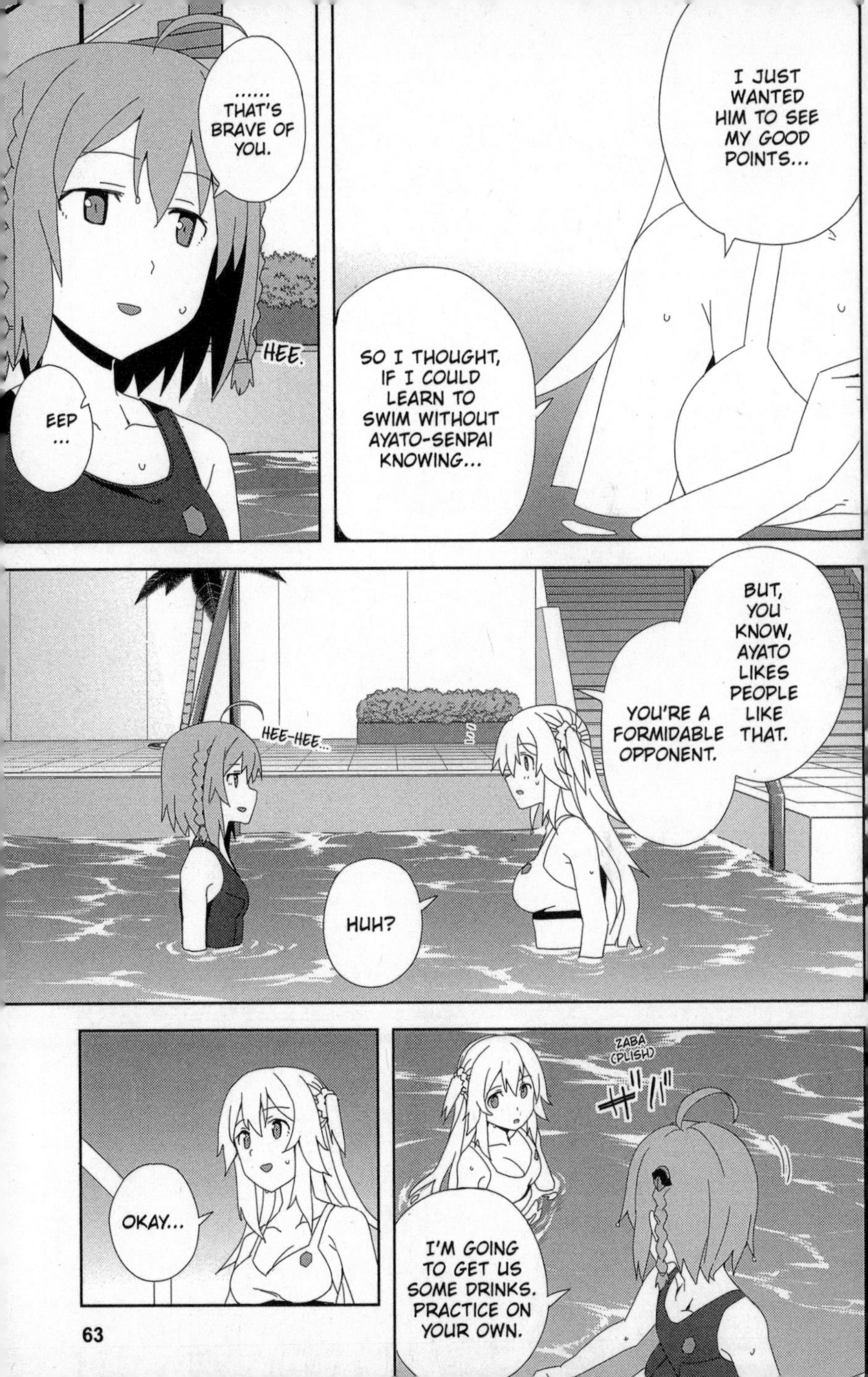
I JUST WANTED HIM TO SEE MY GOOD POINTS...
SO I THOUGHT, IF I COULD LEARN TO SWIM WITHOUT AYATO-SENPAI KNOWING...
...... THAT'S BRAVE OF YOU.
HEE.
EEP ...
BUT, YOU KNOW, AYATO LIKES PEOPLE LIKE THAT.
YOU'RE A FORMIDABLE OPPONENT.
HEE-HEE...
HUH?
ZABA (PLISH)
I'M GOING TO GET US SOME DRINKS. PRACTICE ON YOUR OWN.
OKAY...

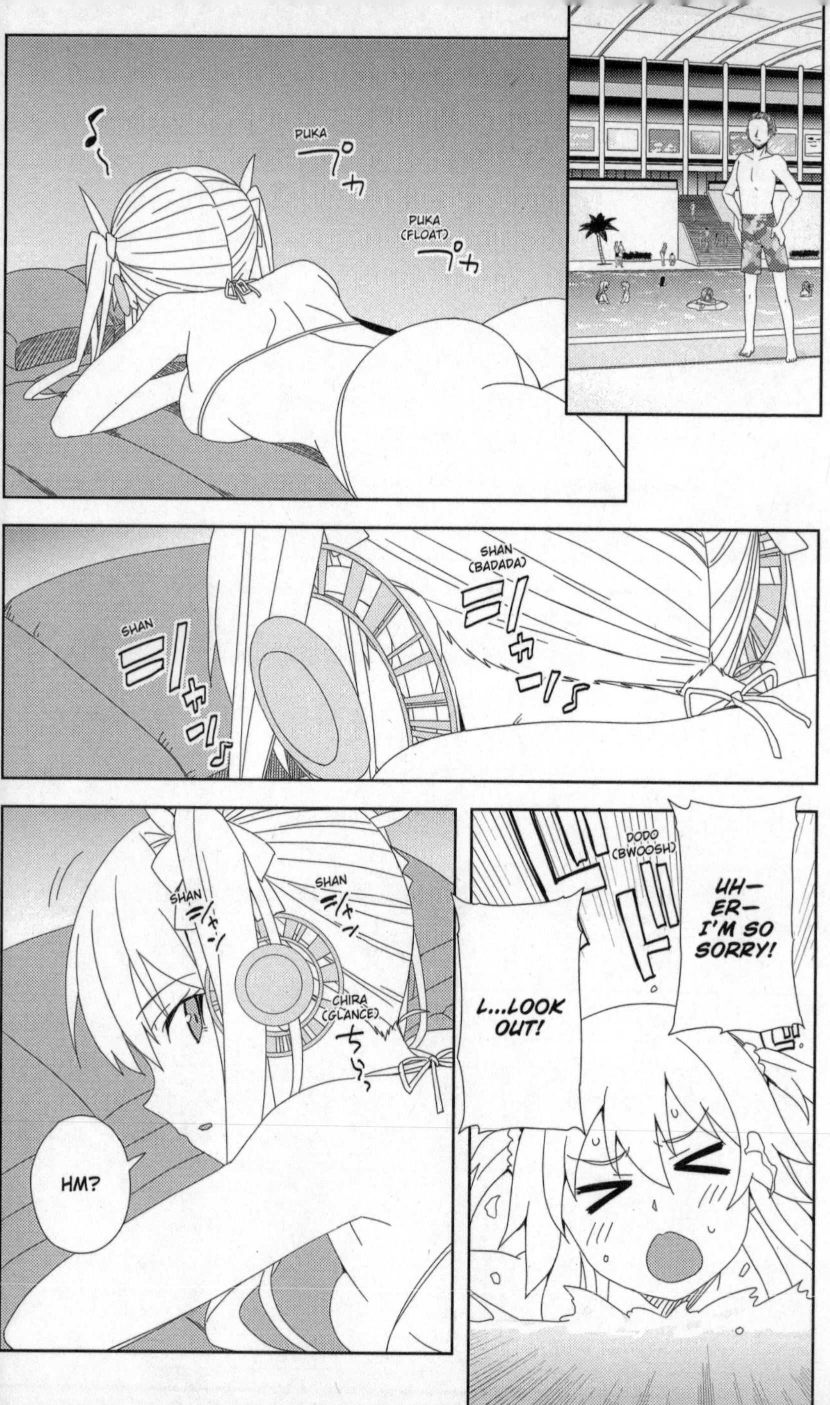
PUKA
PUKA (FLOAT)
SHAN (BADADA)
SHAN
DODO (BWOOSH)
UH— ER— I'M SO SORRY!
L...LOOK OUT!
SHAN
SHAN
CHIRA (GLANCE)
HM?

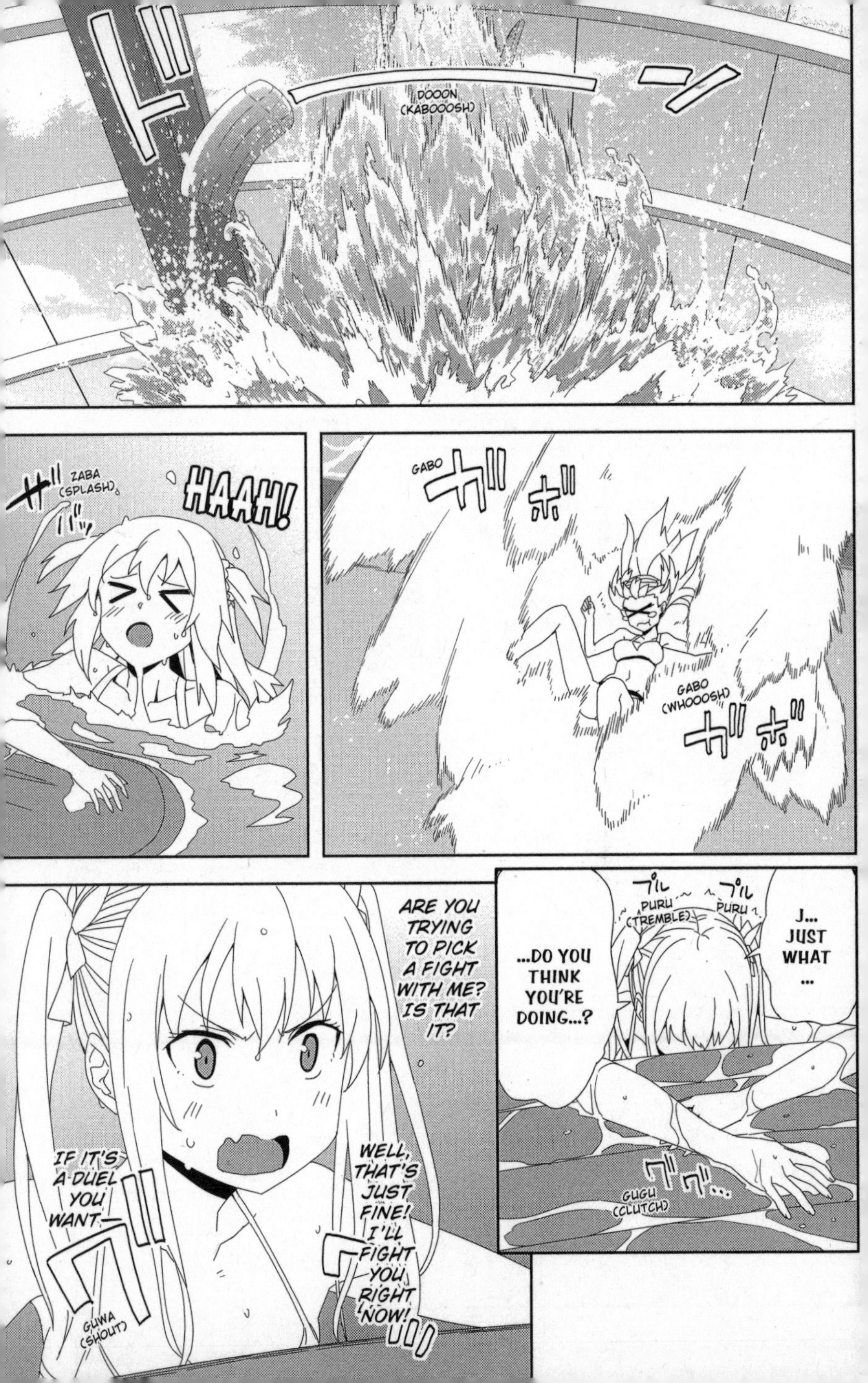
DOOON (KABOOOSH)
GABO
GABO (WHOOOSH)
ZABA (SPLASH)
HAAAH!
PURU (TREMBLE) PURU
J... JUST WHAT ...
...DO YOU THINK YOU'RE DOING...?
GUGU (CLUTCH)
ARE YOU TRYING TO PICK A FIGHT WITH ME? IS THAT IT?
IF IT'S A DUEL YOU WANT—
WELL, THAT'S JUST FINE! I'LL FIGHT YOU RIGHT NOW!
GUWA (SHOUT)

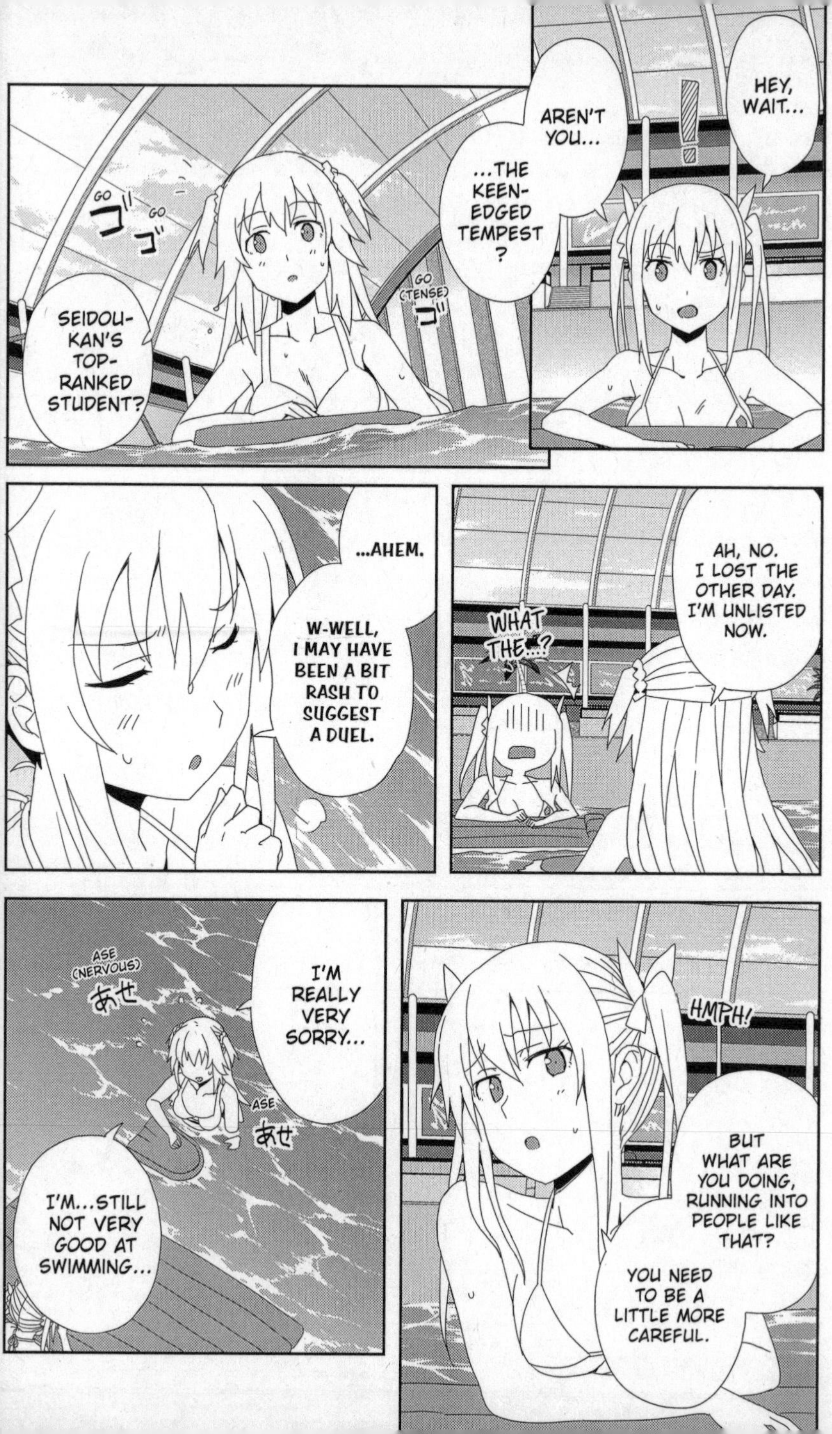
HEY, WAIT...
ARE'NT YOU...
...THE KEEN-EDGED TEMPEST?
!
GO GO ゴゴ
GO (TENSE) ゴ
SEIDOU-KAN'S TOP-RANKED STUDENT?
AH, NO. I LOST THE OTHER DAY. I'M UNLISTED NOW.
WHAT THE...?
...AHEM.
W-WELL, I MAY HAVE BEEN A BIT RASH TO SUGGEST A DUEL.
HMPH!
BUT WHAT ARE YOU DOING, RUNNING INTO PEOPLE LIKE THAT?
YOU NEED TO BE A LITTLE MORE CAREFUL.
I'M REALLY VERY SORRY...
ASE (NERVOUS) あせ
ASE あせ
I'M...STILL NOT VERY GOOD AT SWIMMING...

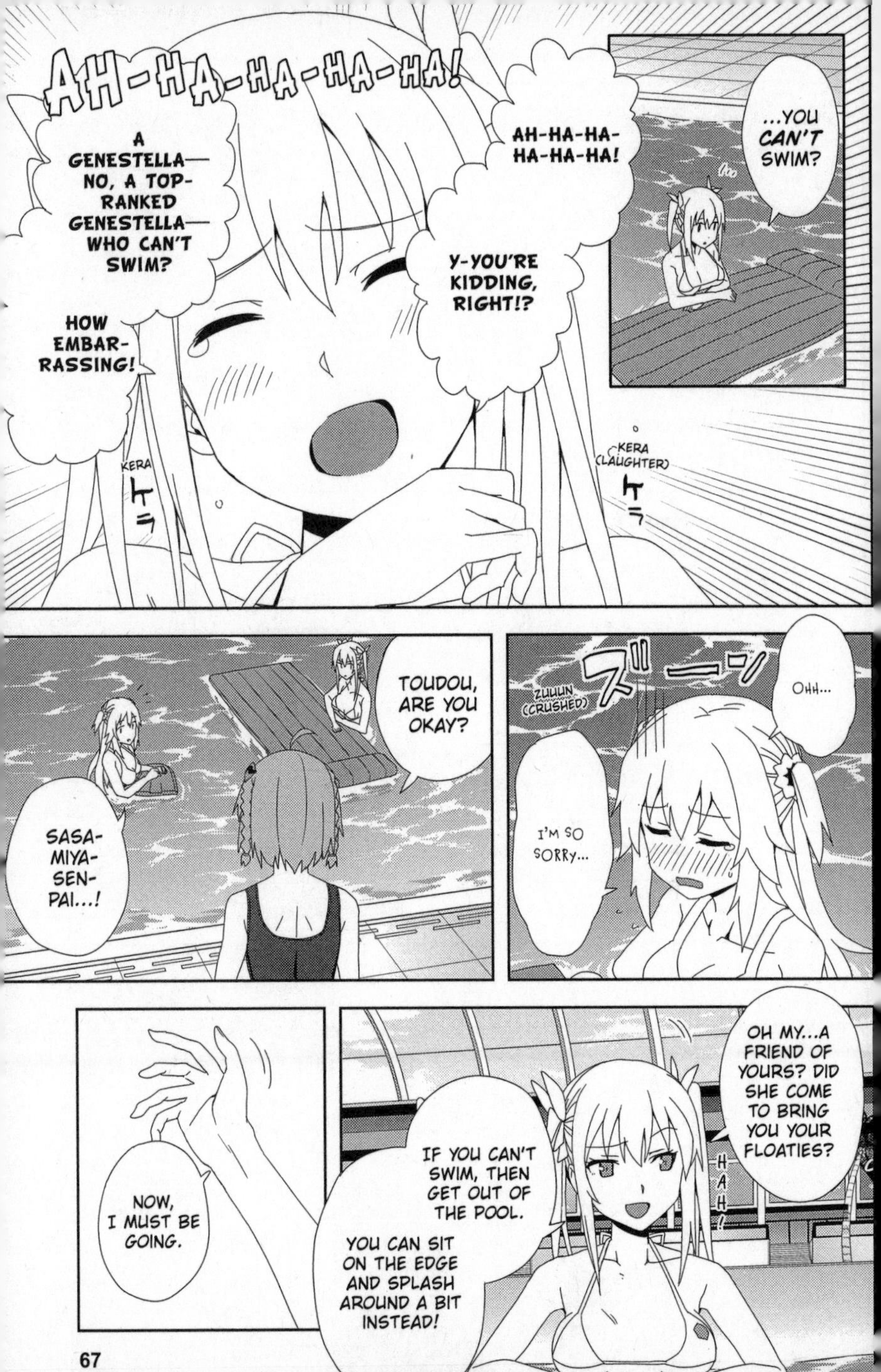
...YOU CAN'T SWIM?
AH-HA-HA-HA-HA-HA!
Y-YOU'RE KIDDING, RIGHT!?
AH-HA-HA-HA-HA!
A GENESTELLA—NO, A TOP-RANKED GENESTELLA—WHO CAN'T SWIM?
HOW EMBARRASSING!
KERA (LAUGHTER)
KERA
OHH...
ZUUUN (CRUSHED)
I'M SO SORRY...
TOUDOU, ARE YOU OKAY?
SASAMIYA-SENPAI...!
OH MY...A FRIEND OF YOURS? DID SHE COME TO BRING YOU YOUR FLOATIES?
HAH!
IF YOU CAN'T SWIM, THEN GET OUT OF THE POOL.
YOU CAN SIT ON THE EDGE AND SPLASH AROUND A BIT INSTEAD!
NOW, I MUST BE GOING.

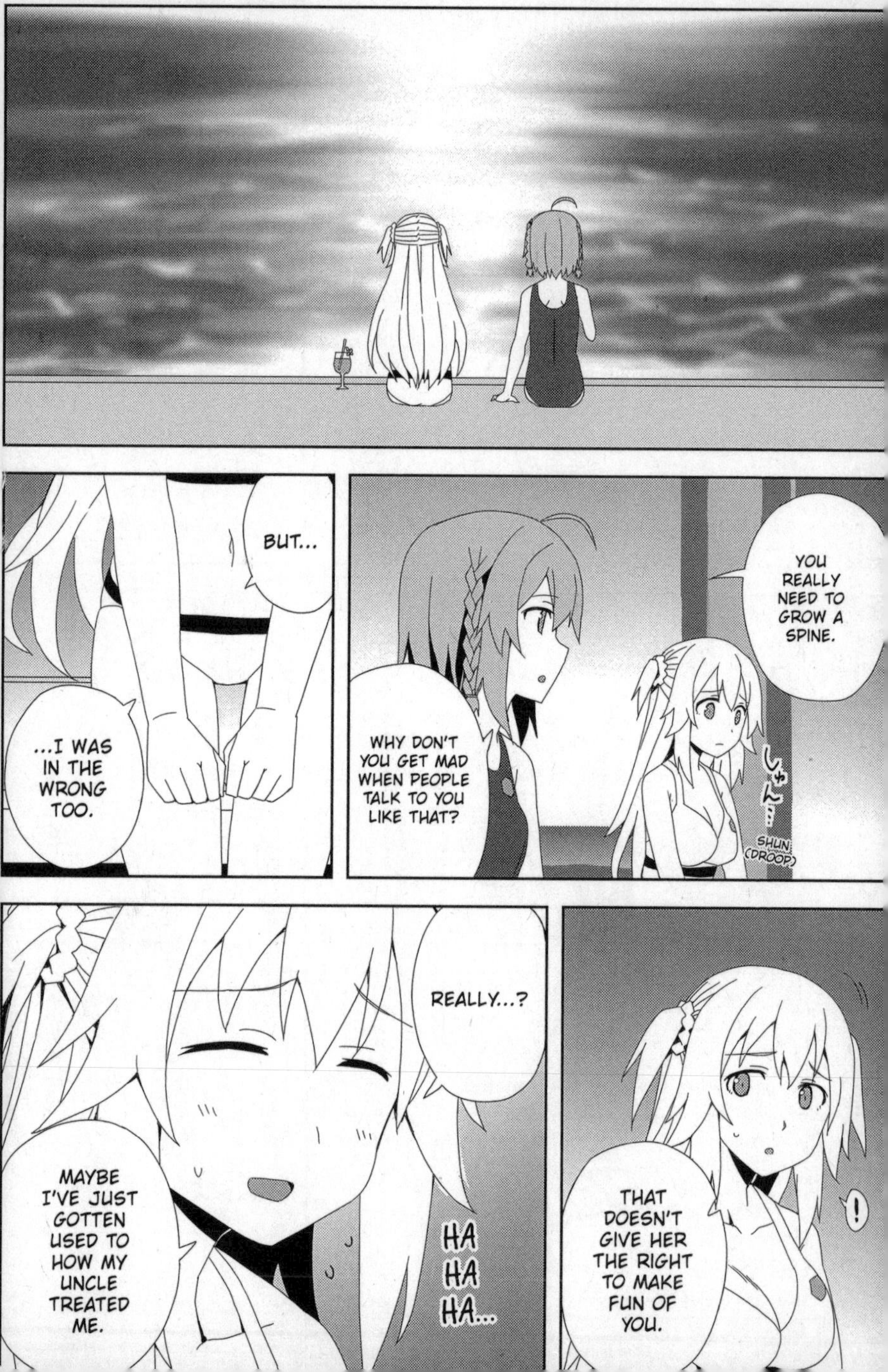
YOU REALLY NEED TO GROW A SPINE.
WHY DON'T YOU GET MAD WHEN PEOPLE TALK TO YOU LIKE THAT?
しゅん…
SHUN (DROOP)
BUT...
...I WAS IN THE WRONG TOO.
!
THAT DOESN'T GIVE HER THE RIGHT TO MAKE FUN OF YOU.
REALLY...?
MAYBE I'VE JUST GOTTEN USED TO HOW MY UNCLE TREATED ME.
HA HA HA...

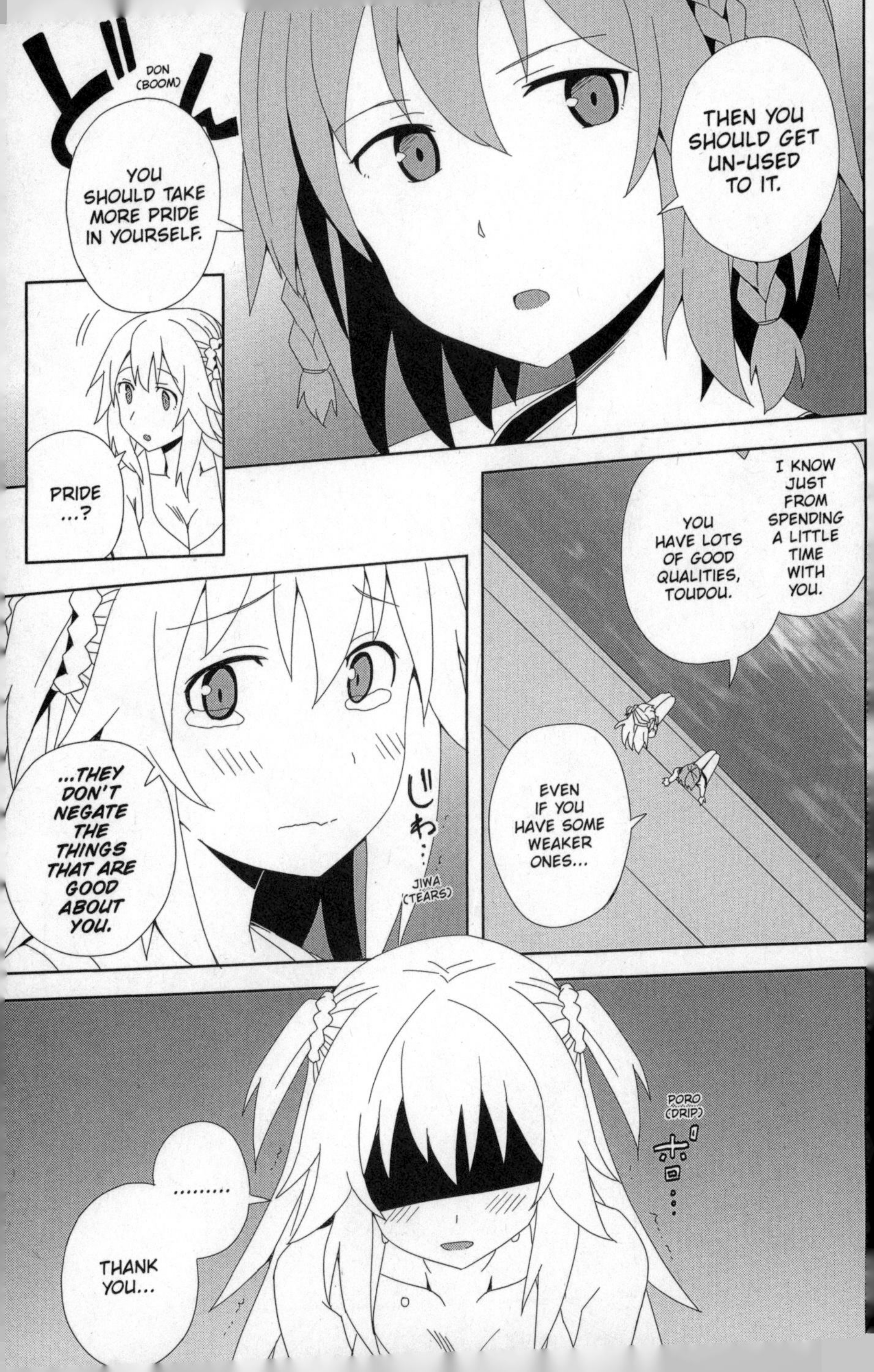
THEN YOU SHOULD GET UN-USED TO IT.
DON (BOOM)
YOU SHOULD TAKE MORE PRIDE IN YOURSELF.
PRIDE ...?
I KNOW JUST FROM SPENDING A LITTLE TIME WITH YOU.
YOU HAVE LOTS OF GOOD QUALITIES, TOUDOU.
EVEN IF YOU HAVE SOME WEAKER ONES...
じわ…
JIWA (TEARS)
...THEY DON'T NEGATE THE THINGS THAT ARE GOOD ABOUT YOU.
ぽろ…
PORO (DRIP)
....
THANK YOU...

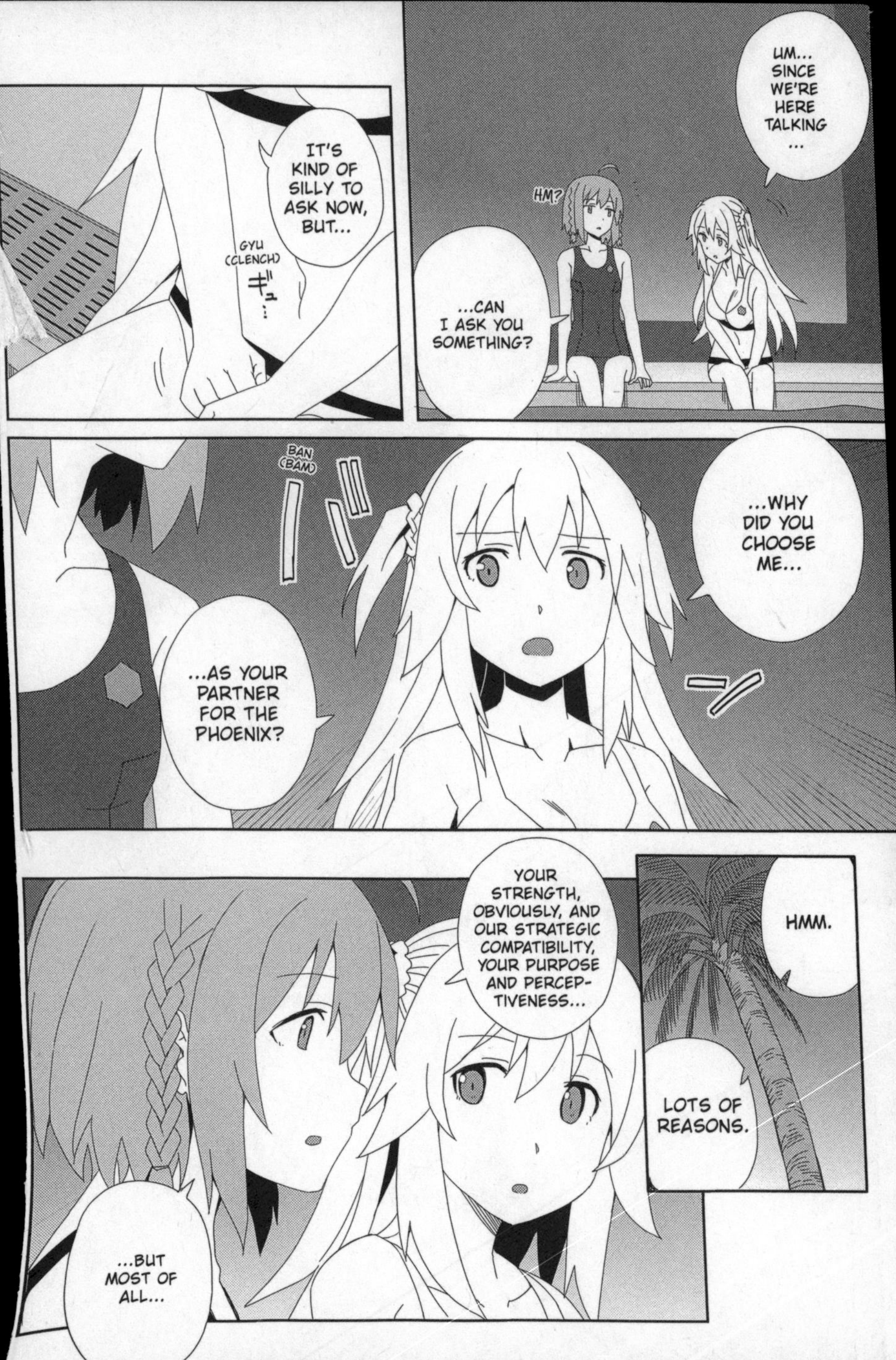
UM... SINCE WE'RE HERE TALKING...
HM?
...CAN I ASK YOU SOMETHING?
IT'S KIND OF SILLY TO ASK NOW, BUT...
GYU (CLENCH)
ギュ…
...WHY DID YOU CHOOSE ME...
BAN (BAM)
...AS YOUR PARTNER FOR THE PHOENIX?
HMM.
YOUR STRENGTH, OBVIOUSLY, AND OUR STRATEGIC COMPATIBILITY, YOUR PURPOSE AND PERCEP-TIVENESS...
LOTS OF REASONS.
...BUT MOST OF ALL...

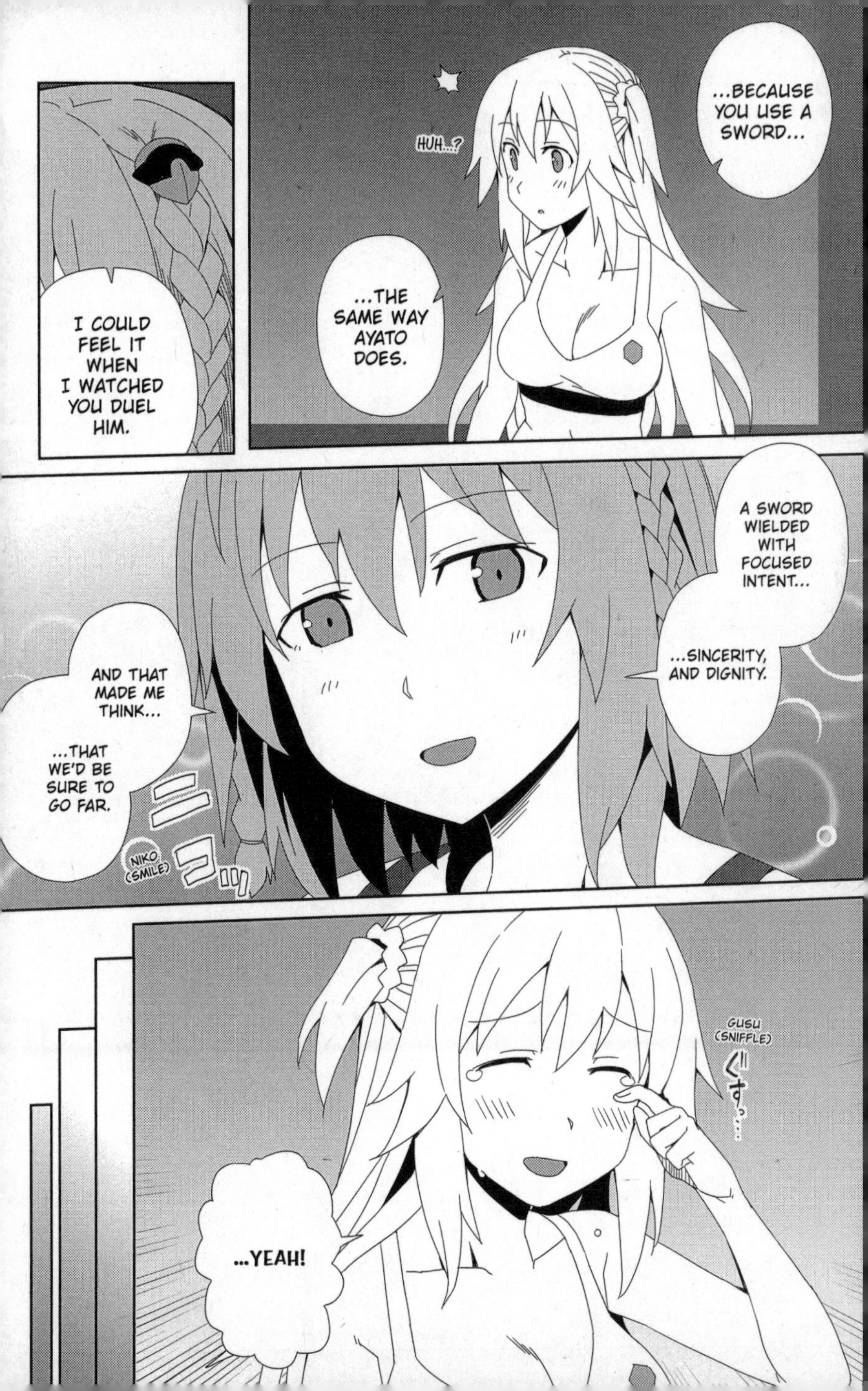
...BECAUSE YOU USE A SWORD...
HUH...?
...THE SAME WAY AYATO DOES.
I COULD FEEL IT WHEN I WATCHED YOU DUEL HIM.
A SWORD WIELDED WITH FOCUSED INTENT...
...SINCERITY, AND DIGNITY.
AND THAT MADE ME THINK...
...THAT WE'D BE SURE TO GO FAR.
ニコッ
NIKO (SMILE)
ぐすっ...
GUSU (SNIFFLE)
...YEAH!

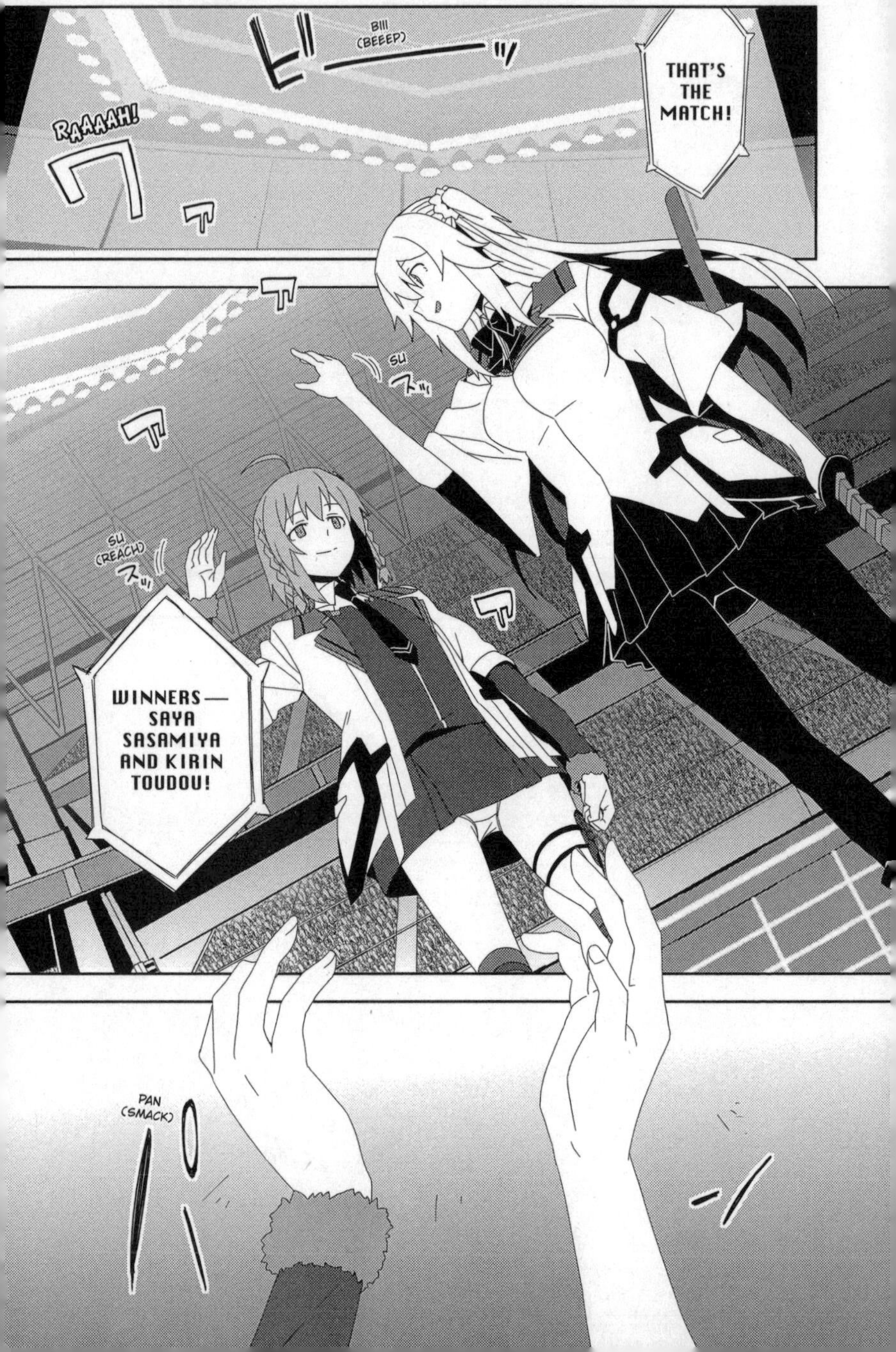
THAT'S THE MATCH!
BIII (BEEEP)
RAAAAH!
SU
SU (REACH)
WINNERS— SAYA SASAMIYA AND KIRIN TOUDOU!
PAN (SMACK)

THE ASTERISK WAR

NO! BAD SISTER!!

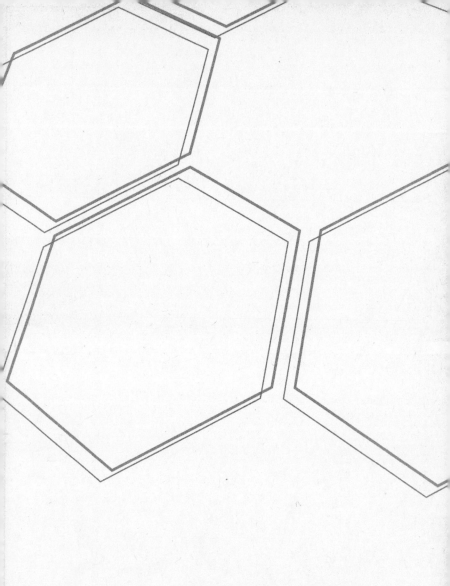

THE
ASTERISK WAR

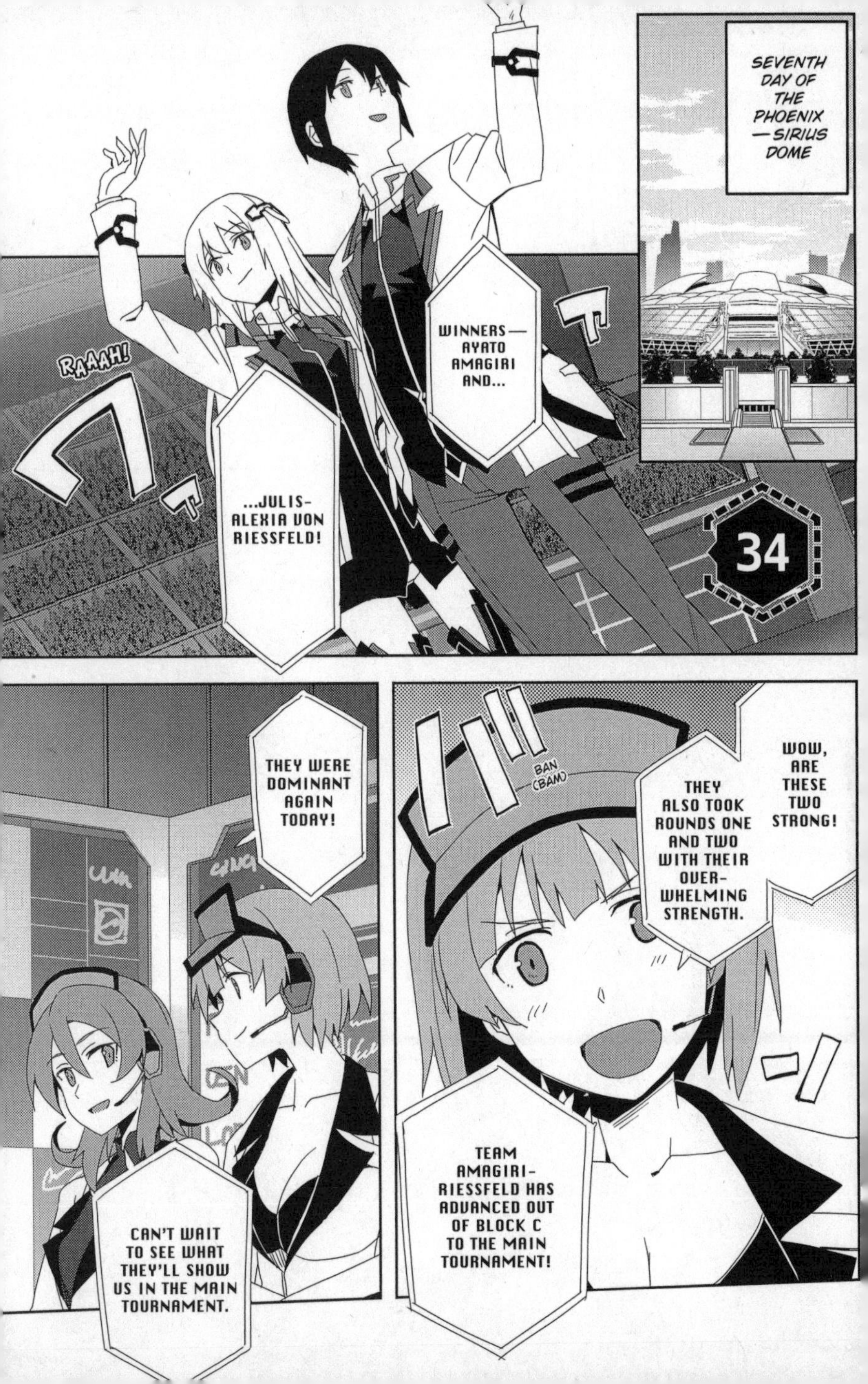
SEVENTH DAY OF THE PHOENIX —SIRIUS DOME
34
WINNERS— AYATO AMAGIRI AND...
...JULIS-ALEXIA VON RIESSFELD!
RAAAH!
WOW, ARE THESE TWO STRONG!
THEY ALSO TOOK ROUNDS ONE AND TWO WITH THEIR OVER-WHELMING STRENGTH.
BAN (BAM)
TEAM AMAGIRI-RIESSFELD HAS ADVANCED OUT OF BLOCK C TO THE MAIN TOURNAMENT!
THEY WERE DOMINANT AGAIN TODAY!
CAN'T WAIT TO SEE WHAT THEY'LL SHOW US IN THE MAIN TOURNAMENT.

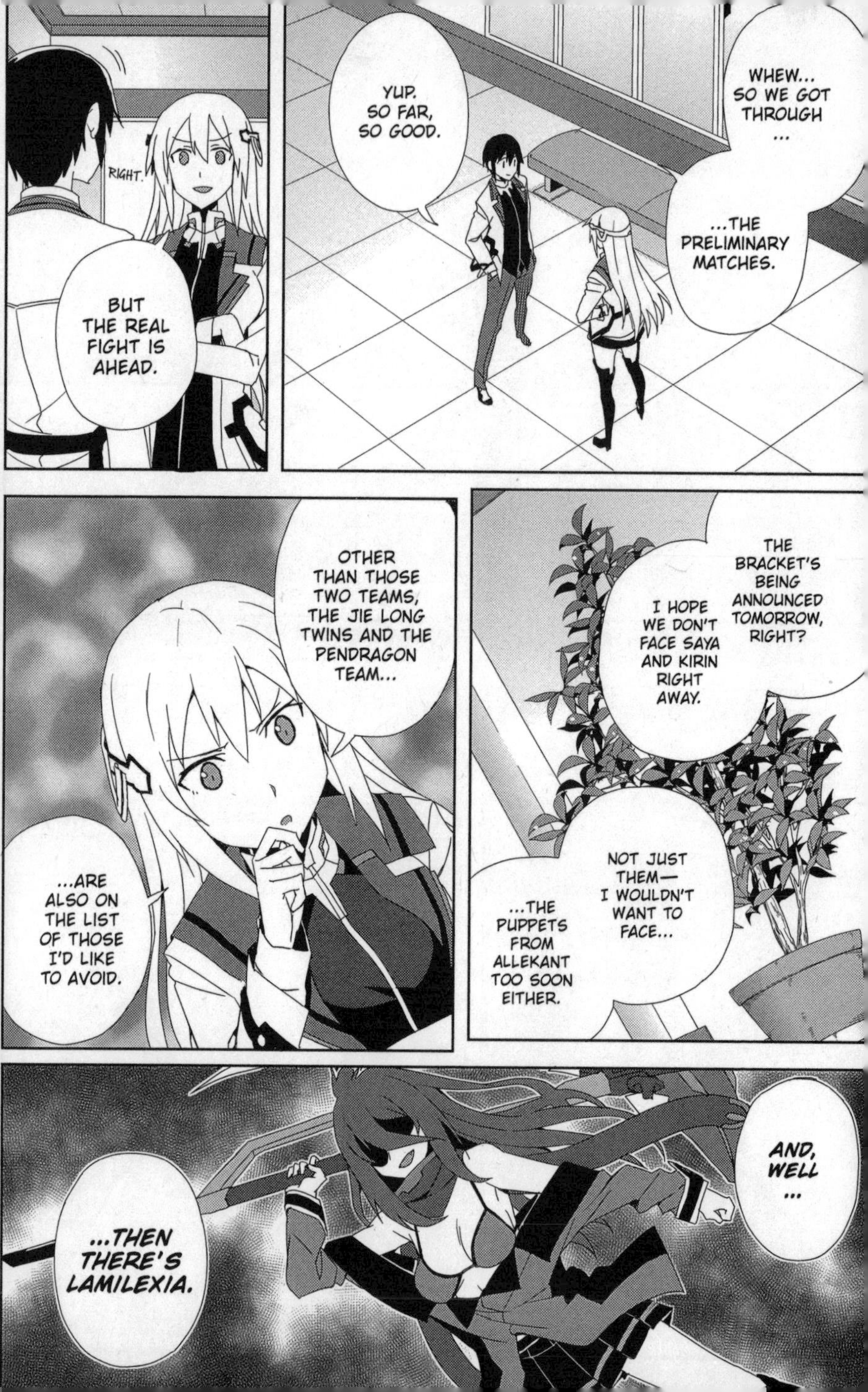
WHEW... SO WE GOT THROUGH ...
...THE PRELIMINARY MATCHES.
YUP. SO FAR, SO GOOD.
RIGHT.
BUT THE REAL FIGHT IS AHEAD.
THE BRACKET'S BEING ANNOUNCED TOMORROW, RIGHT?
I HOPE WE DON'T FACE SAYA AND KIRIN RIGHT AWAY.
NOT JUST THEM— I WOULDN'T WANT TO FACE...
...THE PUPPETS FROM ALLEKANT TOO SOON EITHER.
OTHER THAN THOSE TWO TEAMS, THE JIE LONG TWINS AND THE PENDRAGON TEAM...
...ARE ALSO ON THE LIST OF THOSE I'D LIKE TO AVOID.
AND, WELL ...
...THEN THERE'S LAMILEXIA.

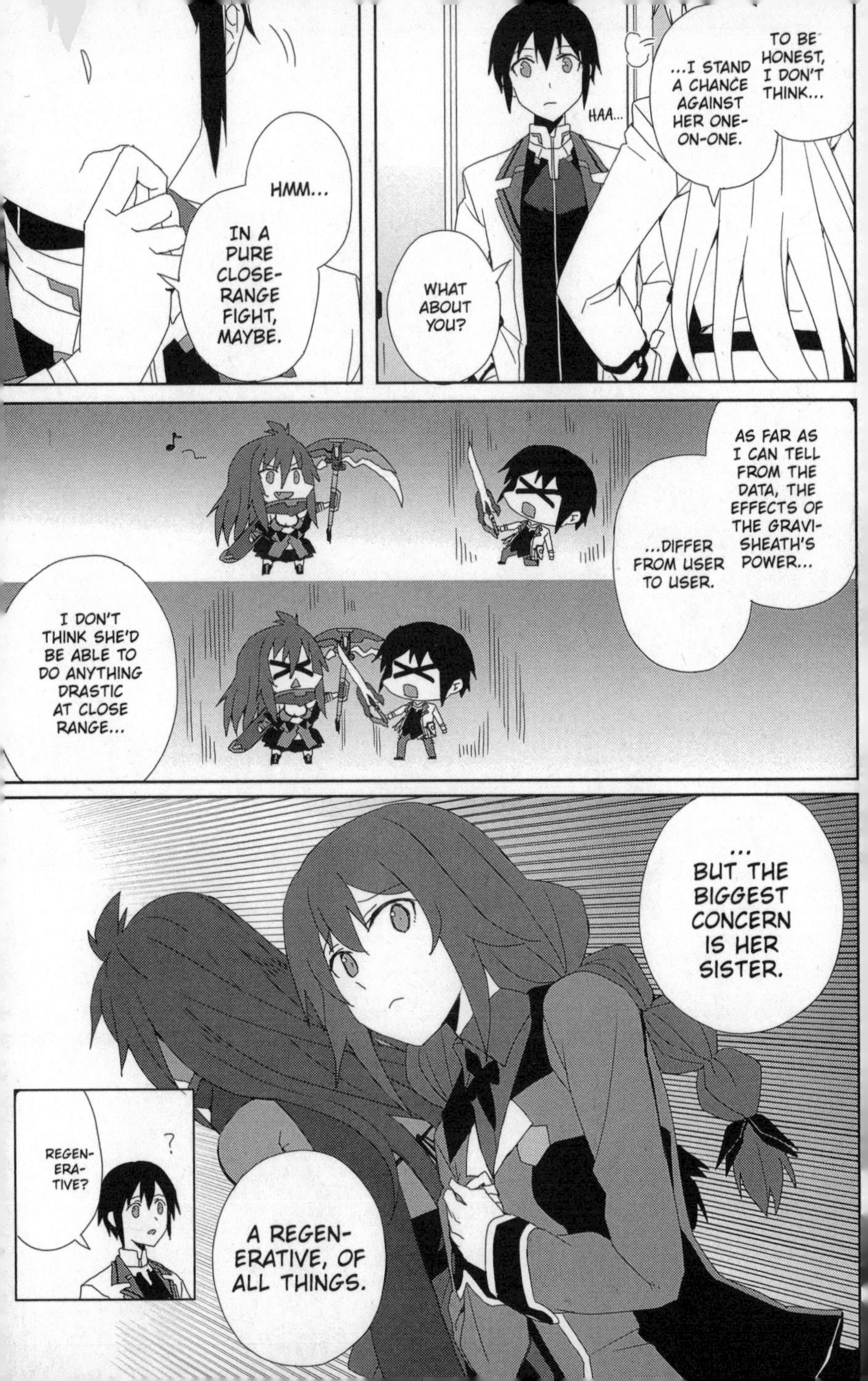
TO BE HONEST, I DON'T THINK...
...I STAND A CHANCE AGAINST HER ONE-ON-ONE.
HAA...
WHAT ABOUT YOU?
HMM...
IN A PURE CLOSE-RANGE FIGHT, MAYBE.
AS FAR AS I CAN TELL FROM THE DATA, THE EFFECTS OF THE GRAVI-SHEATH'S POWER...
...DIFFER FROM USER TO USER.
I DON'T THINK SHE'D BE ABLE TO DO ANYTHING DRASTIC AT CLOSE RANGE...
... BUT THE BIGGEST CONCERN IS HER SISTER.
A REGENERATIVE, OF ALL THINGS.
?
REGENERATIVE?

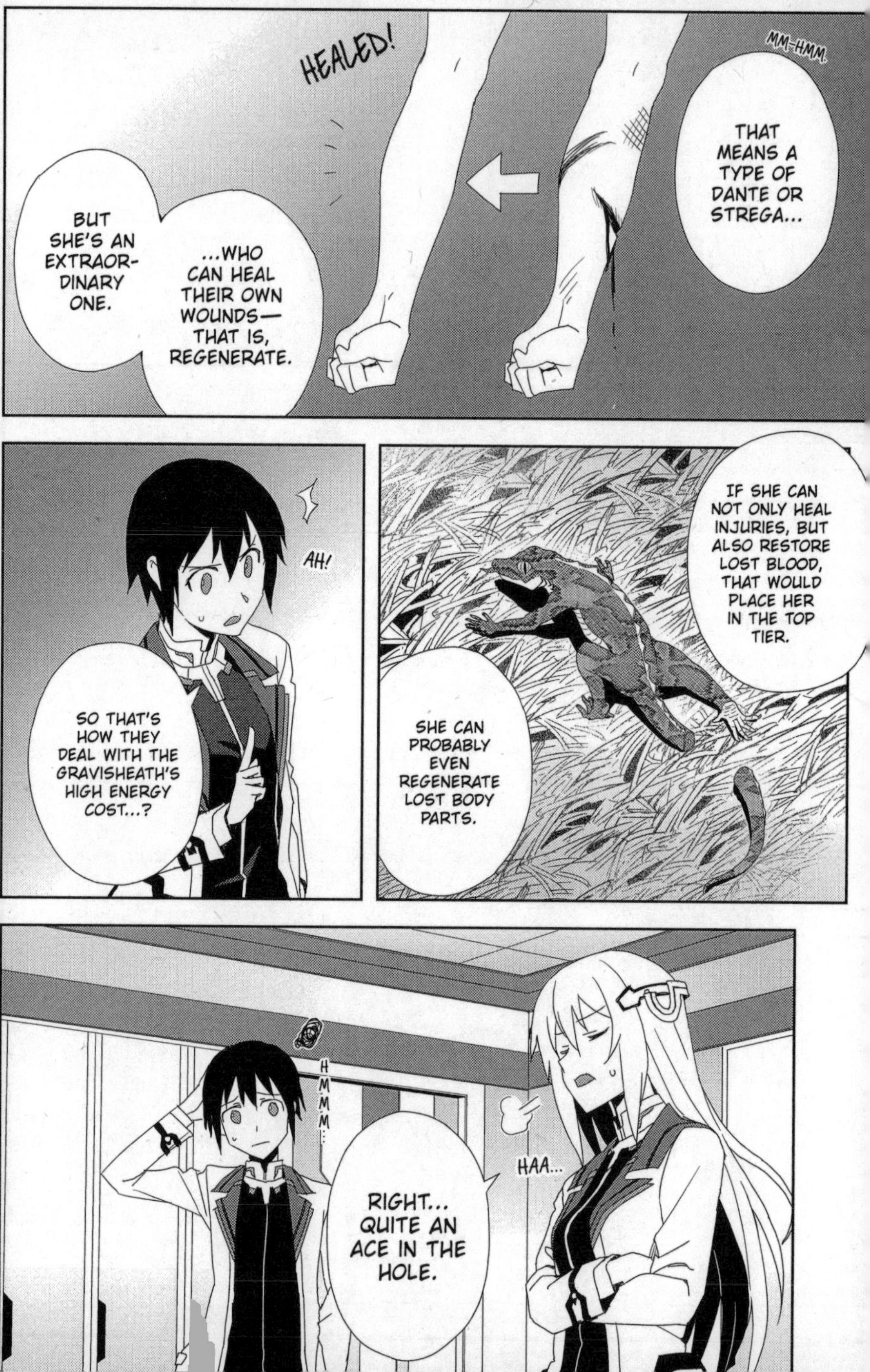
MM-HMM.
THAT MEANS A TYPE OF DANTE OR STREGA...
HEALED!
...WHO CAN HEAL THEIR OWN WOUNDS—THAT IS, REGENERATE.
BUT SHE'S AN EXTRAOR-DINARY ONE.
IF SHE CAN NOT ONLY HEAL INJURIES, BUT ALSO RESTORE LOST BLOOD, THAT WOULD PLACE HER IN THE TOP TIER.
SHE CAN PROBABLY EVEN REGENERATE LOST BODY PARTS.
AH!
SO THAT'S HOW THEY DEAL WITH THE GRAVISHEATH'S HIGH ENERGY COST...?
HAA...
RIGHT... QUITE AN ACE IN THE HOLE.
HMMM...

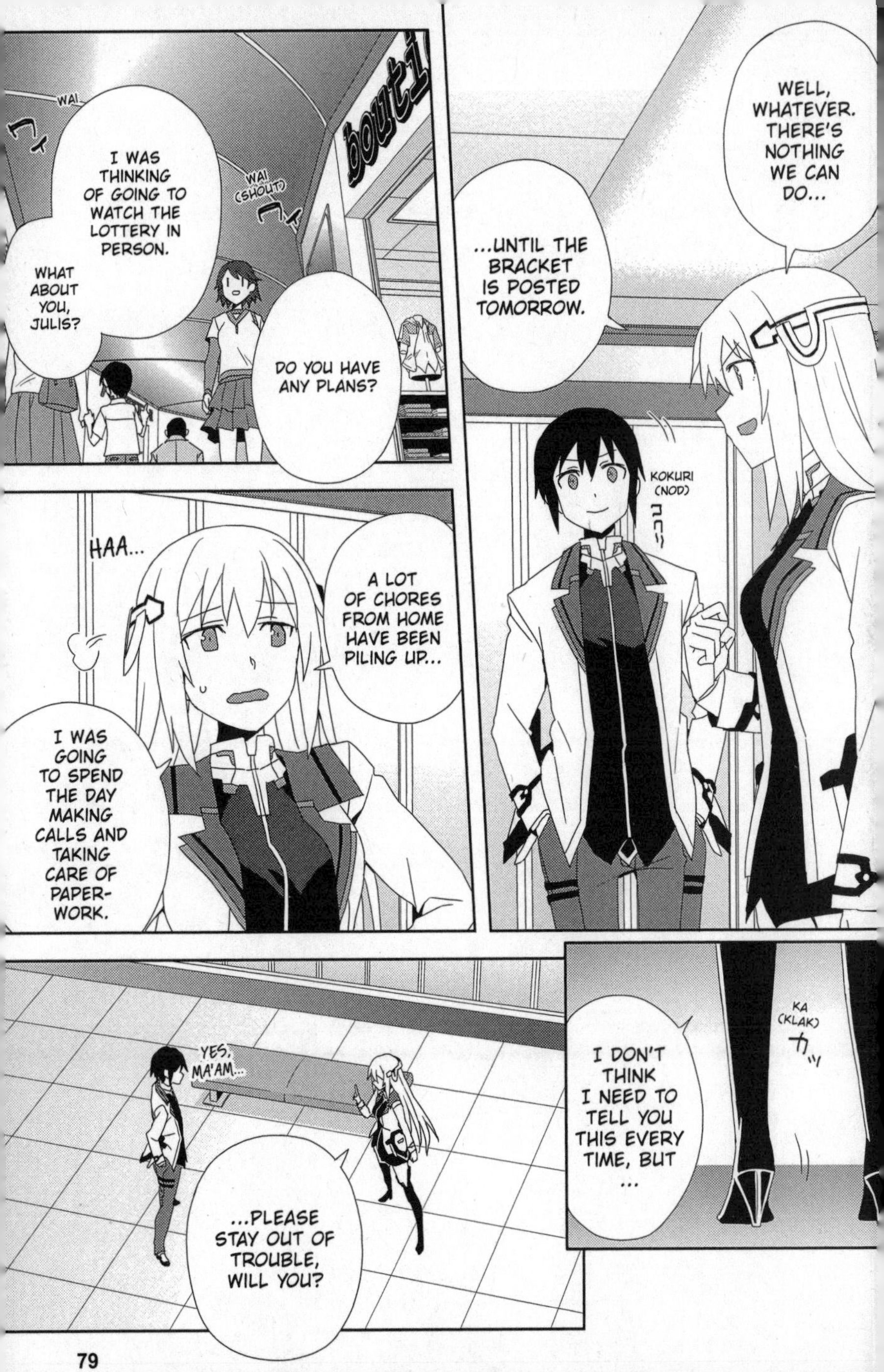
WELL, WHATEVER. THERE'S NOTHING WE CAN DO...
...UNTIL THE BRACKET IS POSTED TOMORROW.
KOKURI (NOD)
WAI
WAI (SHOUT)
I WAS THINKING OF GOING TO WATCH THE LOTTERY IN PERSON.
WHAT ABOUT YOU, JULIS?
DO YOU HAVE ANY PLANS?
A LOT OF CHORES FROM HOME HAVE BEEN PILING UP...
HAA...
I WAS GOING TO SPEND THE DAY MAKING CALLS AND TAKING CARE OF PAPER-WORK.
KA (KLAK)
I DON'T THINK I NEED TO TELL YOU THIS EVERY TIME, BUT ...
...PLEASE STAY OUT OF TROUBLE, WILL YOU?
YES, MA'AM...

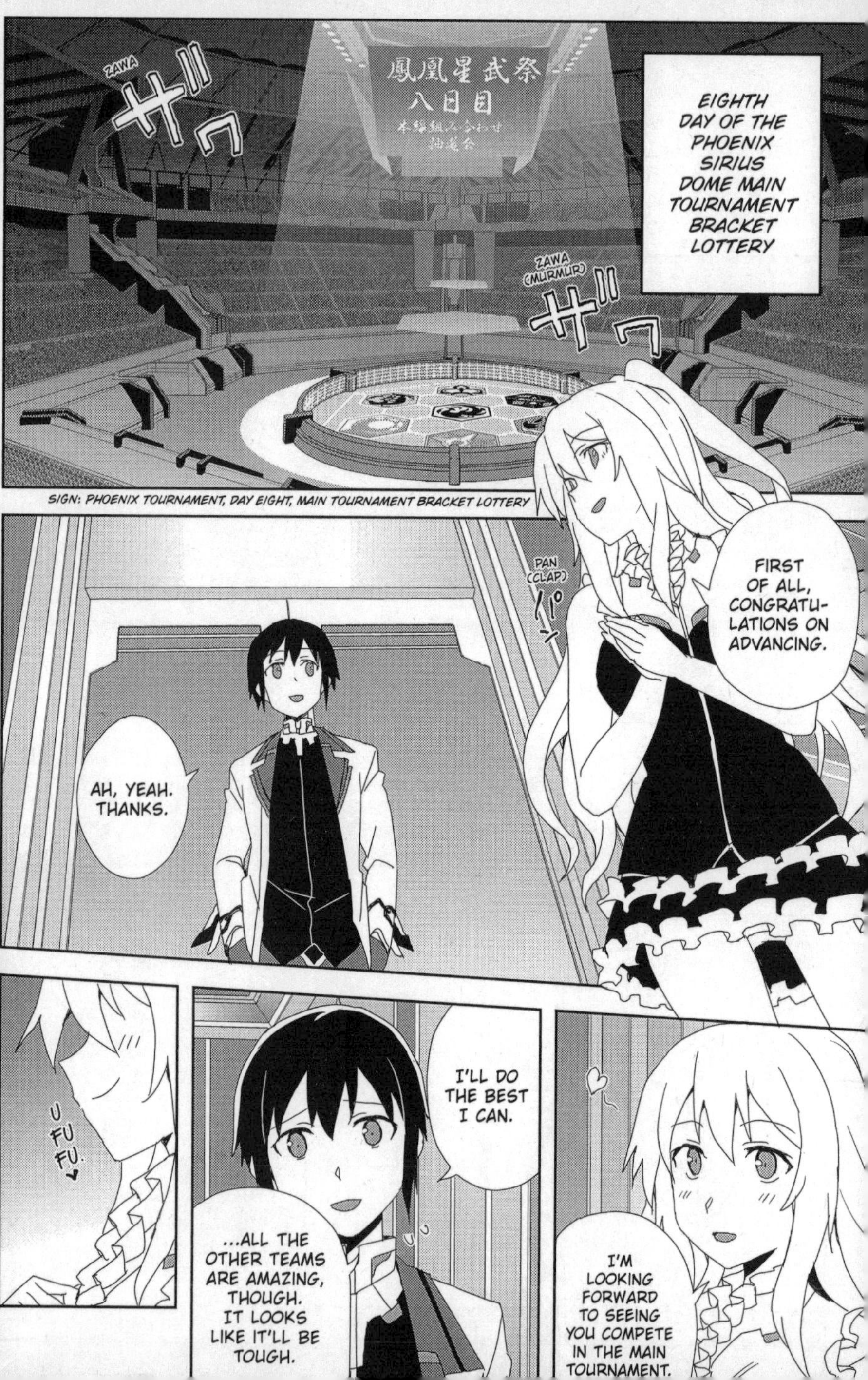
EIGHTH DAY OF THE PHOENIX SIRIUS DOME MAIN TOURNAMENT BRACKET LOTTERY
ZAWA (MURMUR)
鳳凰星武祭
八日目
ZAWA
SIGN: PHOENIX TOURNAMENT, DAY EIGHT, MAIN TOURNAMENT BRACKET LOTTERY
FIRST OF ALL, CONGRATULATIONS ON ADVANCING.
PAN (CLAP)
AH, YEAH. THANKS.
I'M LOOKING FORWARD TO SEEING YOU COMPETE IN THE MAIN TOURNAMENT.
I'LL DO THE BEST I CAN.
...ALL THE OTHER TEAMS ARE AMAZING, THOUGH. IT LOOKS LIKE IT'LL BE TOUGH.
U FU FU.

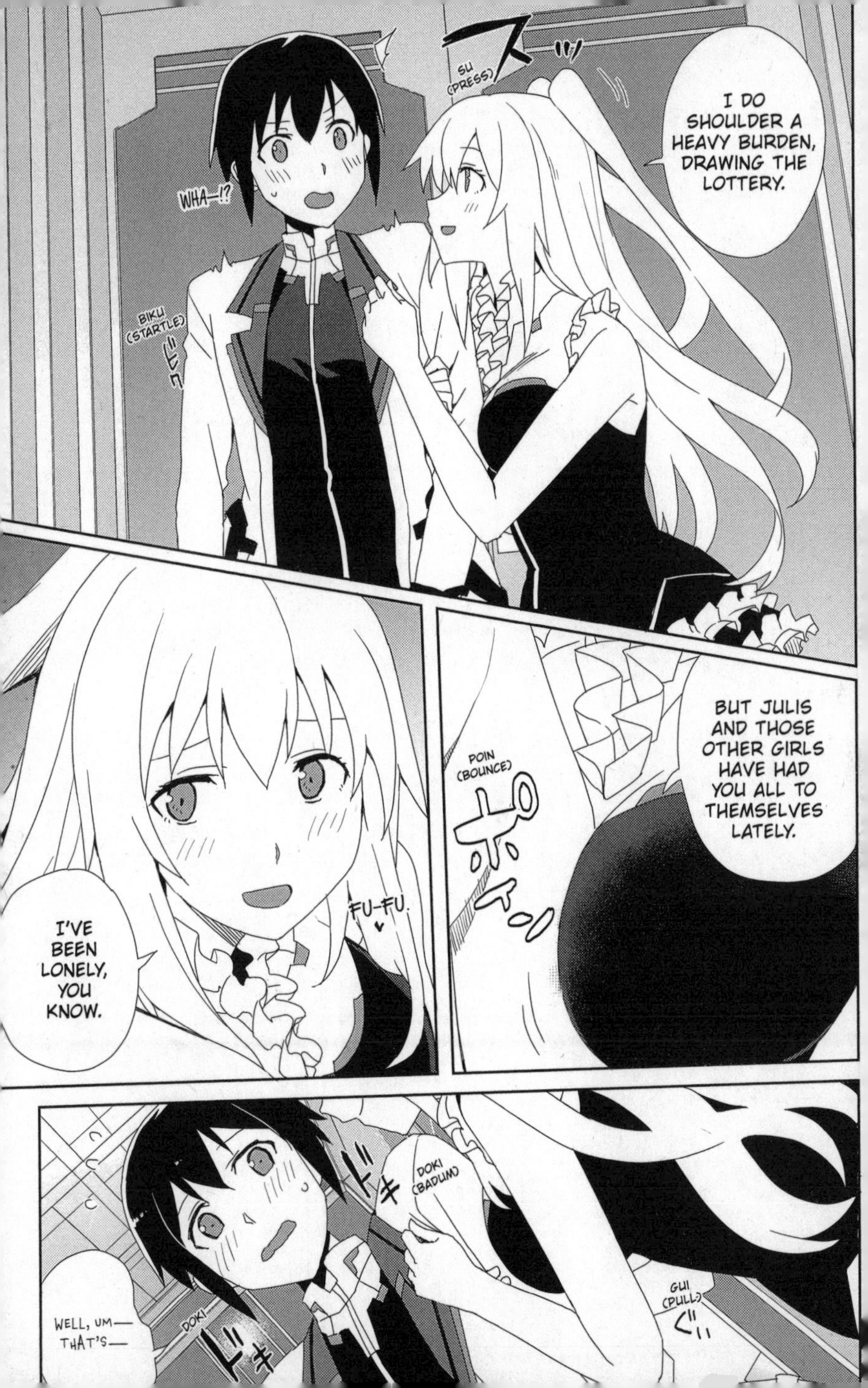
SU (PRESS)
I DO SHOULDER A HEAVY BURDEN, DRAWING THE LOTTERY.
WHA—!?
BIKU (STARTLE)
POIN (BOUNCE)
BUT JULIS AND THOSE OTHER GIRLS HAVE HAD YOU ALL TO THEMSELVES LATELY.
FU-FU.
I'VE BEEN LONELY, YOU KNOW.
GUI (PULL)
DOKI (BADUM)
DOKI
WELL, UM— THAT'S—

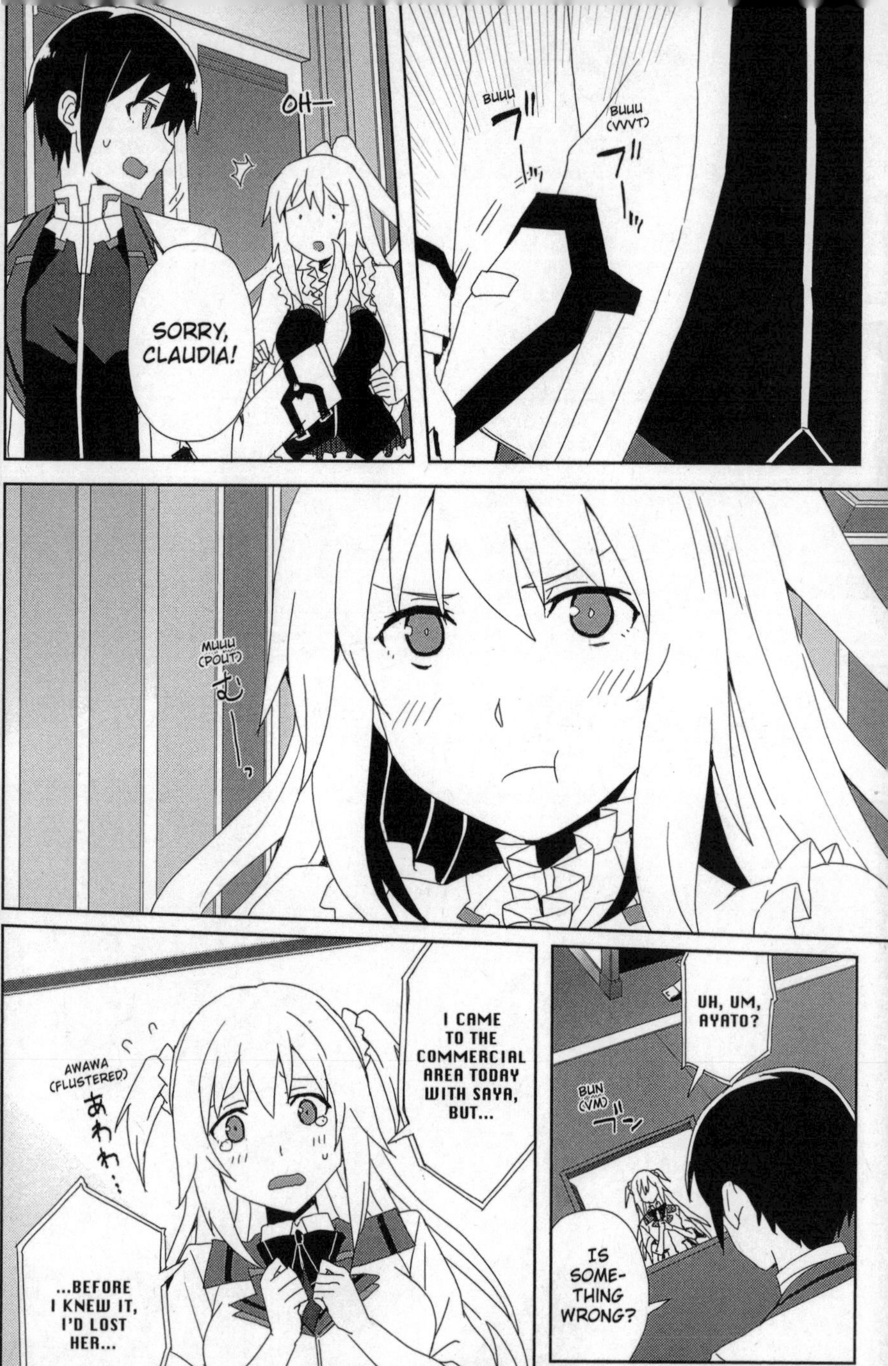
BUUU
ブーッ
BUUU (VVVT)
ブーッ
OH—
SORRY, CLAUDIA!
MUUU (POUT)
むー…っ
UH, UM, AYATO?
BUN (VM)
ブン
IS SOME-THING WRONG?
AWAWA (FLUSTERED)
あわわ…
I CAME TO THE COMMERCIAL AREA TODAY WITH SAYA, BUT…
…BEFORE I KNEW IT, I'D LOST HER…

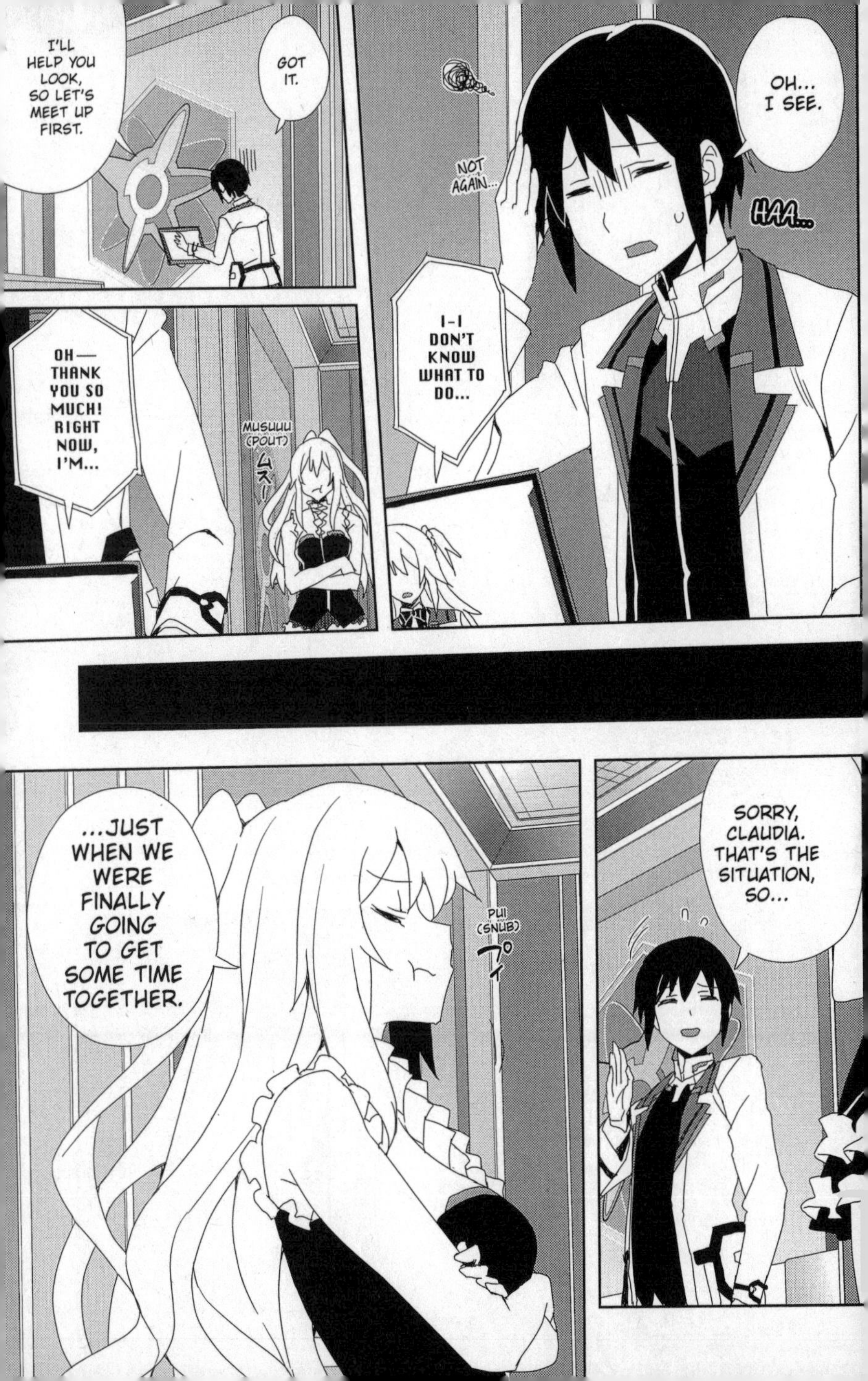
OH... I SEE.
HAA...
NOT AGAIN...
I-I DON'T KNOW WHAT TO DO...
I'LL HELP YOU LOOK, SO LET'S MEET UP FIRST.
GOT IT.
OH— THANK YOU SO MUCH! RIGHT NOW, I'M...
MUSUUU (POUT)
ムスー
SORRY, CLAUDIA. THAT'S THE SITUATION, SO...
PUI (SNUB)
プイ
...JUST WHEN WE WERE FINALLY GOING TO GET SOME TIME TOGETHER.

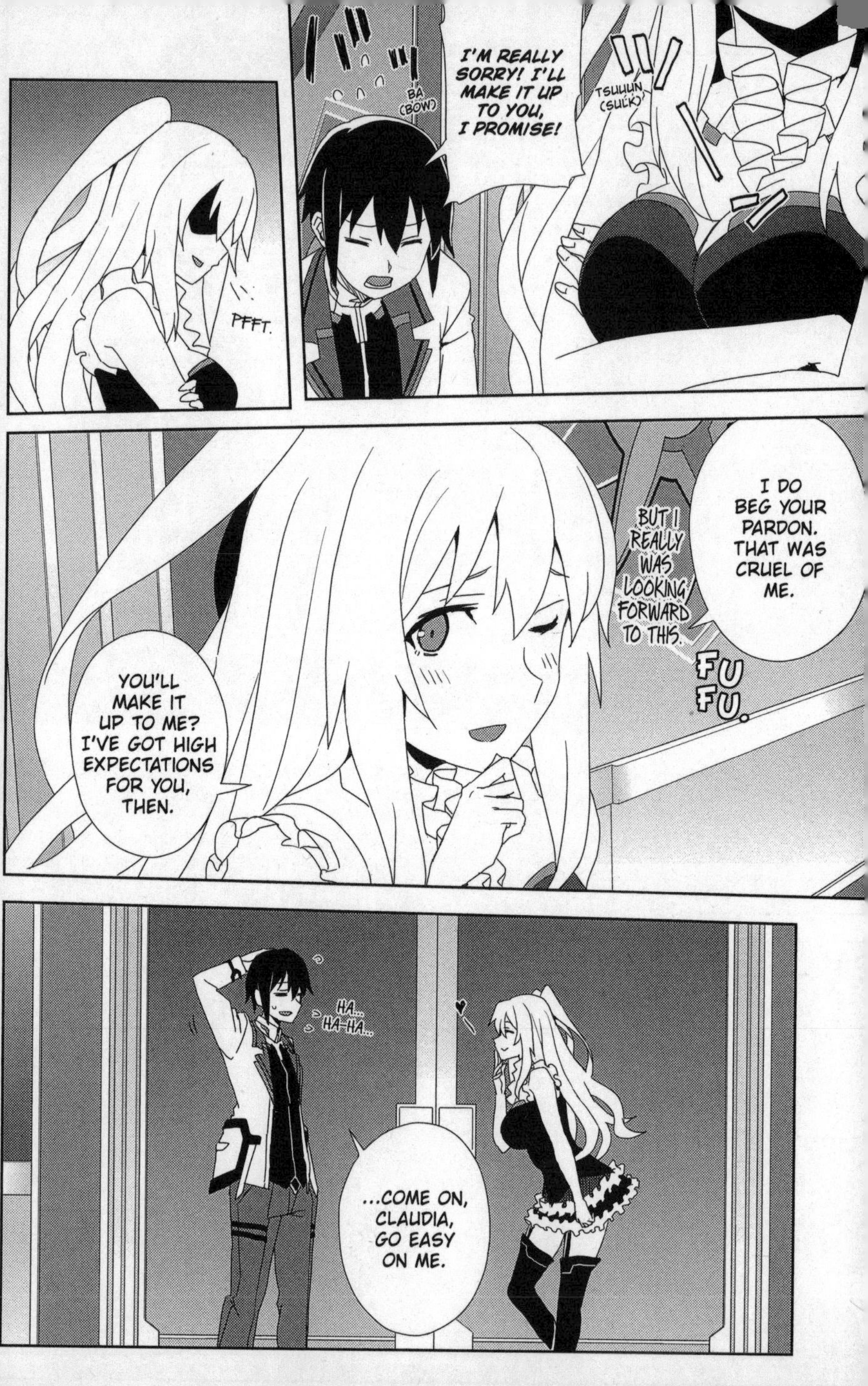
TSUUUN (SULK)
BA (BOW)
I'M REALLY SORRY! I'LL MAKE IT UP TO YOU, I PROMISE!
PFFT.
I DO BEG YOUR PARDON. THAT WAS CRUEL OF ME.
BUT I REALLY WAS LOOKING FORWARD TO THIS.
FU FU.
YOU'LL MAKE IT UP TO ME? I'VE GOT HIGH EXPECTATIONS FOR YOU, THEN.
HA... HA-HA...
...COME ON, CLAUDIA, GO EASY ON ME.

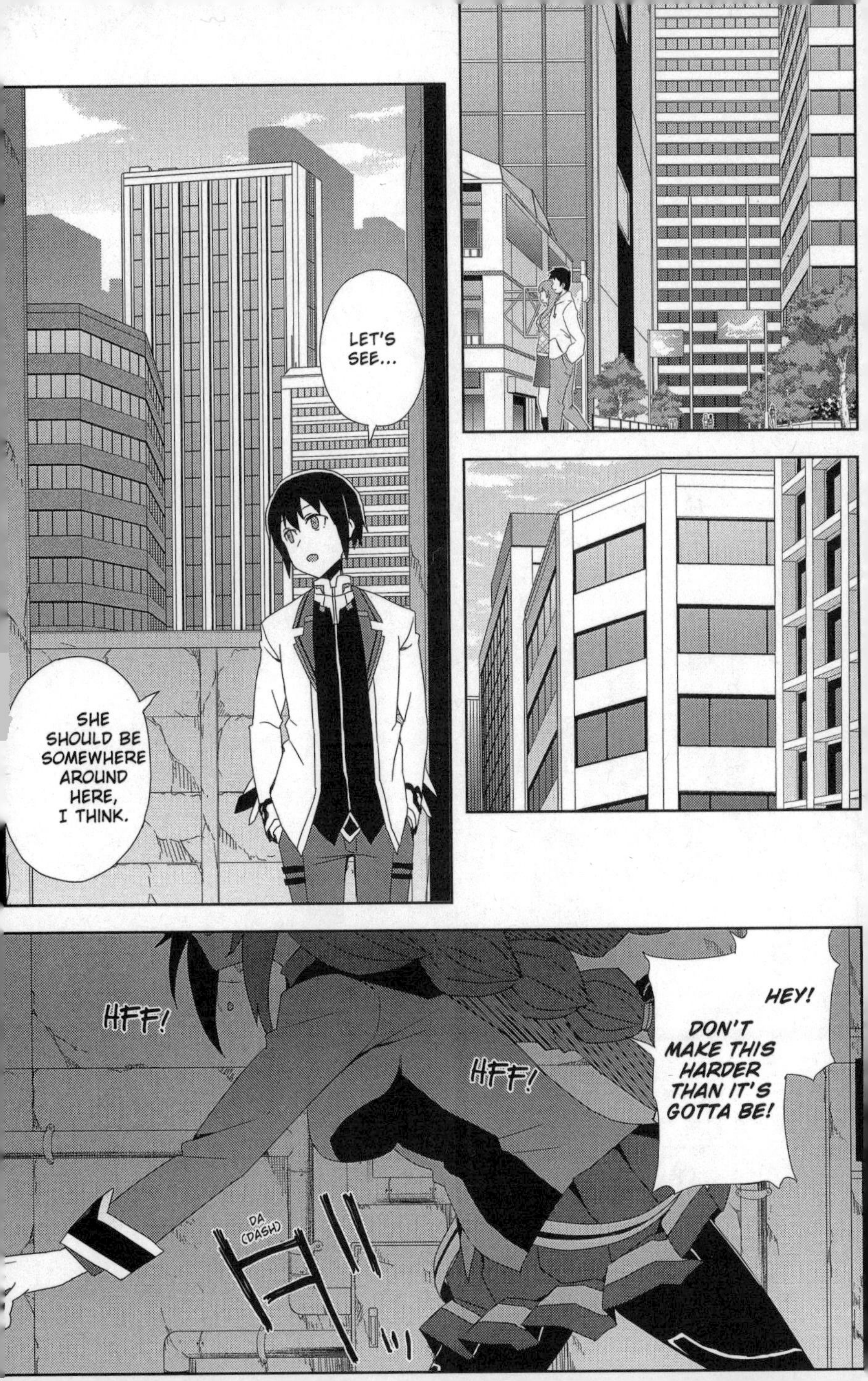
LET'S SEE...
SHE SHOULD BE SOMEWHERE AROUND HERE, I THINK.
HEY! DON'T MAKE THIS HARDER THAN IT'S GOTTA BE!
HFF!
HFF!
DA (DASH)

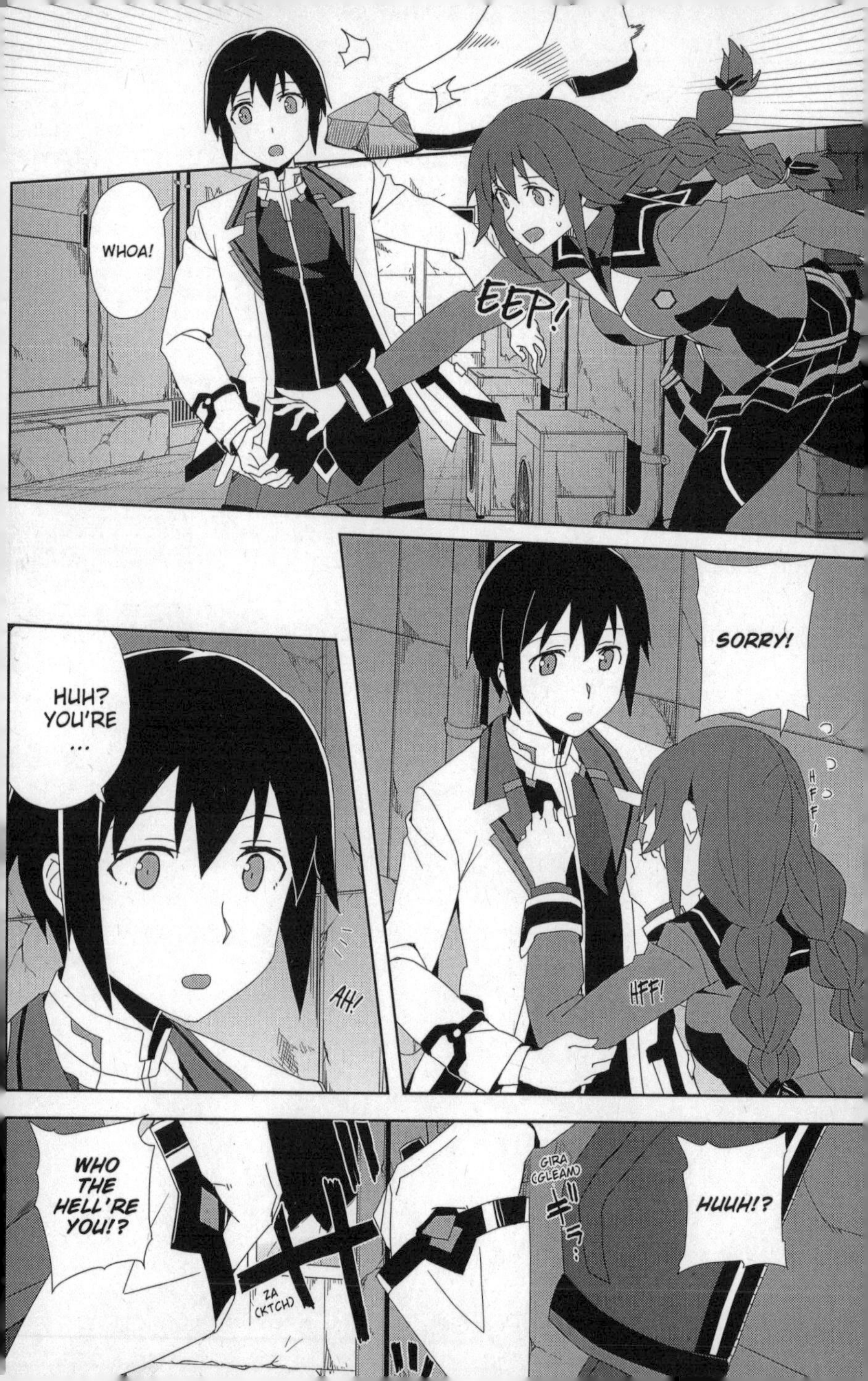
EEP!
WHOA!
SORRY!
HFF!
HFF!
HUH? YOU'RE ...
AH!
HUUH!?
GIRA (GLEAM)
ギラ
WHO THE HELL'RE YOU!?
ZA (KTCH)

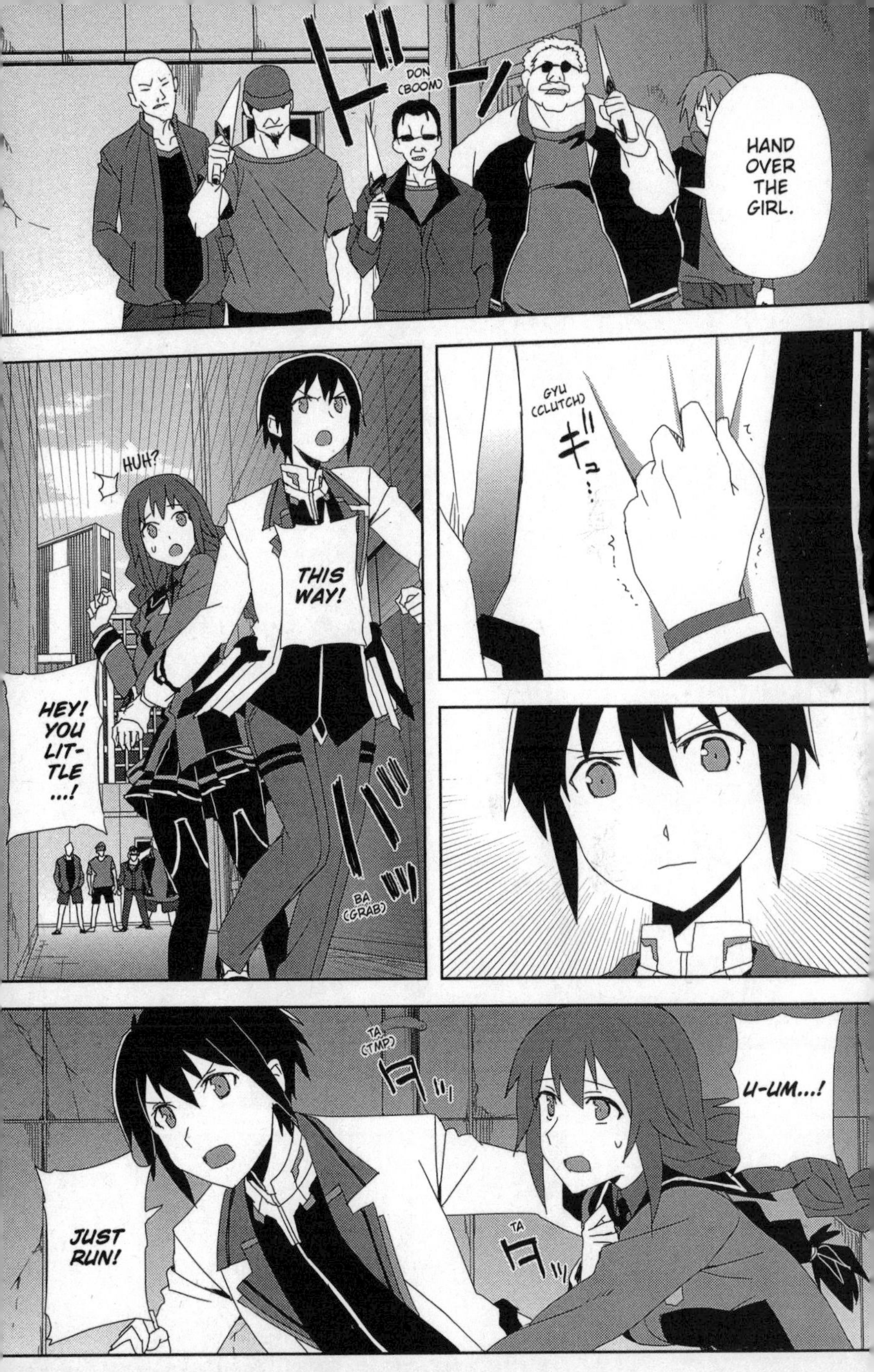
DON (BOOM)
HAND OVER THE GIRL.
GYU (CLUTCH)
HUH?
THIS WAY!
HEY! YOU LIT-TLE ...!
BA (GRAB)
U-UM...!
TA (TMP)
TA
JUST RUN!

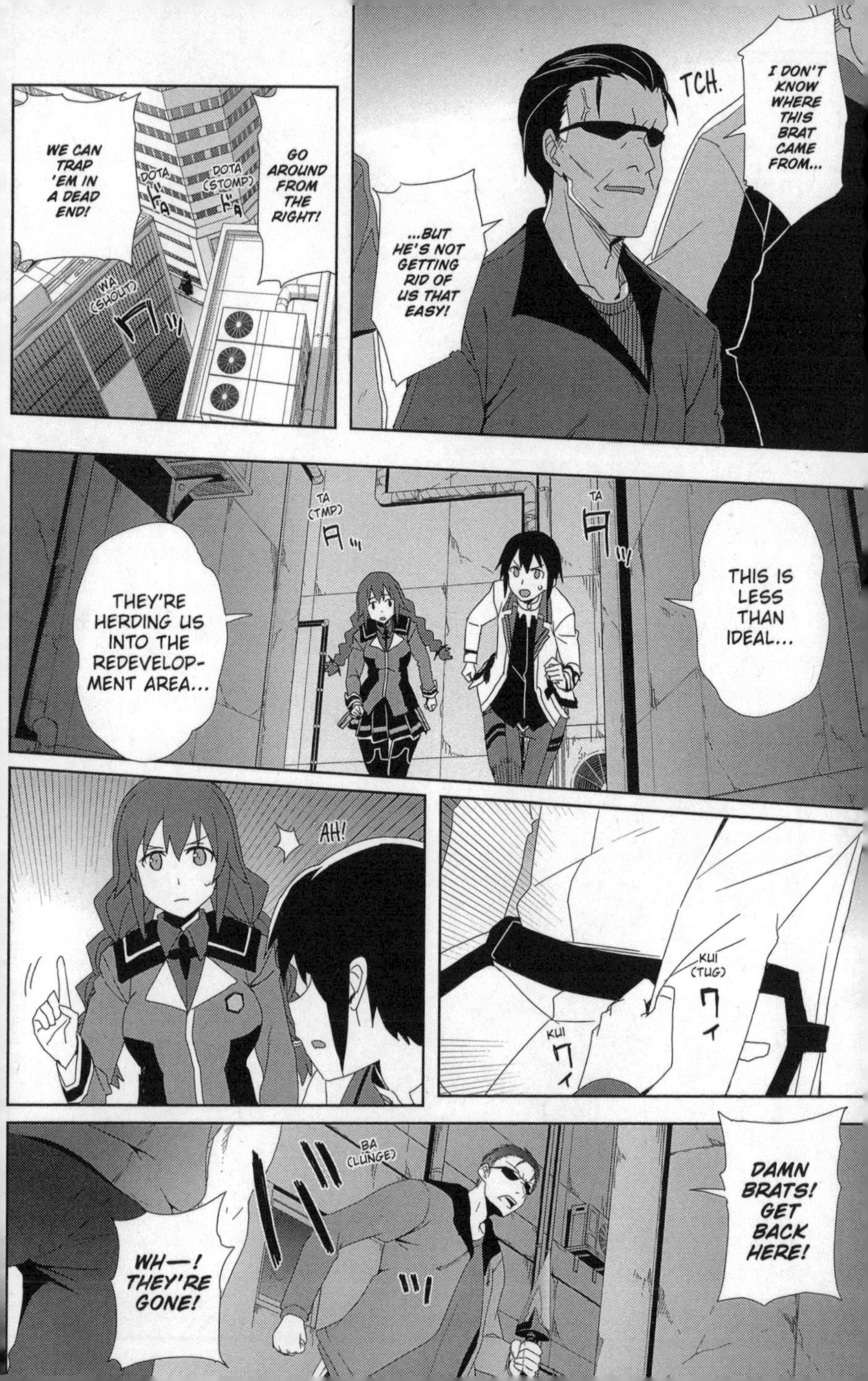
TCH.
I DON'T KNOW WHERE THIS BRAT CAME FROM...
...BUT HE'S NOT GETTING RID OF US THAT EASY!
GO AROUND FROM THE RIGHT!
DOTA (STOMP)
DOTA
WE CAN TRAP 'EM IN A DEAD END!
WA (SHOUT)
THIS IS LESS THAN IDEAL...
TA
TA (TMP)
THEY'RE HERDING US INTO THE REDEVELOPMENT AREA...
KUI (TUG)
KUI
AH!
DAMN BRATS! GET BACK HERE!
BA (LUNGE)
WH—! THEY'RE GONE!

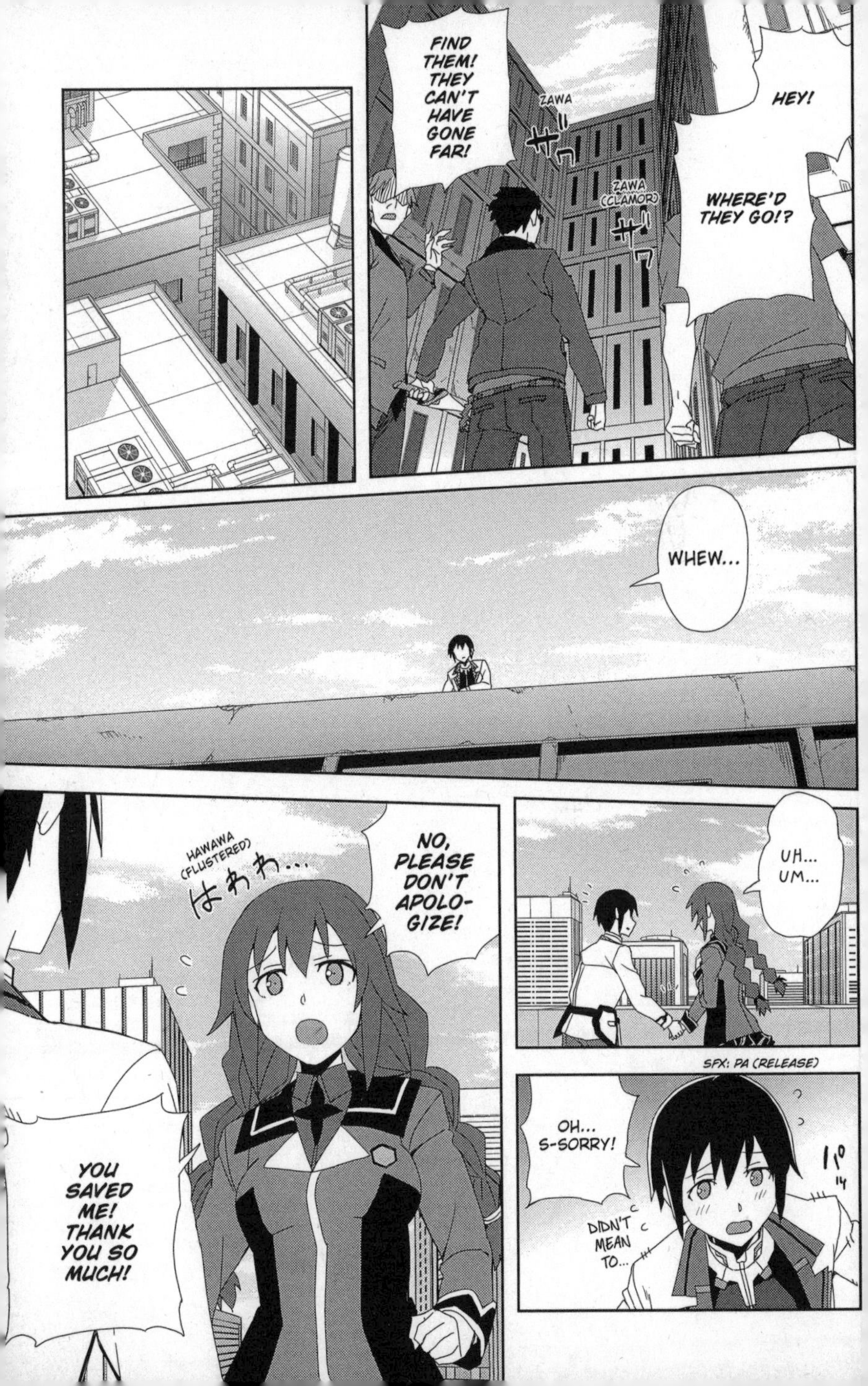
HEY!
FIND THEM! THEY CAN'T HAVE GONE FAR!
ZAWA
WHERE'D THEY GO!?
ZAWA (CLAMOR)
WHEW...
UH... UM...
SFX: PA (RELEASE)
OH... S-SORRY!
DIDN'T MEAN TO...
NO, PLEASE DON'T APOLO-GIZE!
HAWAWA (FLUSTERED)
YOU SAVED ME! THANK YOU SO MUCH!

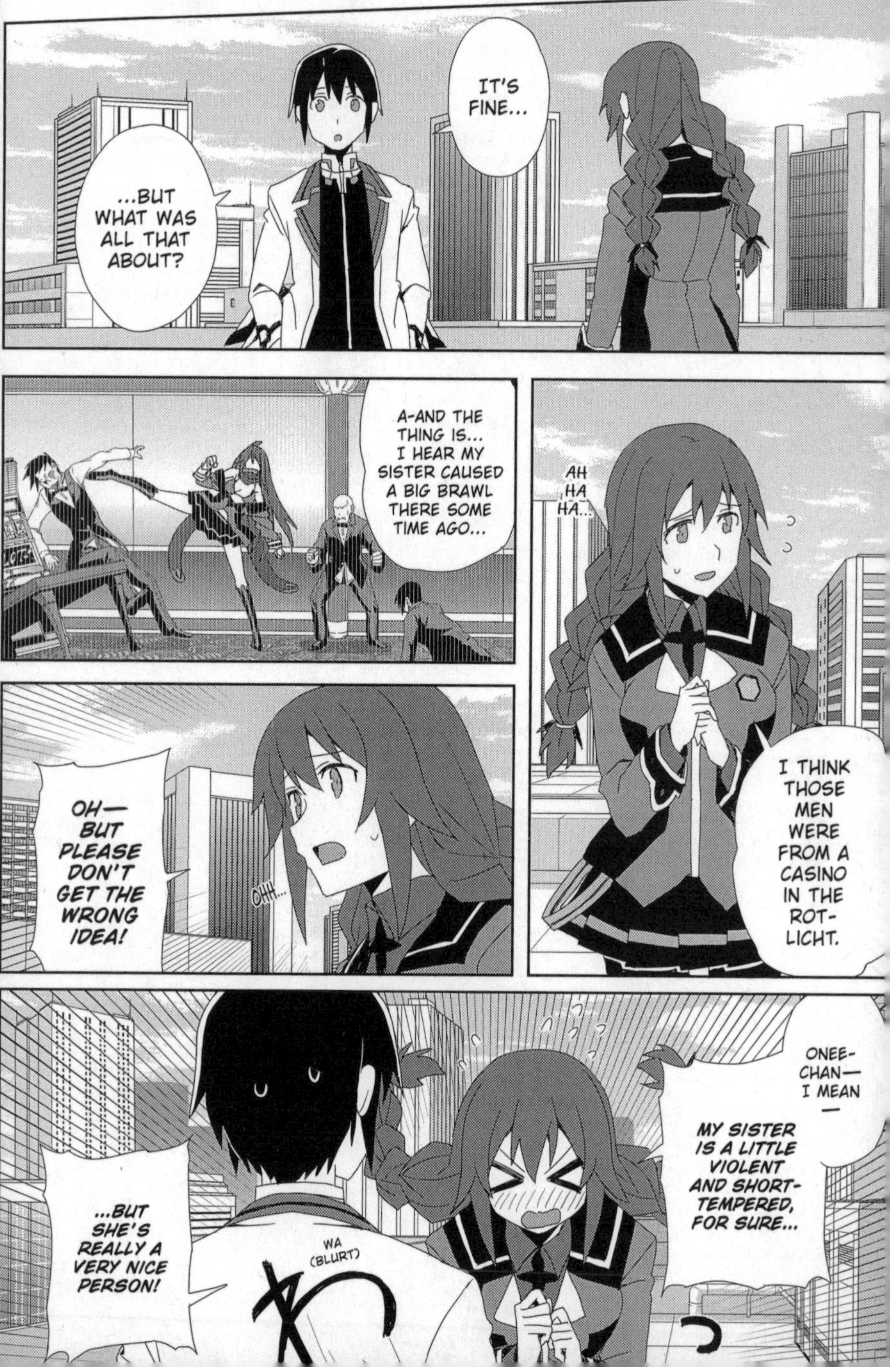
IT'S FINE...
...BUT WHAT WAS ALL THAT ABOUT?
AH HA HA...
I THINK THOSE MEN WERE FROM A CASINO IN THE ROT-LICHT.
A-AND THE THING IS... I HEAR MY SISTER CAUSED A BIG BRAWL THERE SOME TIME AGO...
OH— BUT PLEASE DON'T GET THE WRONG IDEA!
OHHH...
ONEE-CHAN— I MEAN —
MY SISTER IS A LITTLE VIOLENT AND SHORT-TEMPERED, FOR SURE...
WA (BLURT)
...BUT SHE'S REALLY A VERY NICE PERSON!

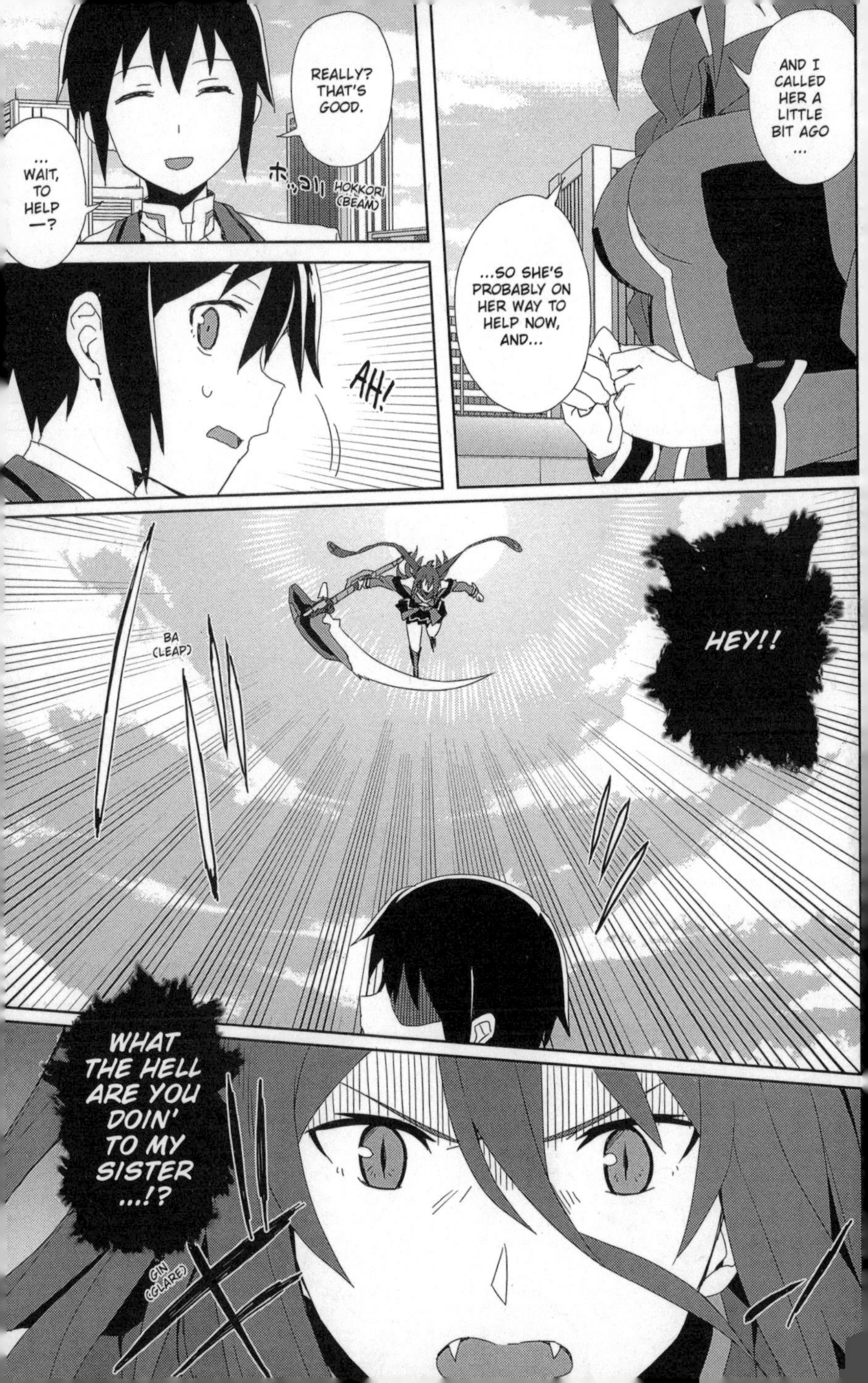

AND I CALLED HER A LITTLE BIT AGO...
...SO SHE'S PROBABLY ON HER WAY TO HELP NOW, AND...
REALLY? THAT'S GOOD.
ホッコリ HOKKORI (BEAM)
... WAIT, TO HELP—?
AH!
HEY!!
BA (LEAP)
WHAT THE HELL ARE YOU DOIN' TO MY SISTER ...!?
GIN (GLARE)

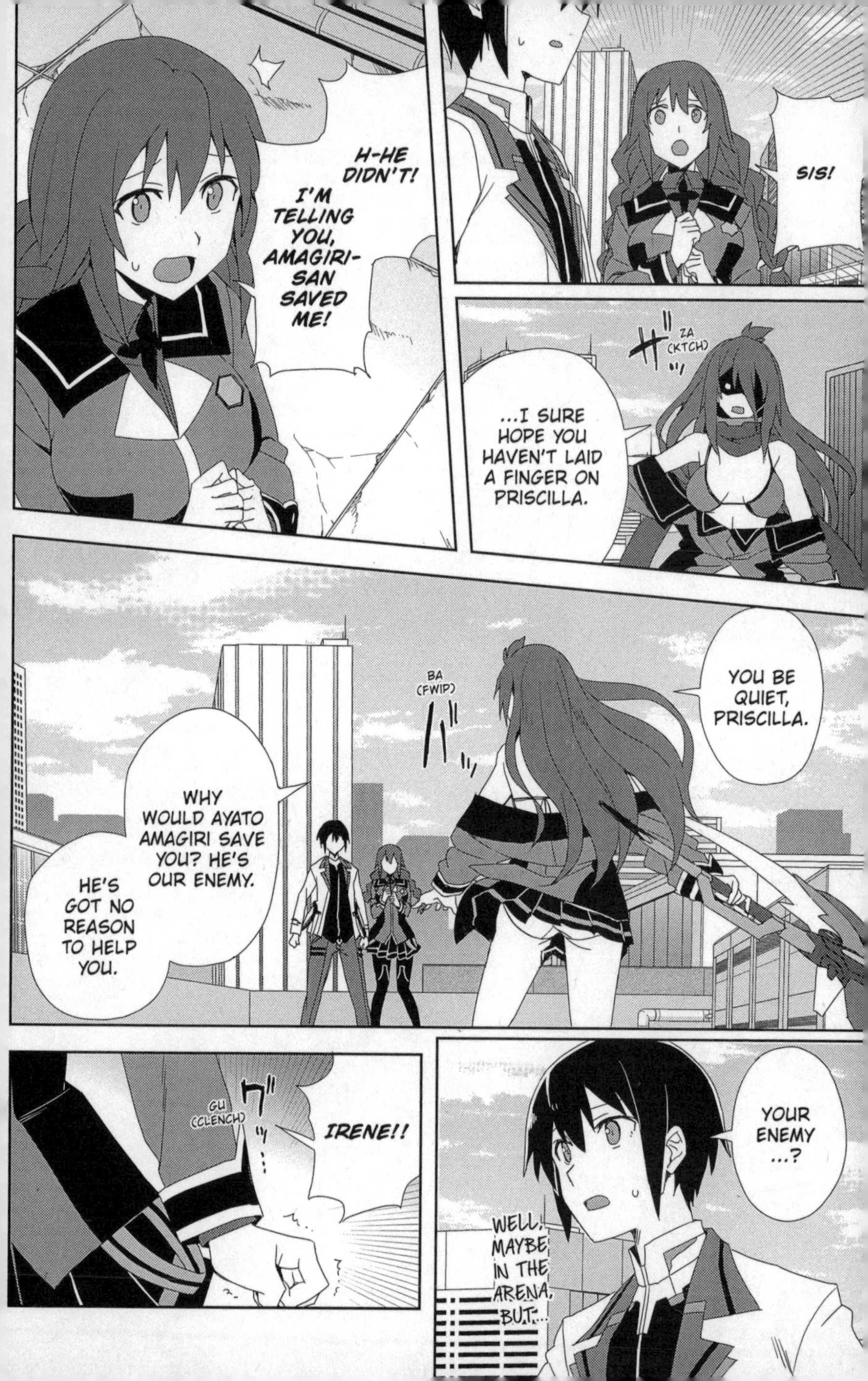
SIS!
ZA (KTCH)
...I SURE HOPE YOU HAVEN'T LAID A FINGER ON PRISCILLA.
H-HE DIDN'T! I'M TELLING YOU, AMAGIRI-SAN SAVED ME!
YOU BE QUIET, PRISCILLA.
BA (FWIP)
WHY WOULD AYATO AMAGIRI SAVE YOU? HE'S OUR ENEMY.
HE'S GOT NO REASON TO HELP YOU.
YOUR ENEMY ...?
WELL, MAYBE IN THE ARENA, BUT...
GU (CLENCH)
IRENE!!

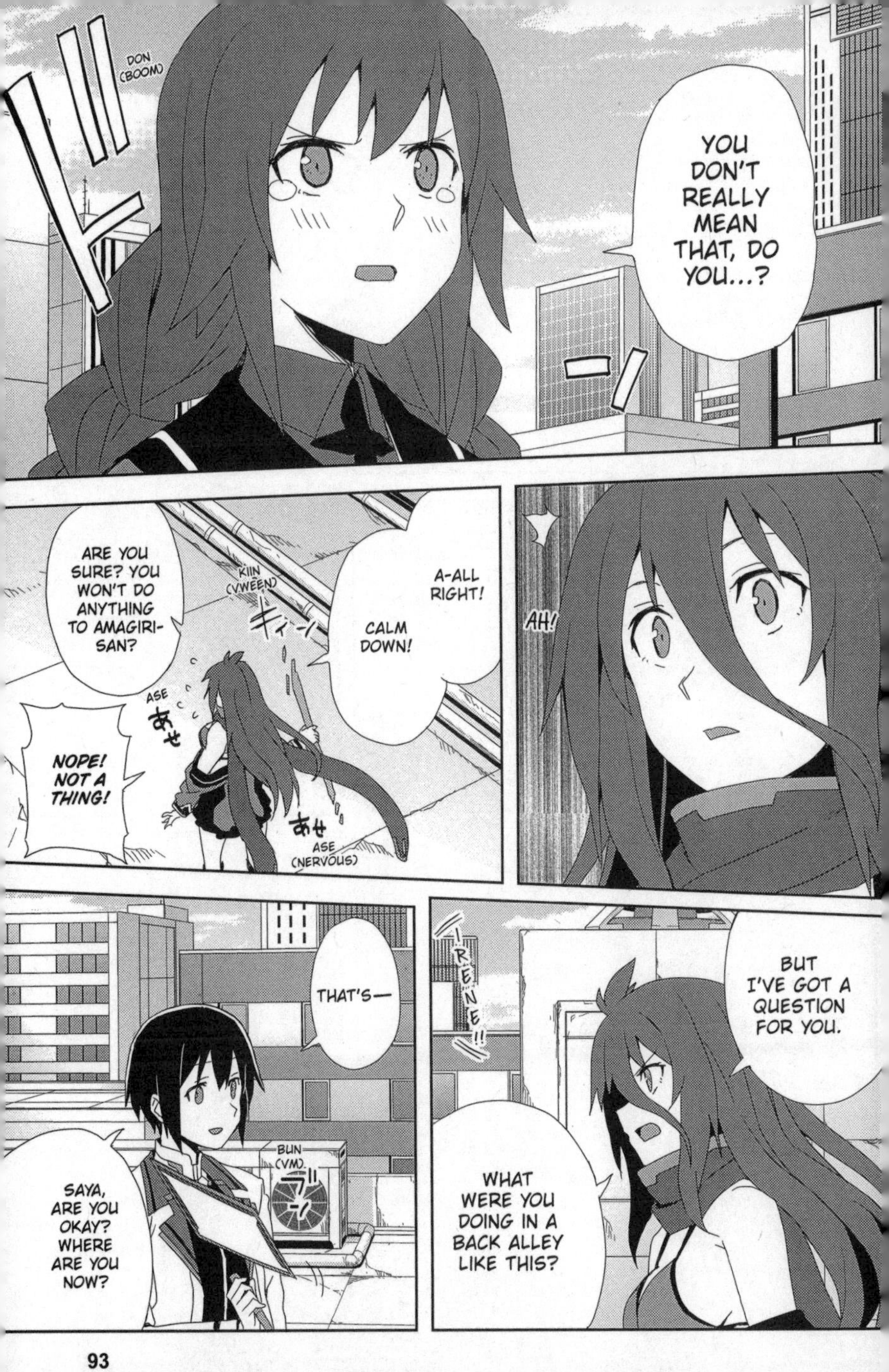
DON (BOOM)
YOU DON'T REALLY MEAN THAT, DO YOU...?
AH!
A-ALL RIGHT! CALM DOWN!
KIIN (VWEEN)
ARE YOU SURE? YOU WON'T DO ANYTHING TO AMAGIRI-SAN?
ASE あせ
NOPE! NOT A THING!
あせ ASE (NERVOUS)
BUT I'VE GOT A QUESTION FOR YOU.
WHAT WERE YOU DOING IN A BACK ALLEY LIKE THIS?
IRENE!!
THAT'S—
BUN (VM)
SAYA, ARE YOU OKAY? WHERE ARE YOU NOW?

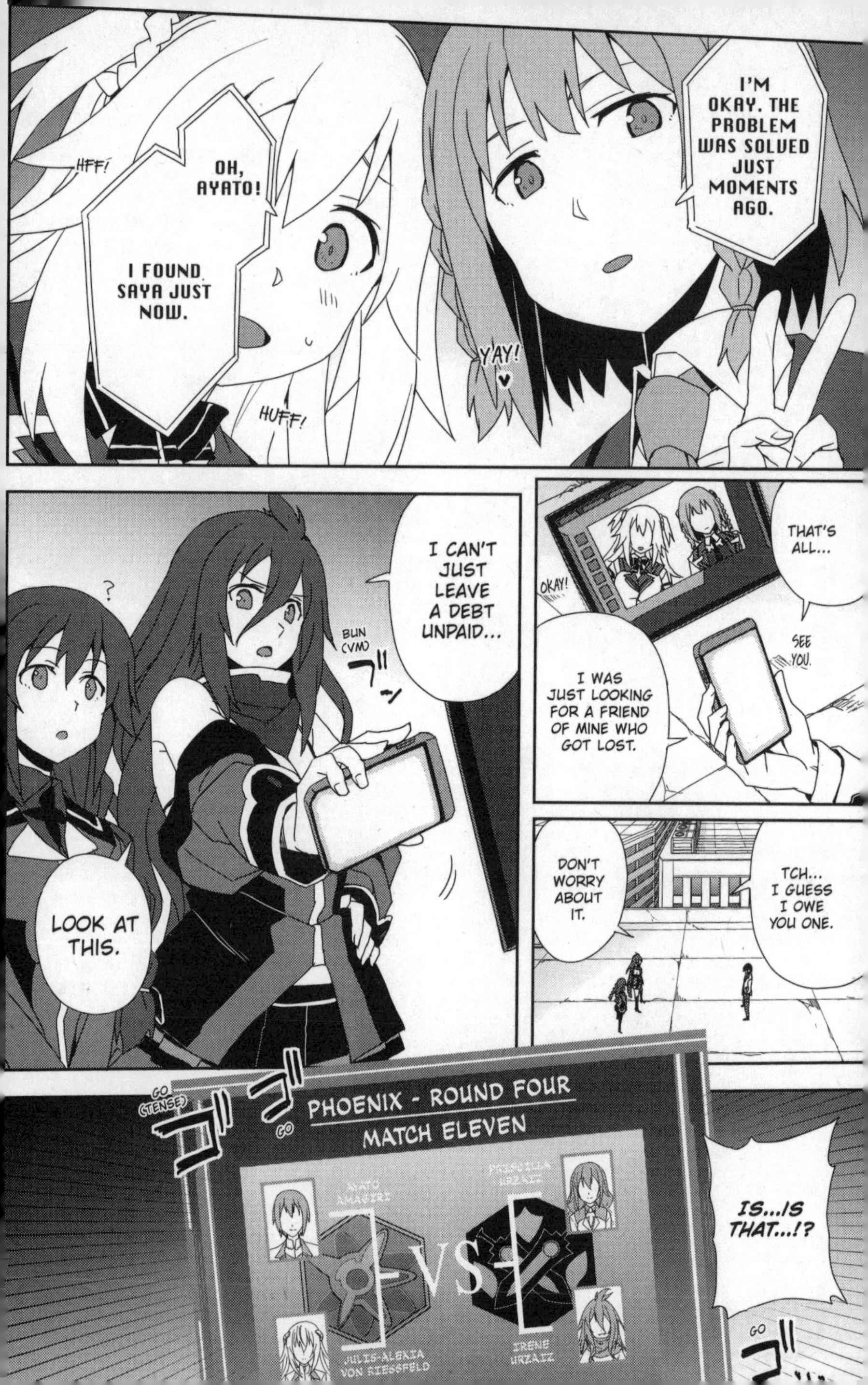
I'M OKAY. THE PROBLEM WAS SOLVED JUST MOMENTS AGO.
YAY! ♥
HFF!
OH, AYATO!
I FOUND SAYA JUST NOW.
HUFF!
THAT'S ALL...
OKAY!
SEE YOU.
I WAS JUST LOOKING FOR A FRIEND OF MINE WHO GOT LOST.
TCH... I GUESS I OWE YOU ONE.
DON'T WORRY ABOUT IT.
I CAN'T JUST LEAVE A DEBT UNPAID...
BUN (VM)
?
LOOK AT THIS.
IS...IS THAT...!?
GO
PHOENIX - ROUND FOUR
MATCH ELEVEN
GO (TENSE)
GO
VS
JULIS-ALEXIA VON RIESSFELD
IRENE URZAIZ

ASTERISK WAR

THE ASTERISK WAR

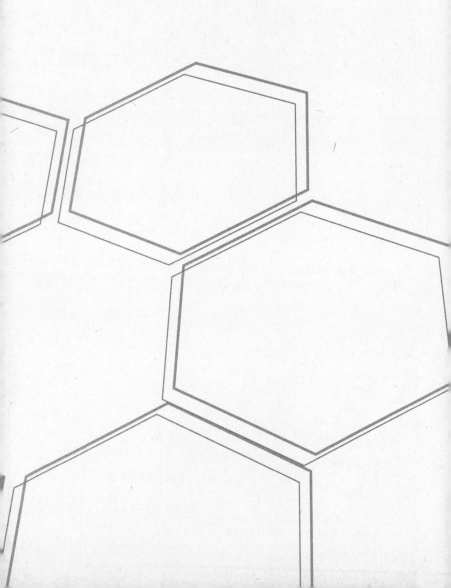

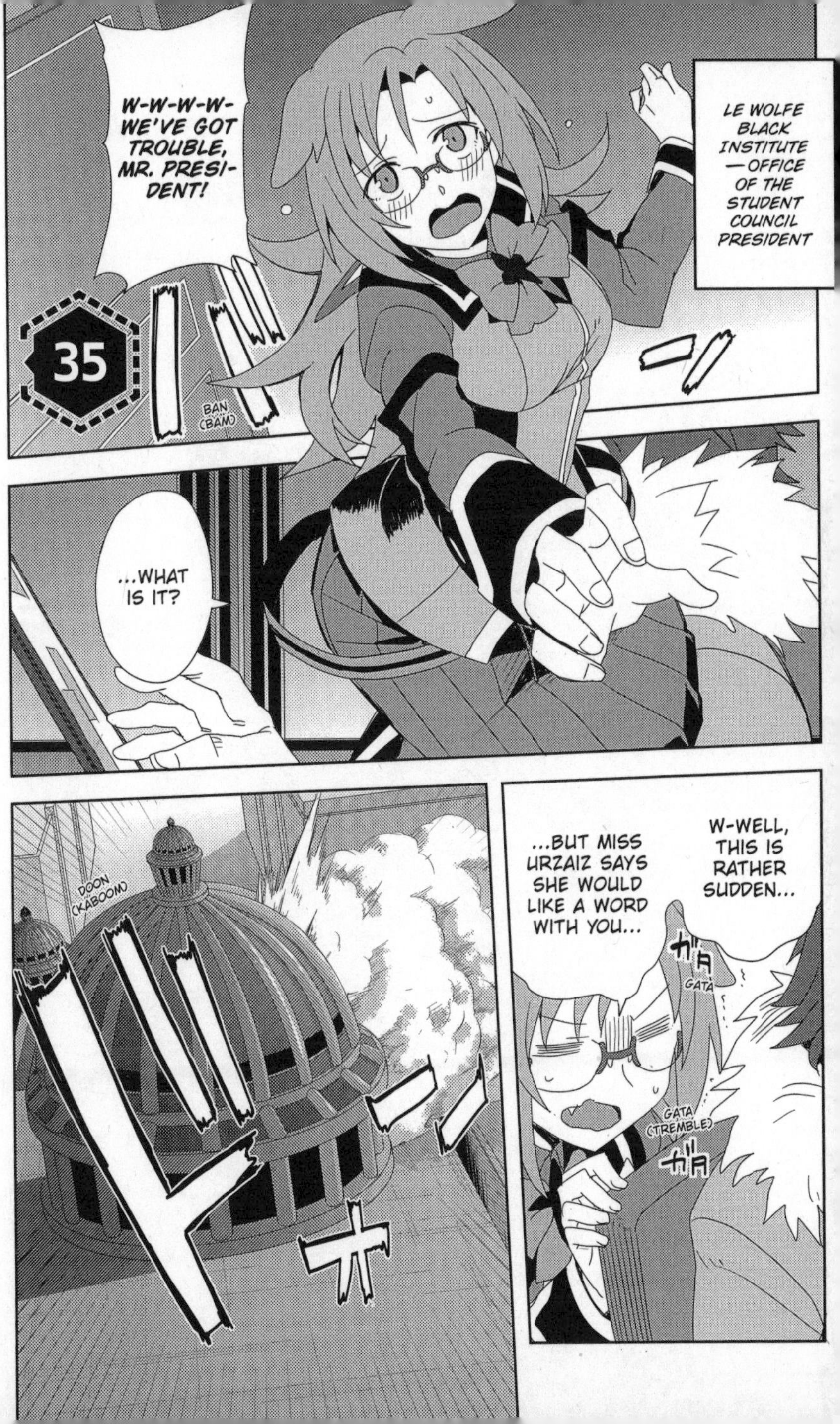

LE WOLFE BLACK INSTITUTE —OFFICE OF THE STUDENT COUNCIL PRESIDENT
W-W-W-W-WE'VE GOT TROUBLE, MR. PRESI-DENT!
35
BAN (BAM)
...WHAT IS IT?
W-WELL, THIS IS RATHER SUDDEN...
...BUT MISS URZAIZ SAYS SHE WOULD LIKE A WORD WITH YOU...
GATA
GATA (TREMBLE)
DOON (KABOOM)

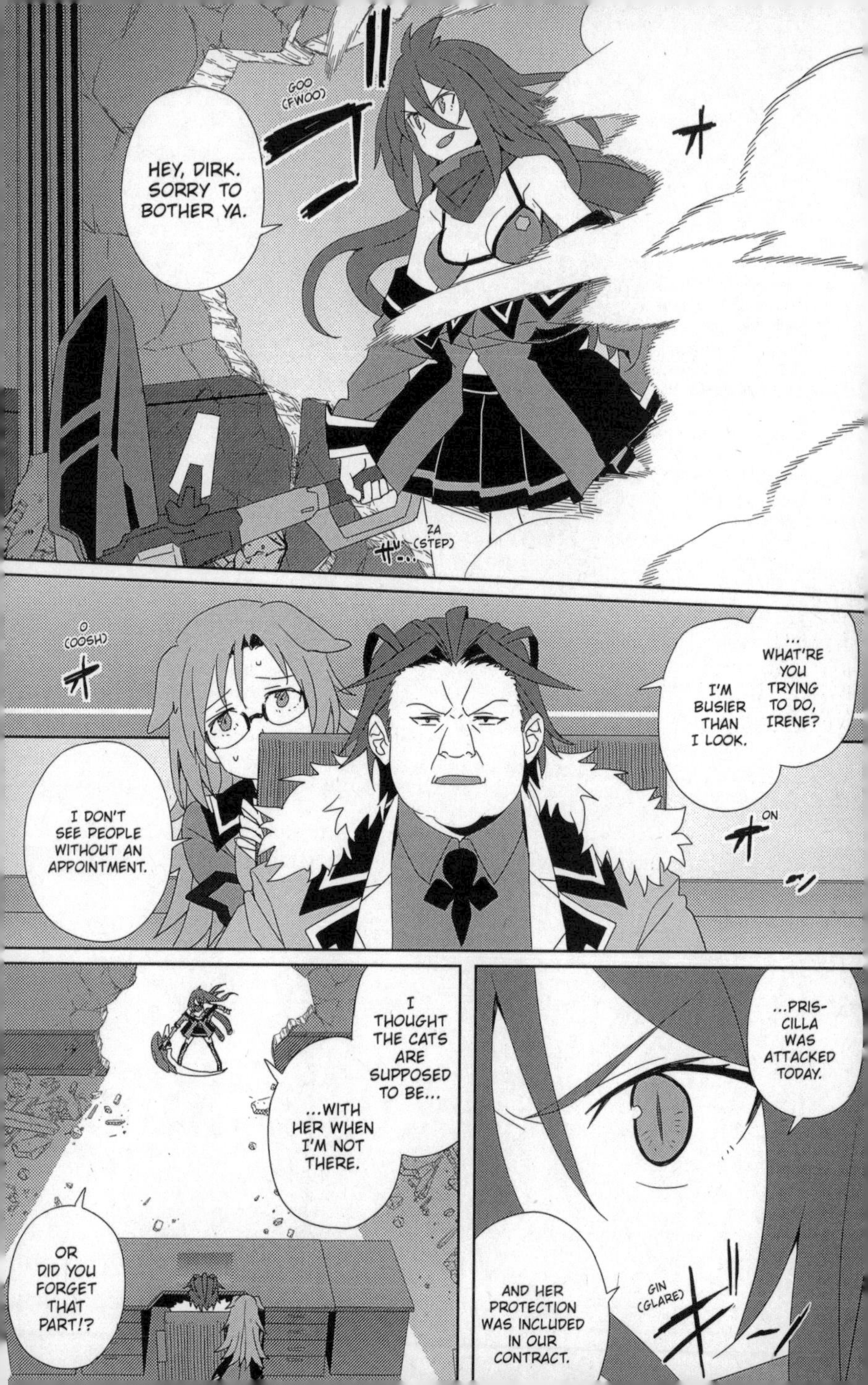
GOO (FWOO)
HEY, DIRK. SORRY TO BOTHER YA.
ZA (STEP)
... WHAT'RE YOU TRYING TO DO, IRENE?
I'M BUSIER THAN I LOOK.
ON
O (OOSH)
I DON'T SEE PEOPLE WITHOUT AN APPOINTMENT.
...PRIS-CILLA WAS ATTACKED TODAY.
GIN (GLARE)
AND HER PROTECTION WAS INCLUDED IN OUR CONTRACT.
I THOUGHT THE CATS ARE SUPPOSED TO BE...
...WITH HER WHEN I'M NOT THERE.
OR DID YOU FORGET THAT PART!?

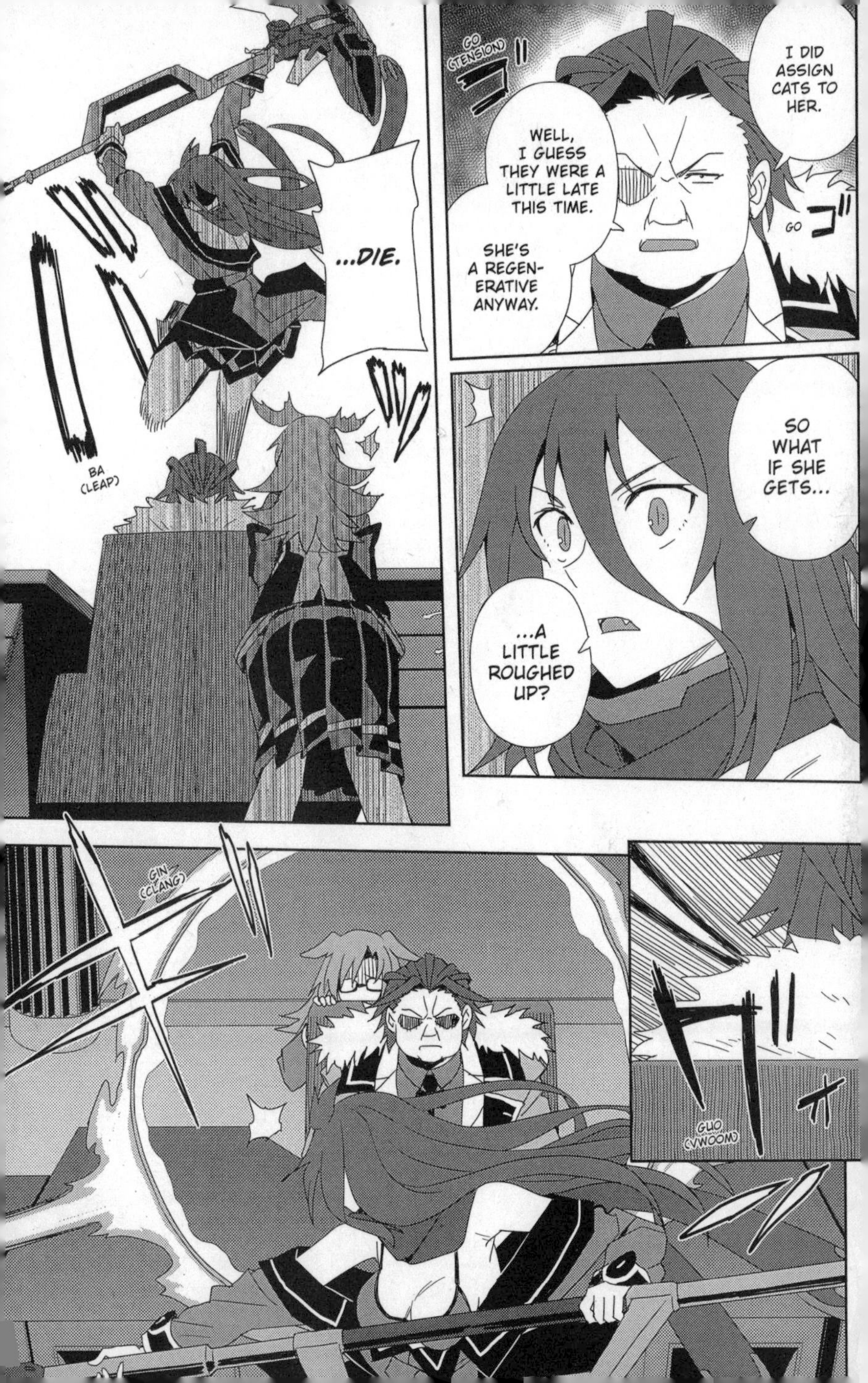
GO (TENSION)
I DID ASSIGN CATS TO HER.
WELL, I GUESS THEY WERE A LITTLE LATE THIS TIME.
GO
SHE'S A REGEN-ERATIVE ANYWAY.
SO WHAT IF SHE GETS...
...A LITTLE ROUGHED UP?
...DIE.
BA (LEAP)
GUO (VWOOM)
GIN (CLANG)

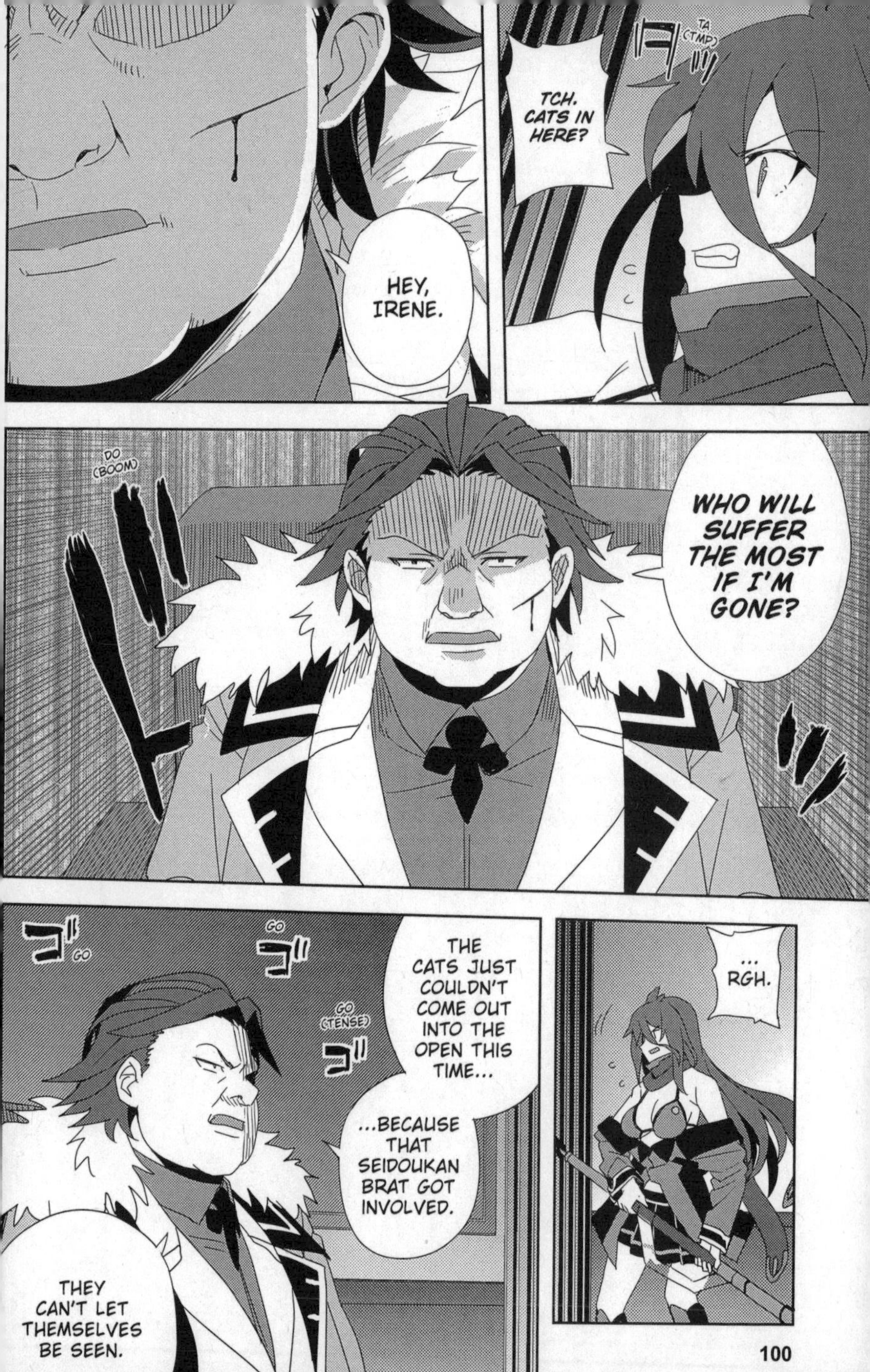
TA (TMP)
TCH. CATS IN HERE?
HEY, IRENE.
DO (BOOM)
WHO WILL SUFFER THE MOST IF I'M GONE?
... RGH.
GO
GO
GO (TENSE)
THE CATS JUST COULDN'T COME OUT INTO THE OPEN THIS TIME...
...BECAUSE THAT SEIDOUKAN BRAT GOT INVOLVED.
THEY CAN'T LET THEMSELVES BE SEEN.

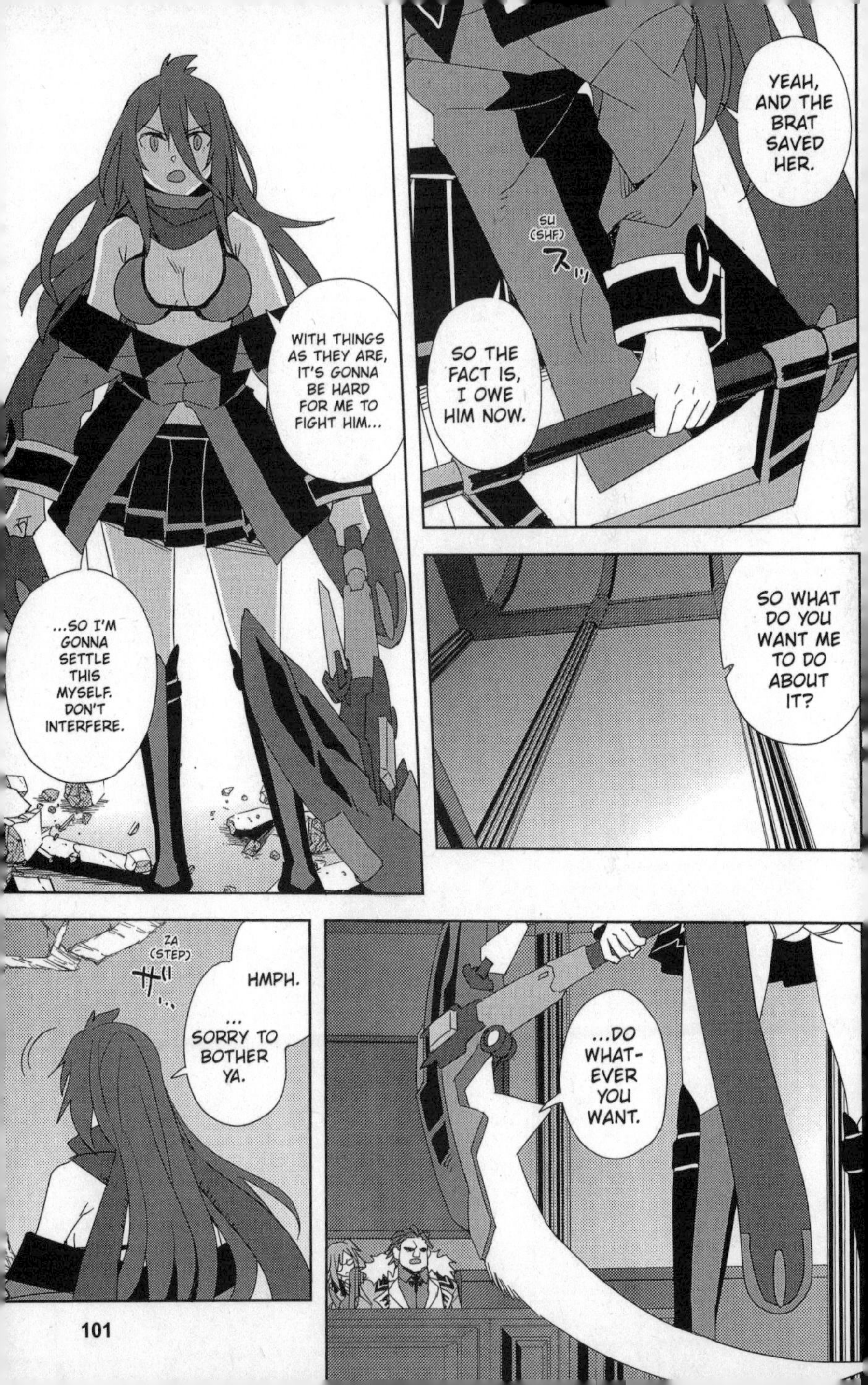
YEAH, AND THE BRAT SAVED HER.
SU (SHF)
SO THE FACT IS, I OWE HIM NOW.
SO WHAT DO YOU WANT ME TO DO ABOUT IT?
WITH THINGS AS THEY ARE, IT'S GONNA BE HARD FOR ME TO FIGHT HIM...
...SO I'M GONNA SETTLE THIS MYSELF. DON'T INTERFERE.
...DO WHAT-EVER YOU WANT.
ZA (STEP)
HMPH.
... SORRY TO BOTHER YA.

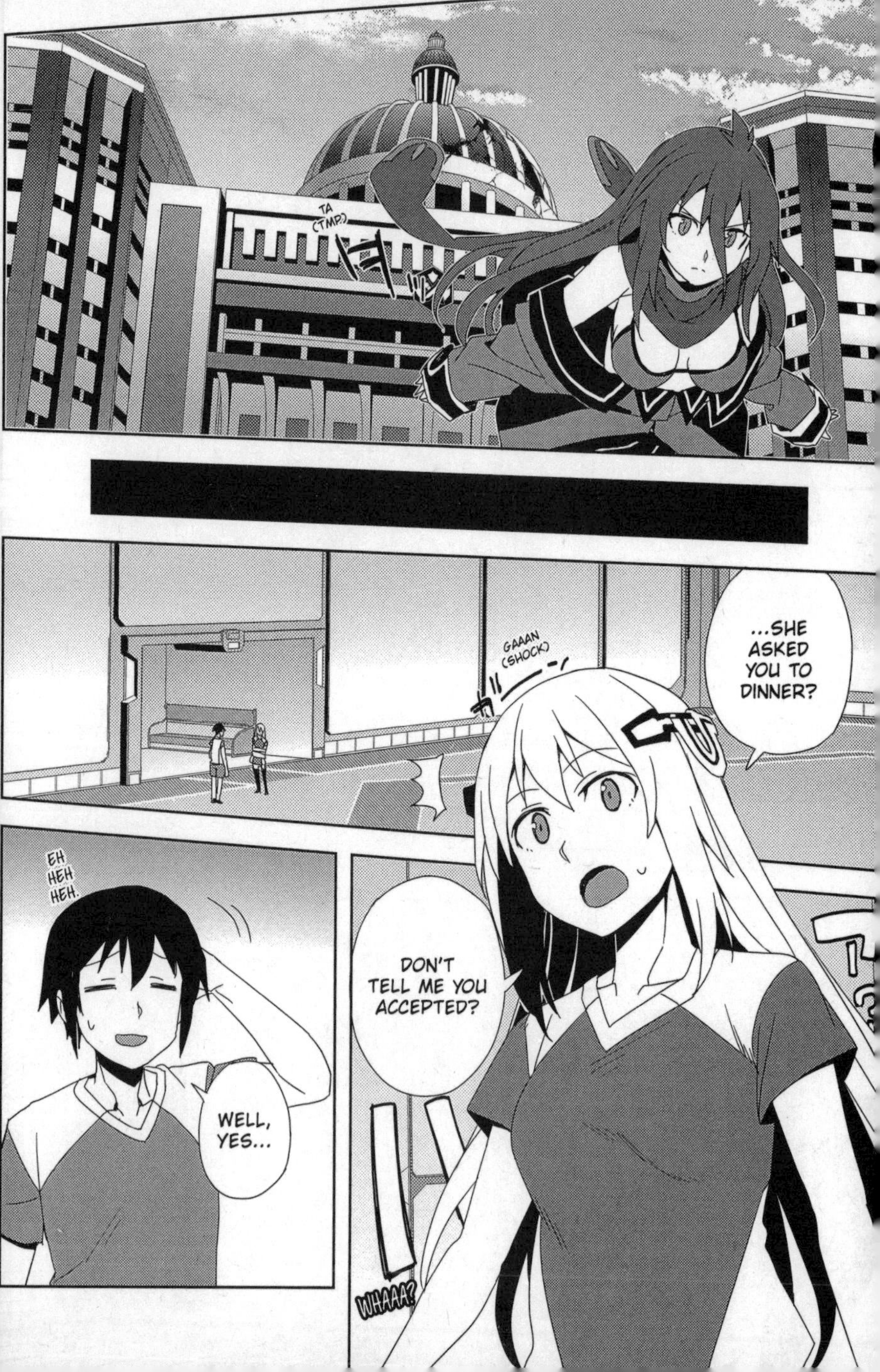
TA (TMP)
GAAAN (SHOCK)
...SHE ASKED YOU TO DINNER?
DON'T TELL ME YOU ACCEPTED?
WHAAA?
EH HEH HEH.
WELL, YES...

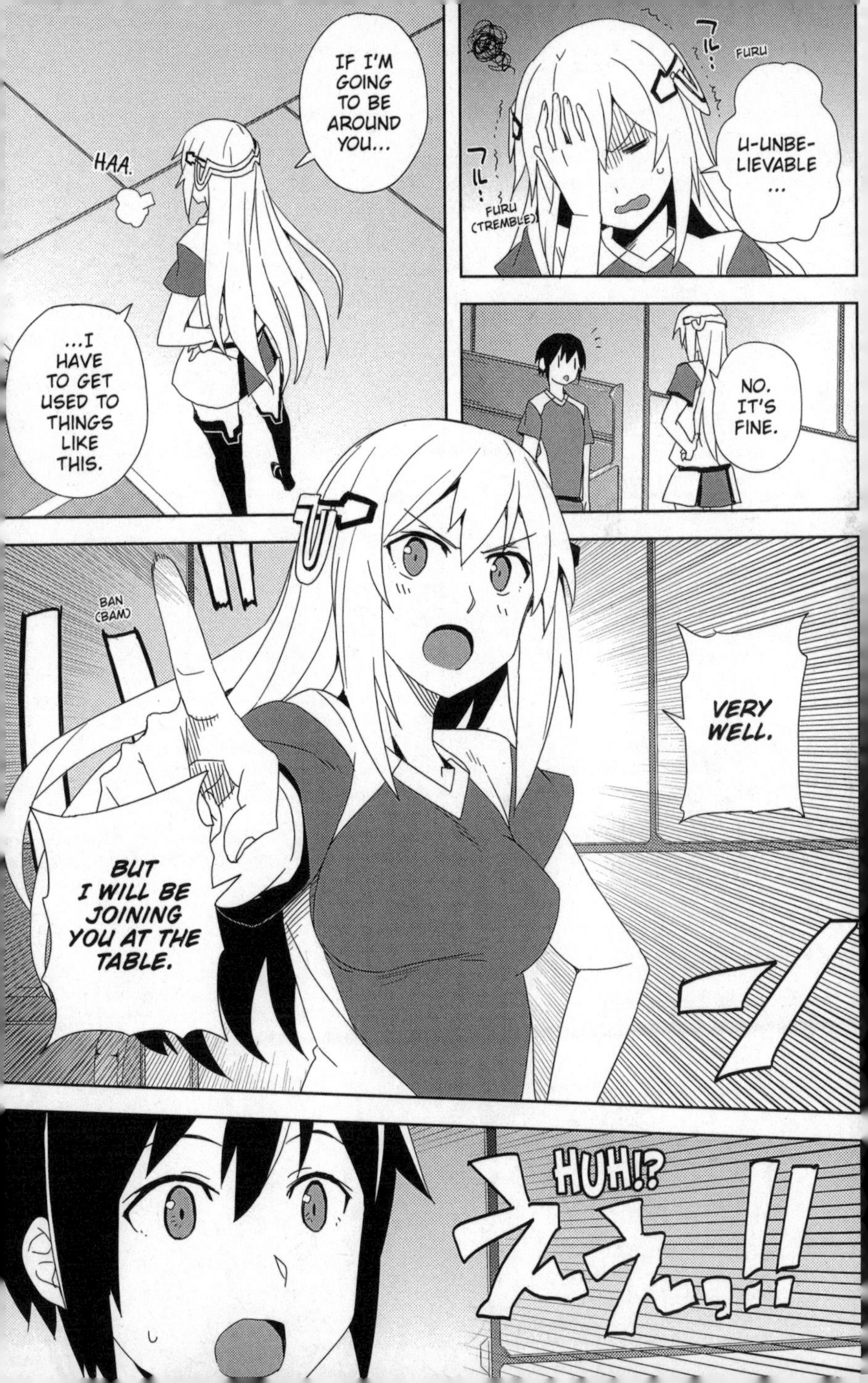
FURU
U-UNBELIEVABLE...
FURU (TREMBLE)
NO. IT'S FINE.
IF I'M GOING TO BE AROUND YOU...
HAA.
...I HAVE TO GET USED TO THINGS LIKE THIS.
VERY WELL.
BAN (BAM)
BUT I WILL BE JOINING YOU AT THE TABLE.
HUH!?

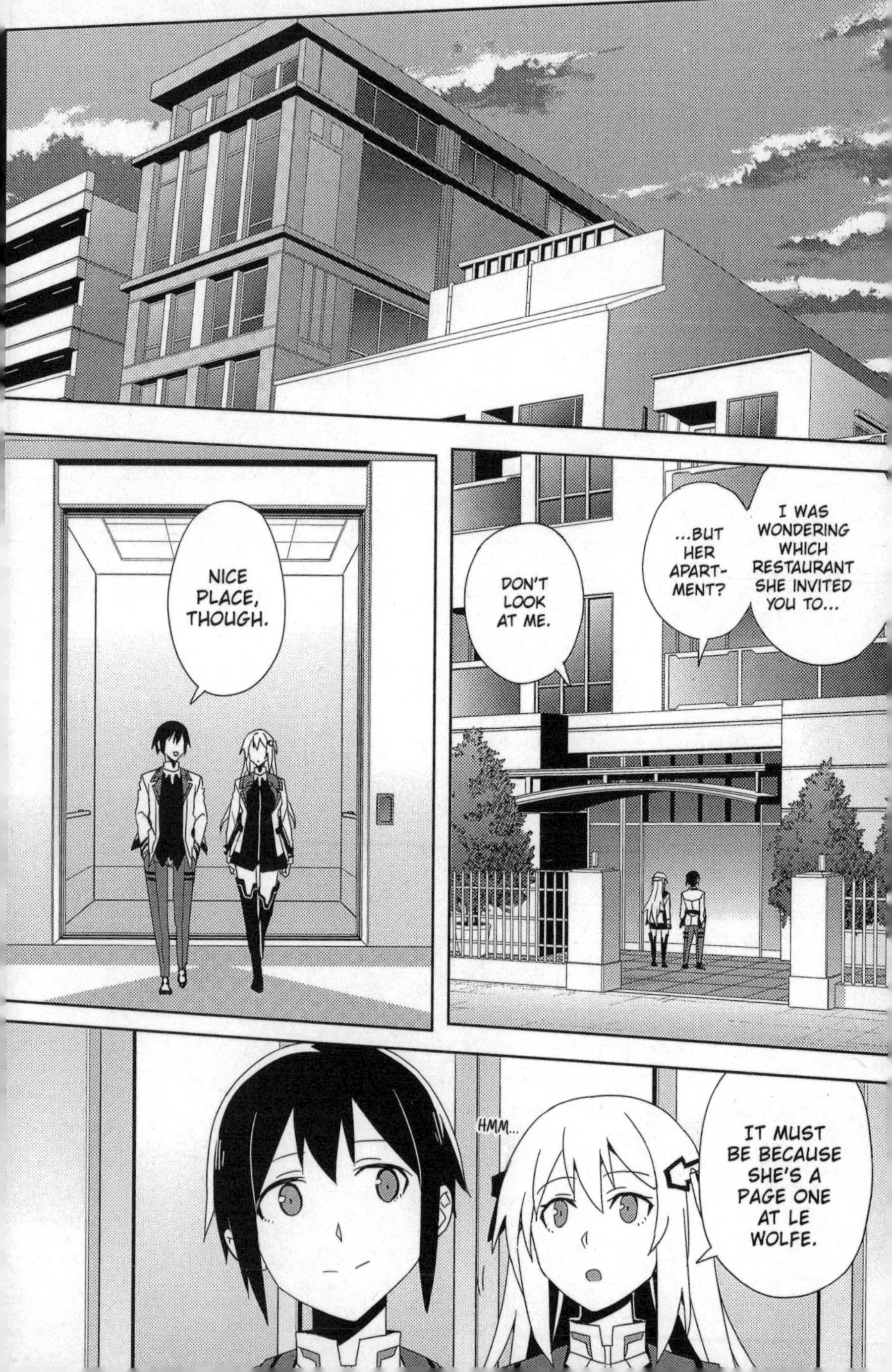
I WAS WONDERING WHICH RESTAURANT SHE INVITED YOU TO...
...BUT HER APARTMENT?
DON'T LOOK AT ME.
NICE PLACE, THOUGH.
IT MUST BE BECAUSE SHE'S A PAGE ONE AT LE WOLFE.
HMM...

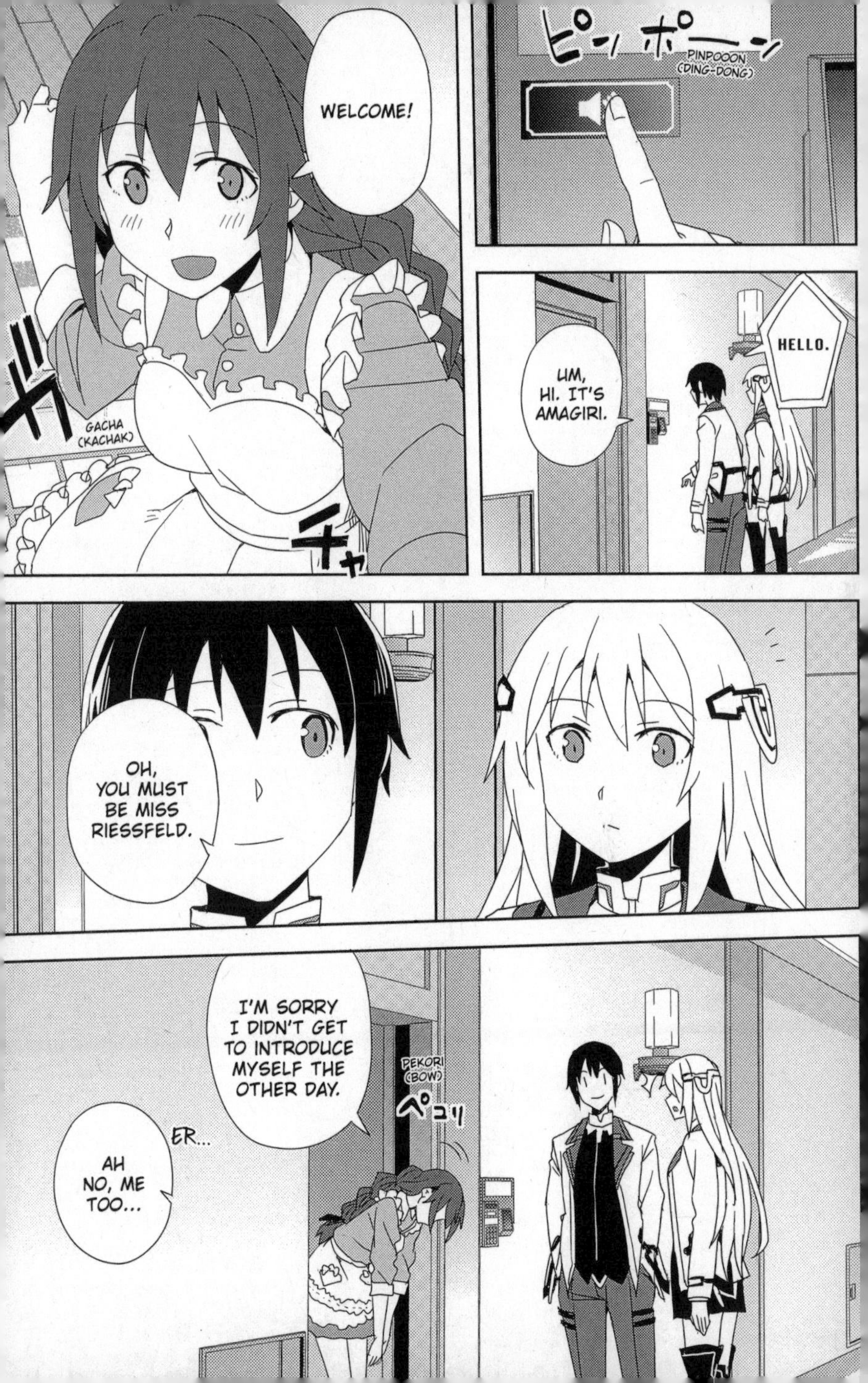
ピンポーン
PINPOOON (DING-DONG)
HELLO.
UM, HI. IT'S AMAGIRI.
WELCOME!
ガチャ
GACHA (KACHAK)
OH, YOU MUST BE MISS RIESSFELD.
I'M SORRY I DIDN'T GET TO INTRODUCE MYSELF THE OTHER DAY.
ペコリ
PEKORI (BOW)
ER...
AH NO, ME TOO...

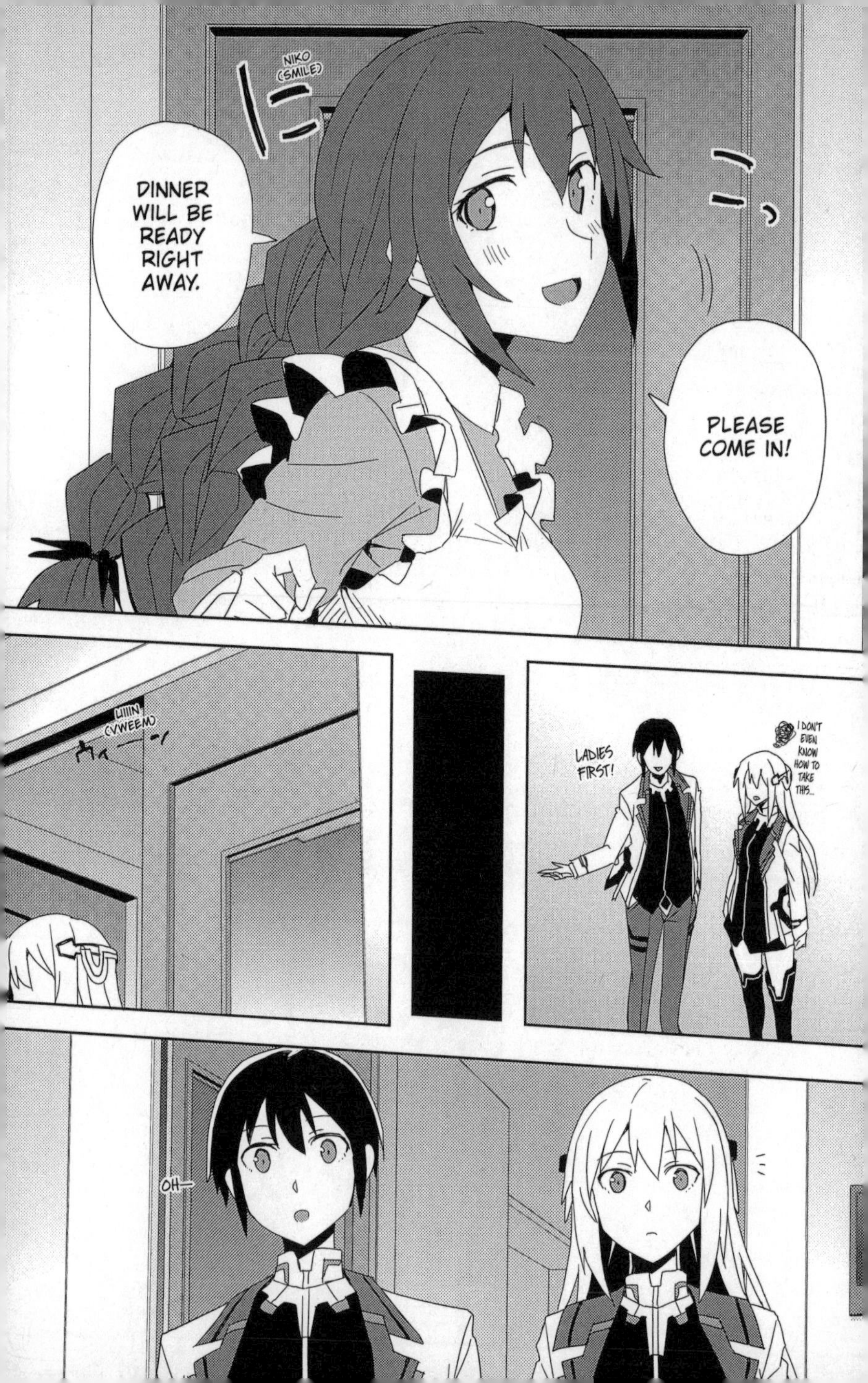
NIKO (SMILE)
PLEASE COME IN!
DINNER WILL BE READY RIGHT AWAY.
I DON'T EVEN KNOW HOW TO TAKE THIS...
LADIES FIRST!
LIIIN (VWEEM)
OH—

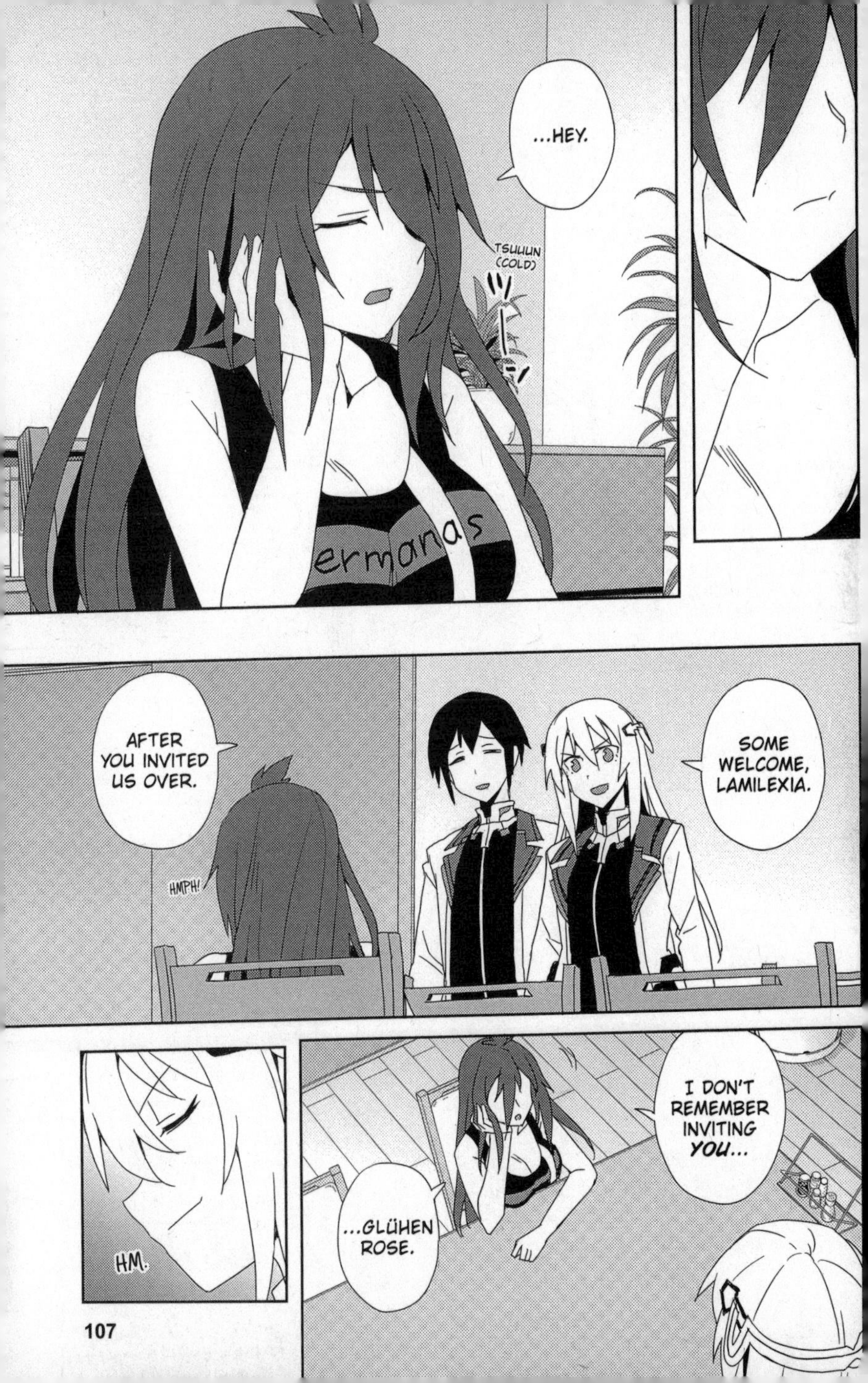
...HEY.
TSUUUN (COLD)
SOME WELCOME, LAMILEXIA.
AFTER YOU INVITED US OVER.
HMPH!
I DON'T REMEMBER INVITING *YOU*...
...GLÜHEN ROSE.
HM.

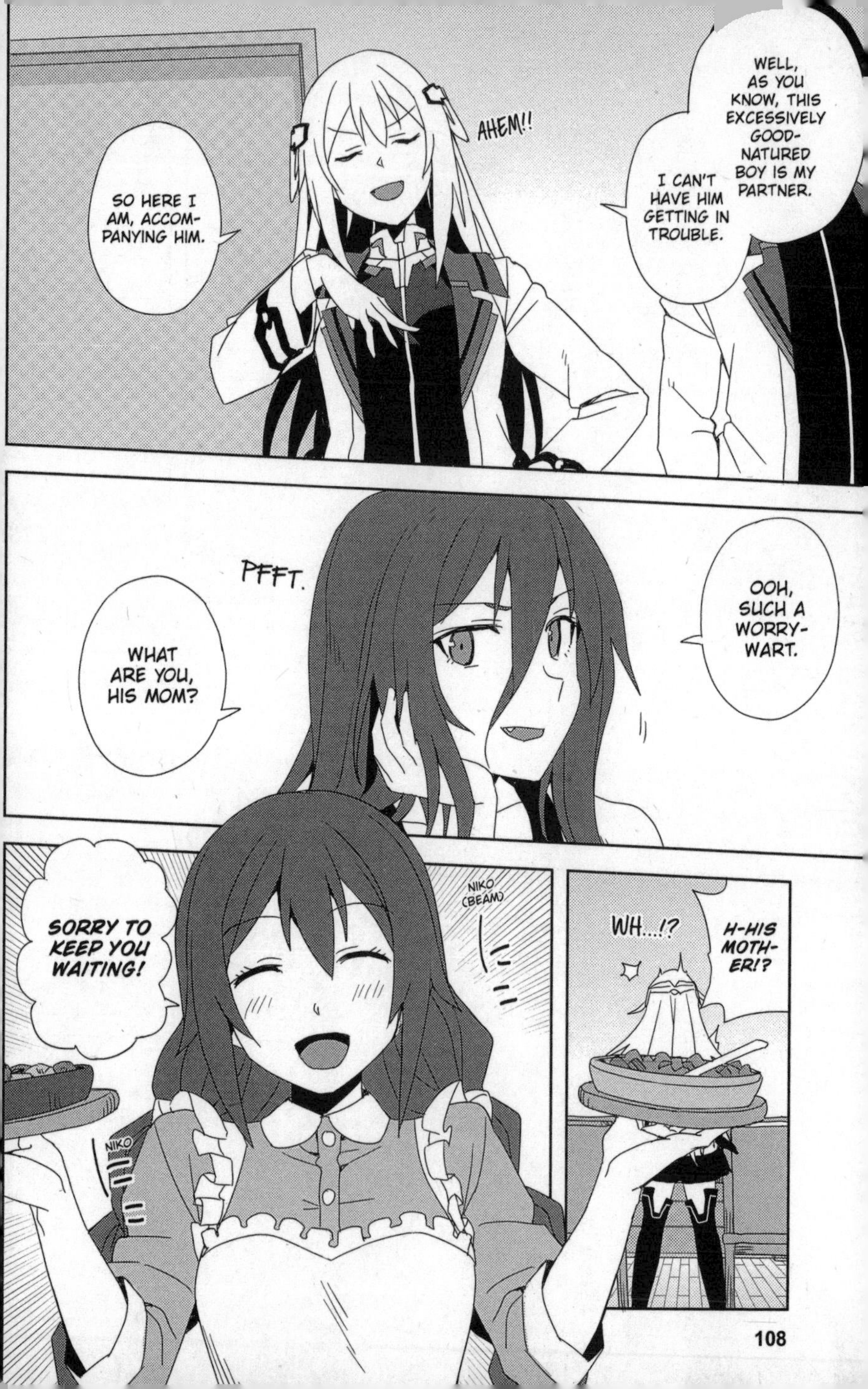
WELL, AS YOU KNOW, THIS EXCESSIVELY GOOD-NATURED BOY IS MY PARTNER.
I CAN'T HAVE HIM GETTING IN TROUBLE.
AHEM!!
SO HERE I AM, ACCOMPANYING HIM.
OOH, SUCH A WORRY-WART.
PFFT.
WHAT ARE YOU, HIS MOM?
H-HIS MOTHER!?
WH...!?
NIKO (BEAM)
SORRY TO KEEP YOU WAITING!
NIKO

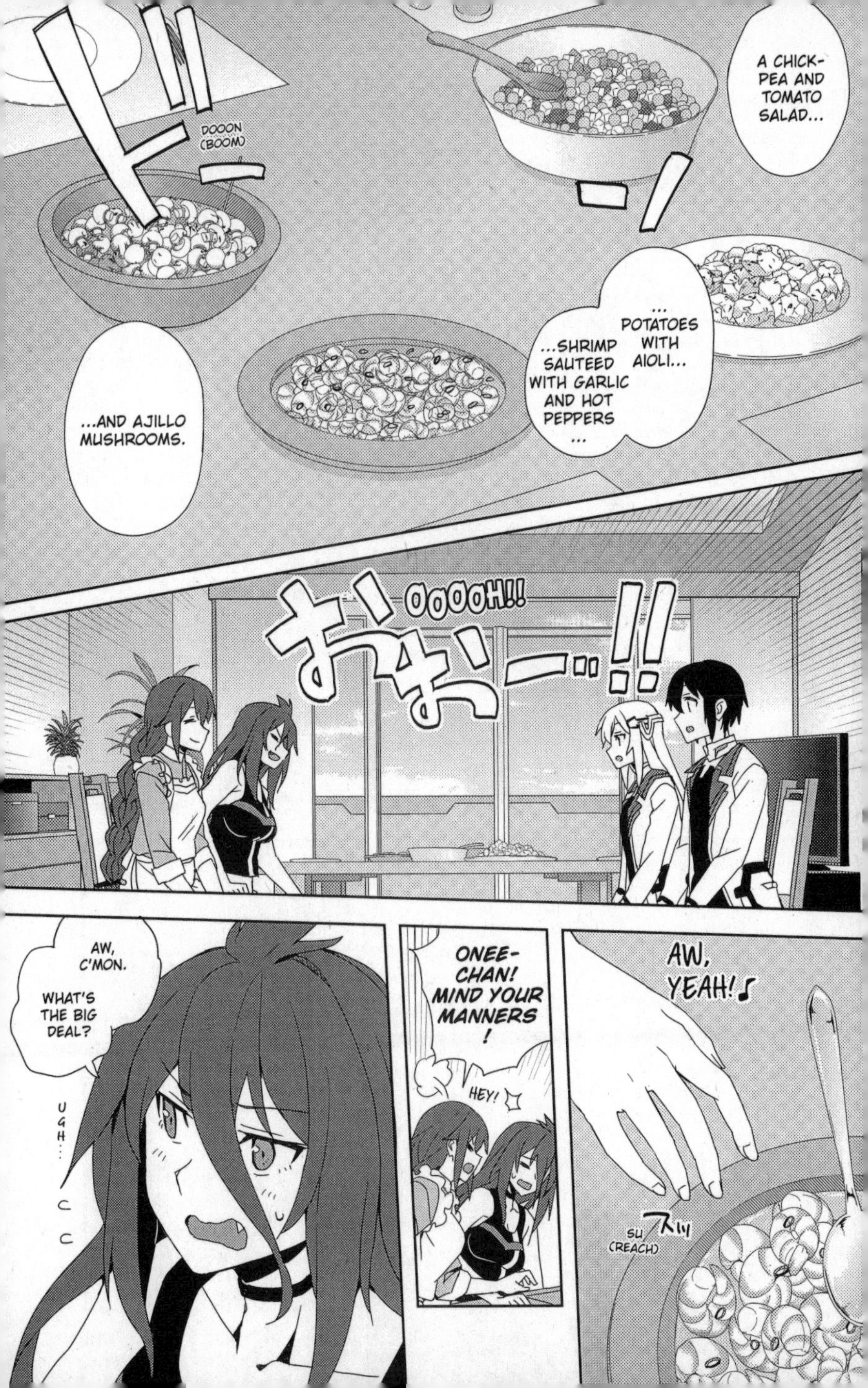

A CHICK-PEA AND TOMATO SALAD...
DOOON (BOOM)
...POTATOES WITH AIOLI...
...SHRIMP SAUTEED WITH GARLIC AND HOT PEPPERS...
...AND AJILLO MUSHROOMS.
OOOOH!!
AW, YEAH!♪
スッ
SU (REACH)
ONEE-CHAN! MIND YOUR MANNERS!
HEY!
AW, C'MON.
WHAT'S THE BIG DEAL?
UGH...

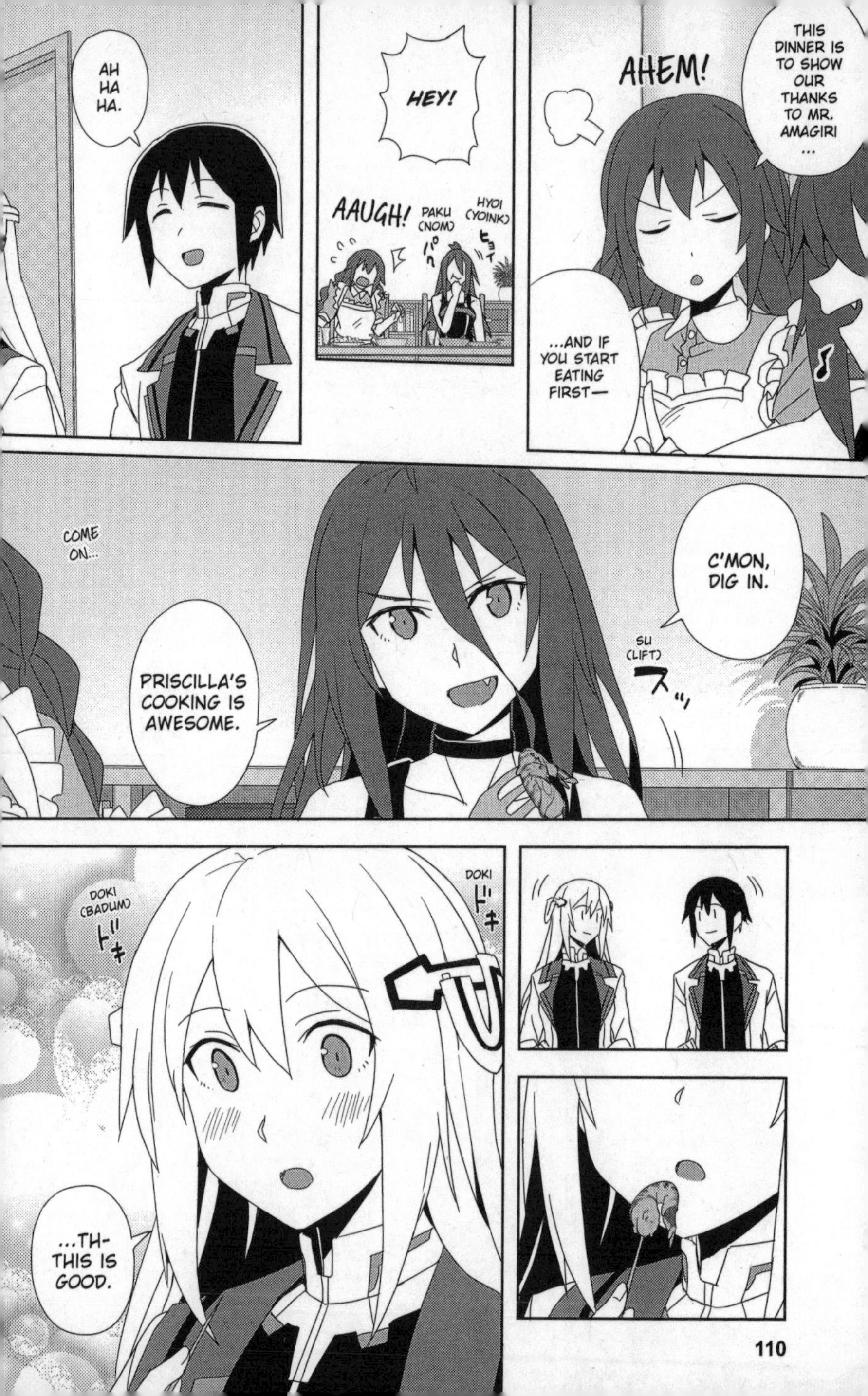
AHEM!
THIS DINNER IS TO SHOW OUR THANKS TO MR. AMAGIRI...
...AND IF YOU START EATING FIRST—
HEY!
HYOI (YOINK)
ヒョイ
PAKU (NOM)
パク
AAUGH!
AH HA HA.
C'MON, DIG IN.
SU (LIFT)
スッ
PRISCILLA'S COOKING IS AWESOME.
COME ON...
DOKI
ドキ
DOKI (BADUM)
ドキ
...TH-THIS IS GOOD.

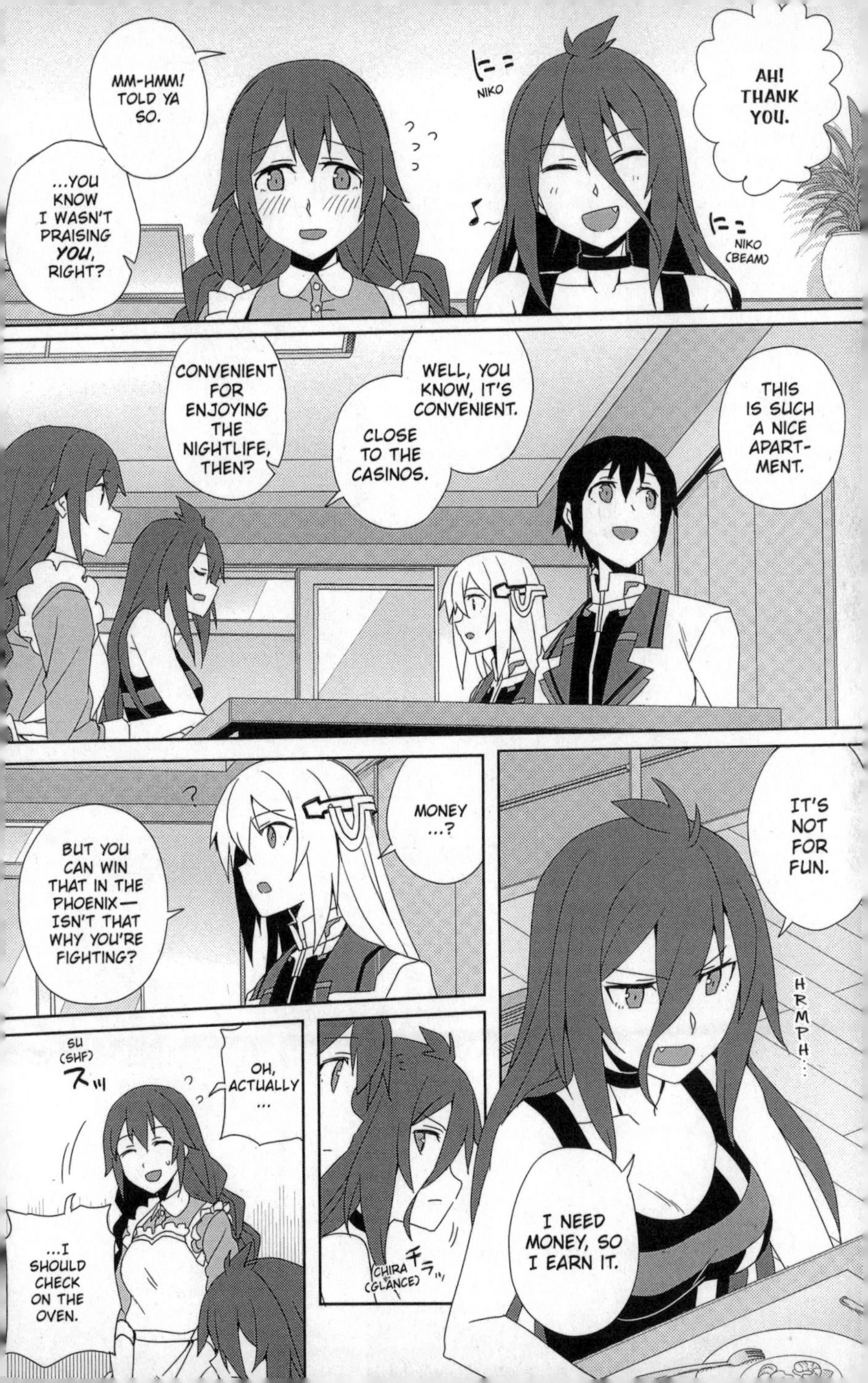
AH! THANK YOU.
ニコ
NIKO (BEAM)
ニコ
NIKO
MM-HMM! TOLD YA SO.
...YOU KNOW I WASN'T PRAISING *YOU*, RIGHT?
THIS IS SUCH A NICE APARTMENT.
WELL, YOU KNOW, IT'S CONVENIENT.
CLOSE TO THE CASINOS.
CONVENIENT FOR ENJOYING THE NIGHTLIFE, THEN?
IT'S NOT FOR FUN.
HRMPH...
I NEED MONEY, SO I EARN IT.
MONEY ...?
BUT YOU CAN WIN THAT IN THE PHOENIX—ISN'T THAT WHY YOU'RE FIGHTING?
チラッ
CHIRA (GLANCE)
OH, ACTUALLY ...
スッ
SU (SHF)
...I SHOULD CHECK ON THE OVEN.

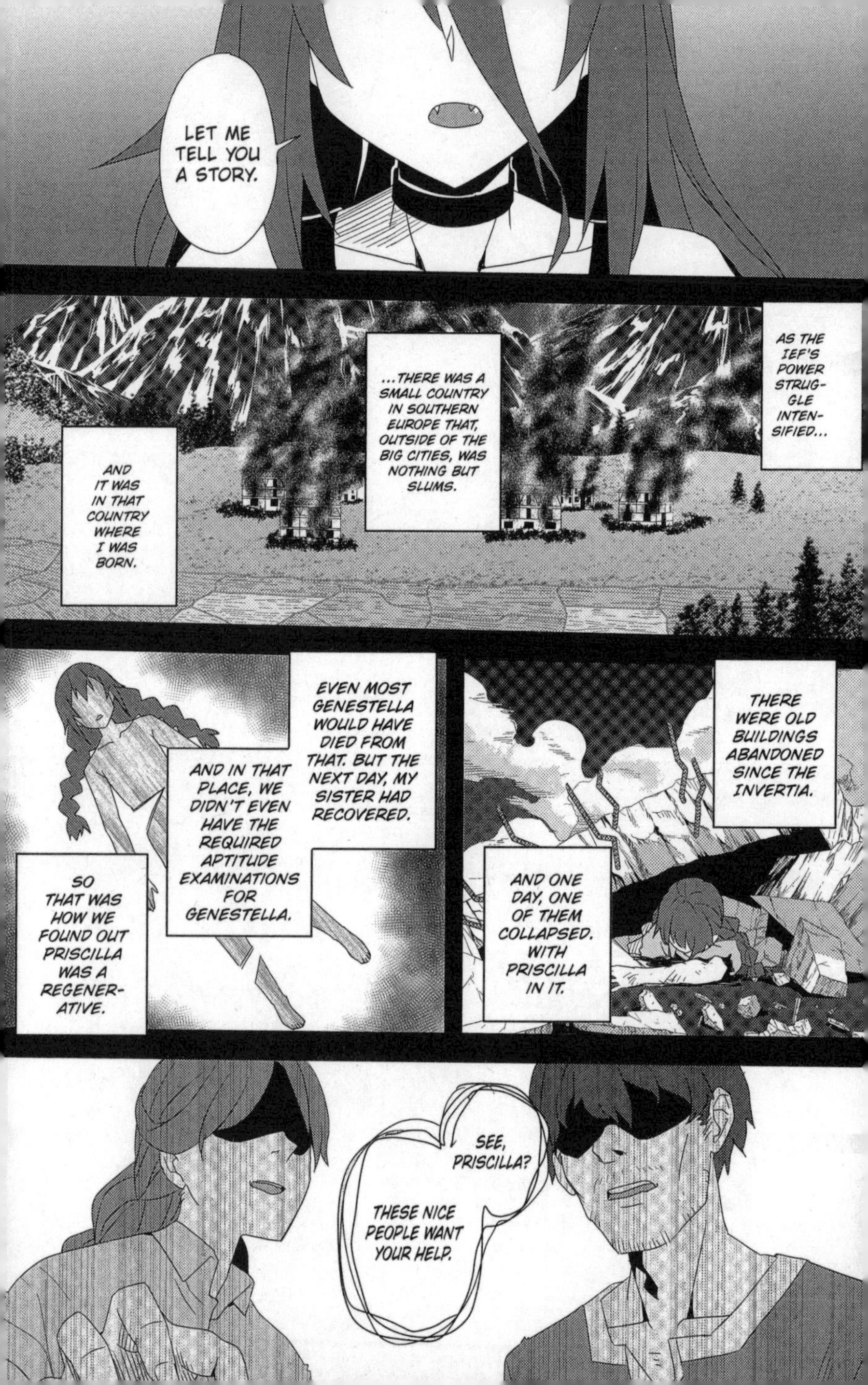
LET ME TELL YOU A STORY.
AS THE IEF'S POWER STRUG-GLE INTEN-SIFIED...
...THERE WAS A SMALL COUNTRY IN SOUTHERN EUROPE THAT, OUTSIDE OF THE BIG CITIES, WAS NOTHING BUT SLUMS.
AND IT WAS IN THAT COUNTRY WHERE I WAS BORN.
THERE WERE OLD BUILDINGS ABANDONED SINCE THE INVERTIA.
AND ONE DAY, ONE OF THEM COLLAPSED. WITH PRISCILLA IN IT.
EVEN MOST GENESTELLA WOULD HAVE DIED FROM THAT. BUT THE NEXT DAY, MY SISTER HAD RECOVERED.
AND IN THAT PLACE, WE DIDN'T EVEN HAVE THE REQUIRED APTITUDE EXAMINATIONS FOR GENESTELLA.
SO THAT WAS HOW WE FOUND OUT PRISCILLA WAS A REGENER-ATIVE.
SEE, PRISCILLA?
THESE NICE PEOPLE WANT YOUR HELP.

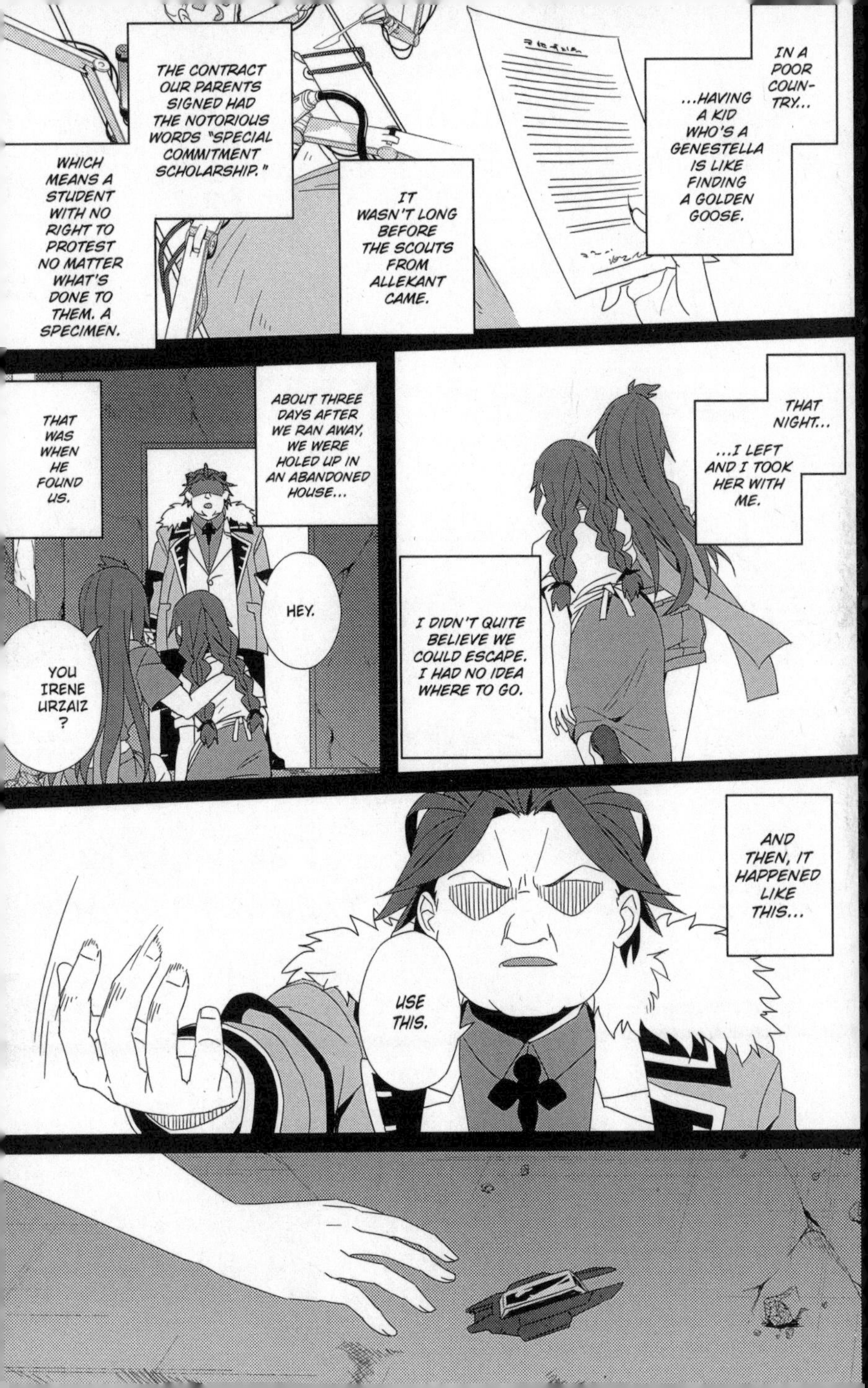
IN A POOR COUNTRY...
...HAVING A KID WHO'S A GENESTELLA IS LIKE FINDING A GOLDEN GOOSE.
IT WASN'T LONG BEFORE THE SCOUTS FROM ALLEKANT CAME.
THE CONTRACT OUR PARENTS SIGNED HAD THE NOTORIOUS WORDS "SPECIAL COMMITMENT SCHOLARSHIP."
WHICH MEANS A STUDENT WITH NO RIGHT TO PROTEST NO MATTER WHAT'S DONE TO THEM. A SPECIMEN.
THAT NIGHT...
...I LEFT AND I TOOK HER WITH ME.
I DIDN'T QUITE BELIEVE WE COULD ESCAPE. I HAD NO IDEA WHERE TO GO.
ABOUT THREE DAYS AFTER WE RAN AWAY, WE WERE HOLED UP IN AN ABANDONED HOUSE...
THAT WAS WHEN HE FOUND US.
HEY.
YOU IRENE URZAIZ?
AND THEN, IT HAPPENED LIKE THIS...
USE THIS.

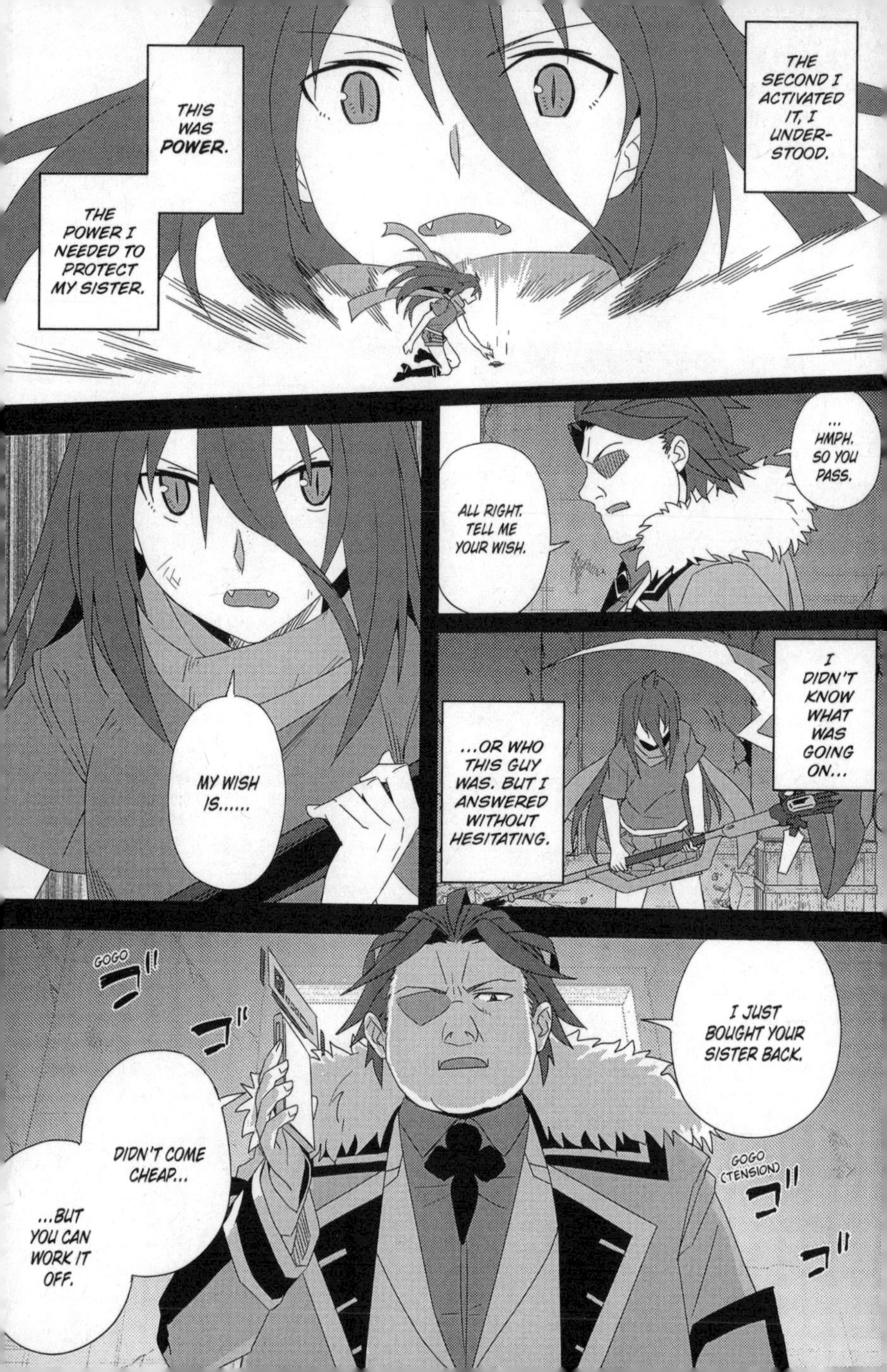
THE SECOND I ACTIVATED IT, I UNDER-STOOD.
THIS WAS POWER.
THE POWER I NEEDED TO PROTECT MY SISTER.
... HMPH. SO YOU PASS.
ALL RIGHT. TELL ME YOUR WISH.
I DIDN'T KNOW WHAT WAS GOING ON...
...OR WHO THIS GUY WAS. BUT I ANSWERED WITHOUT HESITATING.
MY WISH IS......
GOGO (TENSION)
I JUST BOUGHT YOUR SISTER BACK.
GOGO
DIDN'T COME CHEAP...
...BUT YOU CAN WORK IT OFF.

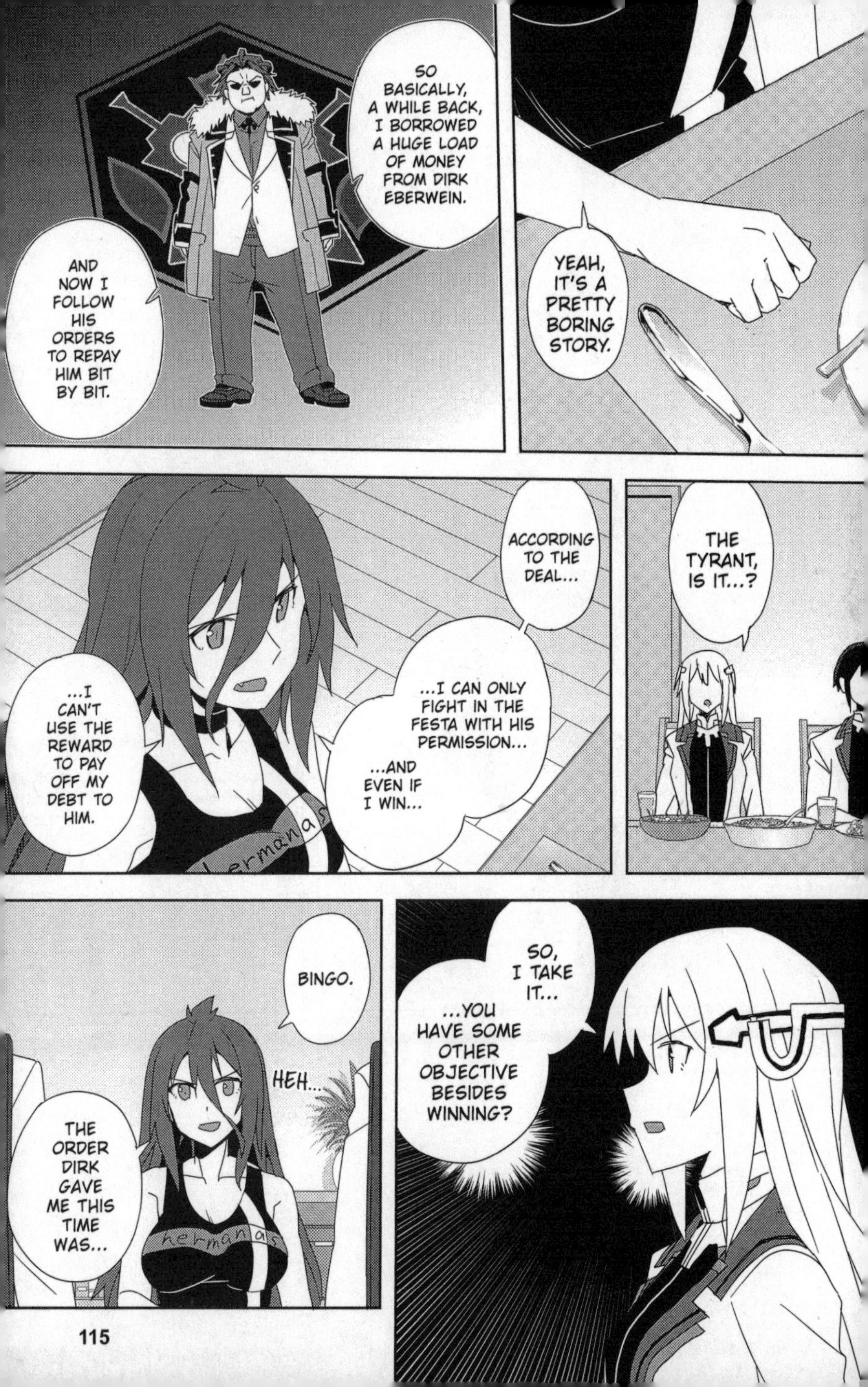
YEAH, IT'S A PRETTY BORING STORY.
SO BASICALLY, A WHILE BACK, I BORROWED A HUGE LOAD OF MONEY FROM DIRK EBERWEIN.
AND NOW I FOLLOW HIS ORDERS TO REPAY HIM BIT BY BIT.
THE TYRANT, IS IT...?
ACCORDING TO THE DEAL...
...I CAN ONLY FIGHT IN THE FESTA WITH HIS PERMISSION...
...AND EVEN IF I WIN...
...I CAN'T USE THE REWARD TO PAY OFF MY DEBT TO HIM.
SO, I TAKE IT...
...YOU HAVE SOME OTHER OBJECTIVE BESIDES WINNING?
BINGO.
HEH...
THE ORDER DIRK GAVE ME THIS TIME WAS...

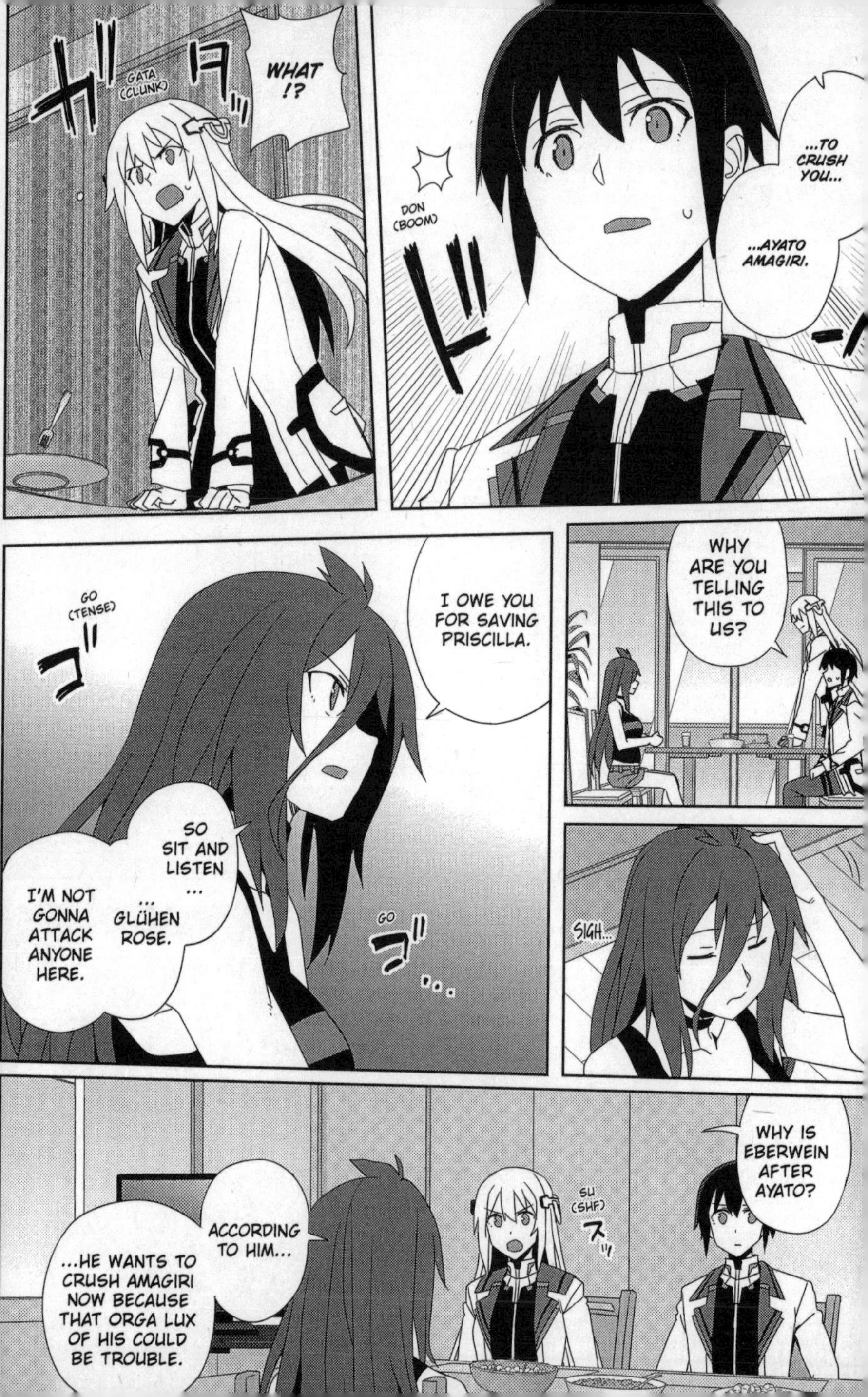
...TO CRUSH YOU...
...AYATO AMAGIRI.
DON (BOOM)
GATA (CLUNK)
WHAT!?
WHY ARE YOU TELLING THIS TO US?
SIGH...
I OWE YOU FOR SAVING PRISCILLA.
GO (TENSE)
SO SIT AND LISTEN... ...GLÜHEN ROSE.
I'M NOT GONNA ATTACK ANYONE HERE.
GO
...
WHY IS EBERWEIN AFTER AYATO?
SU (SHF)
ACCORDING TO HIM...
...HE WANTS TO CRUSH AMAGIRI NOW BECAUSE THAT ORGA LUX OF HIS COULD BE TROUBLE.

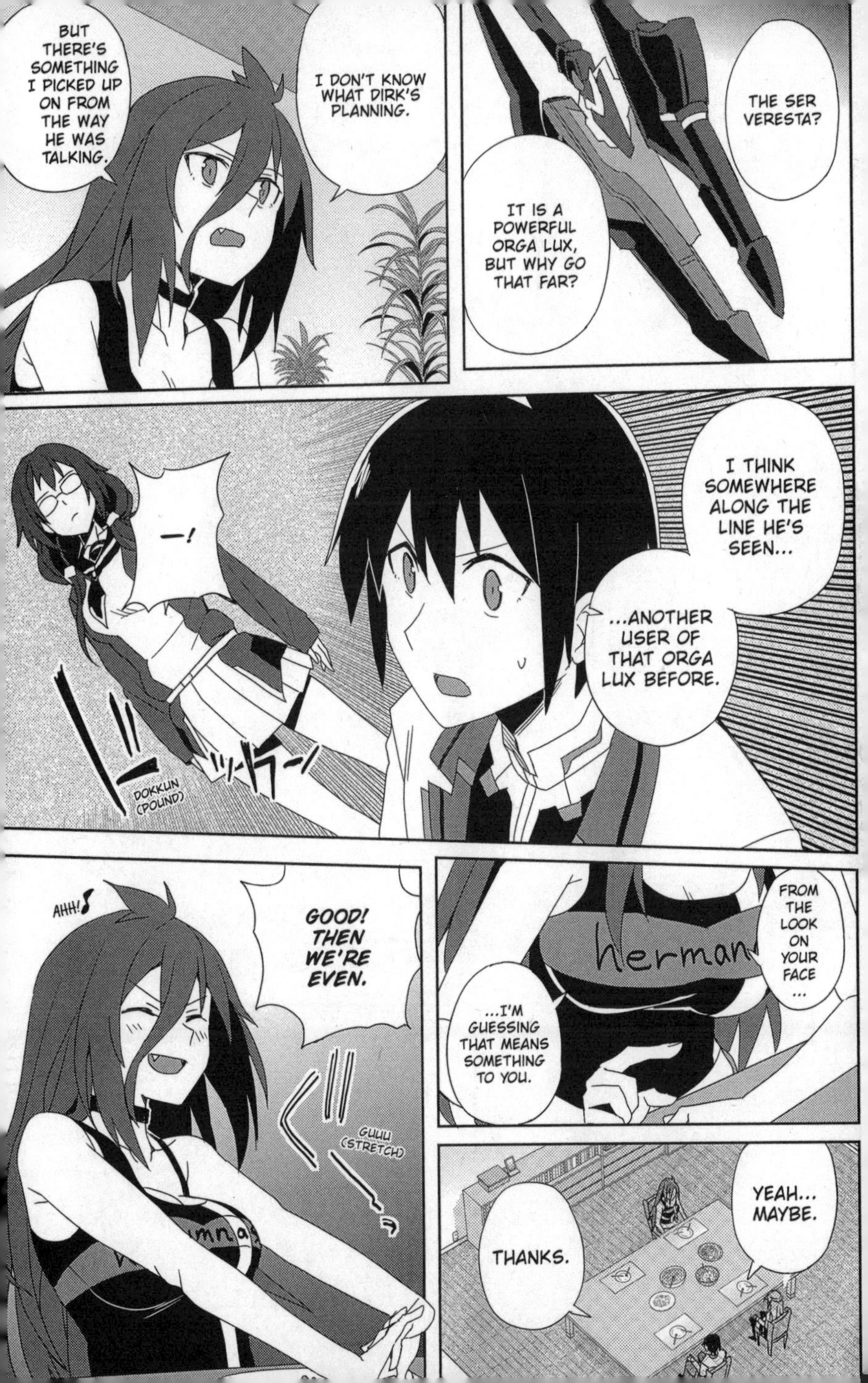
THE SER VERESTA?
IT IS A POWERFUL ORGA LUX, BUT WHY GO THAT FAR?
I DON'T KNOW WHAT DIRK'S PLANNING.
BUT THERE'S SOMETHING I PICKED UP ON FROM THE WAY HE WAS TALKING.
I THINK SOMEWHERE ALONG THE LINE HE'S SEEN...
...ANOTHER USER OF THAT ORGA LUX BEFORE.
—!
DOKKUN (POUND)
FROM THE LOOK ON YOUR FACE...
...I'M GUESSING THAT MEANS SOMETHING TO YOU.
YEAH... MAYBE.
THANKS.
GOOD! THEN WE'RE EVEN.
AHH!♪
GUUU (STRETCH)

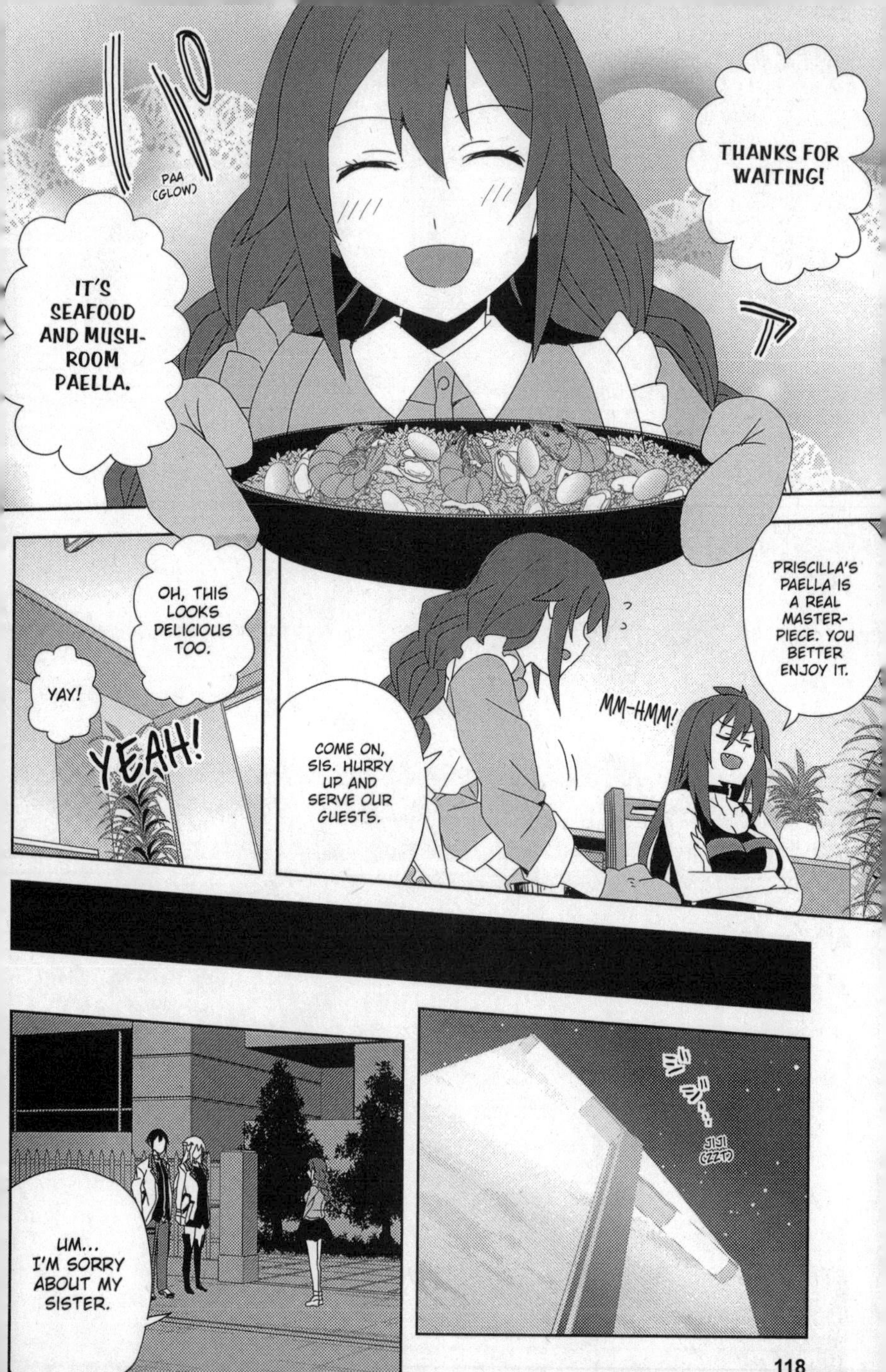
THANKS FOR WAITING!
PAA (GLOW)
IT'S SEAFOOD AND MUSH-ROOM PAELLA.
PRISCILLA'S PAELLA IS A REAL MASTER-PIECE. YOU BETTER ENJOY IT.
MM-HMM!
COME ON, SIS. HURRY UP AND SERVE OUR GUESTS.
OH, THIS LOOKS DELICIOUS TOO.
YAY!
YEAH!
JIJI (ZZZT)
UM... I'M SORRY ABOUT MY SISTER.

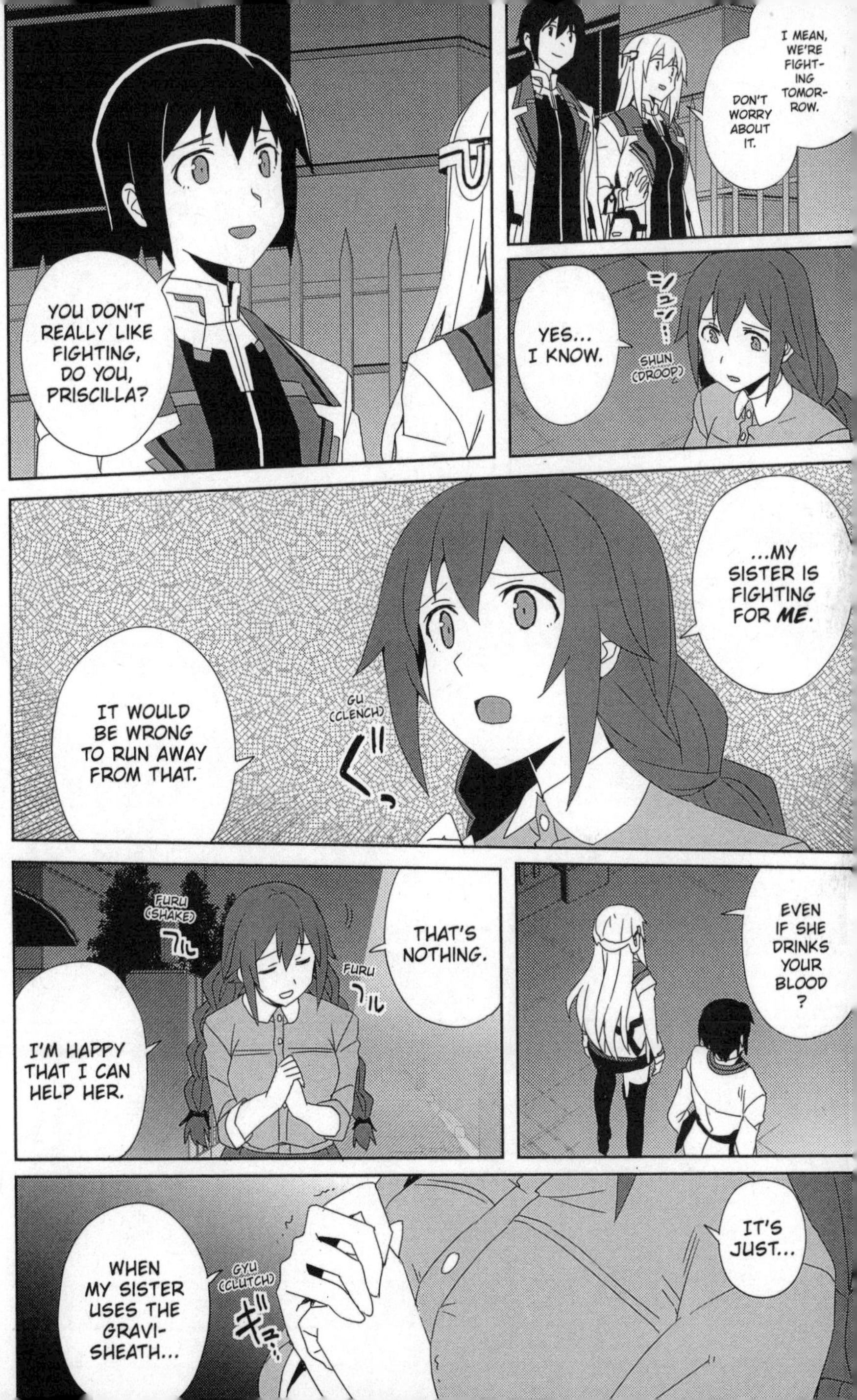
I MEAN, WE'RE FIGHTING TOMORROW.
DON'T WORRY ABOUT IT.
YES... I KNOW.
SHUN (DROOP)
YOU DON'T REALLY LIKE FIGHTING, DO YOU, PRISCILLA?
...MY SISTER IS FIGHTING FOR *ME*.
GU (CLENCH)
IT WOULD BE WRONG TO RUN AWAY FROM THAT.
EVEN IF SHE DRINKS YOUR BLOOD?
THAT'S NOTHING.
FURU (SHAKE)
FURU
I'M HAPPY THAT I CAN HELP HER.
IT'S JUST...
GYU (CLUTCH)
WHEN MY SISTER USES THE GRAVI-SHEATH...

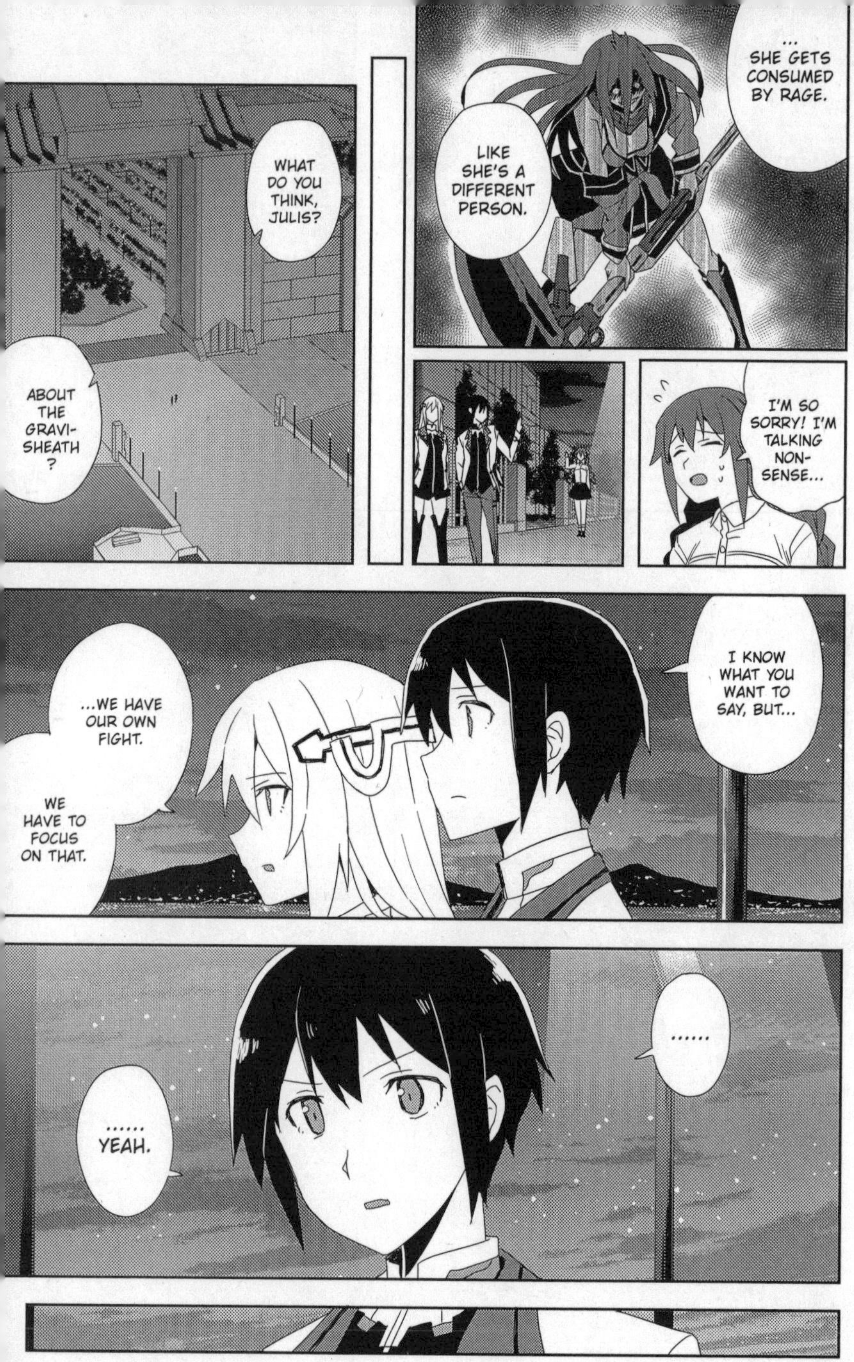
...SHE GETS CONSUMED BY RAGE.
LIKE SHE'S A DIFFERENT PERSON.
I'M SO SORRY! I'M TALKING NON-SENSE...
WHAT DO YOU THINK, JULIS?
ABOUT THE GRAVI-SHEATH?
I KNOW WHAT YOU WANT TO SAY, BUT...
...WE HAVE OUR OWN FIGHT.
WE HAVE TO FOCUS ON THAT.
......
......YEAH.

THE
ASTERISK WAR

GRAVITY SPHERE

I WONDER IF I CAN...?

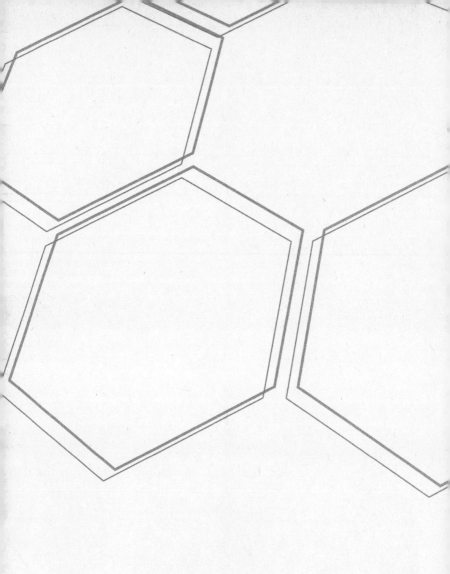

THE
ASTERISK WAR

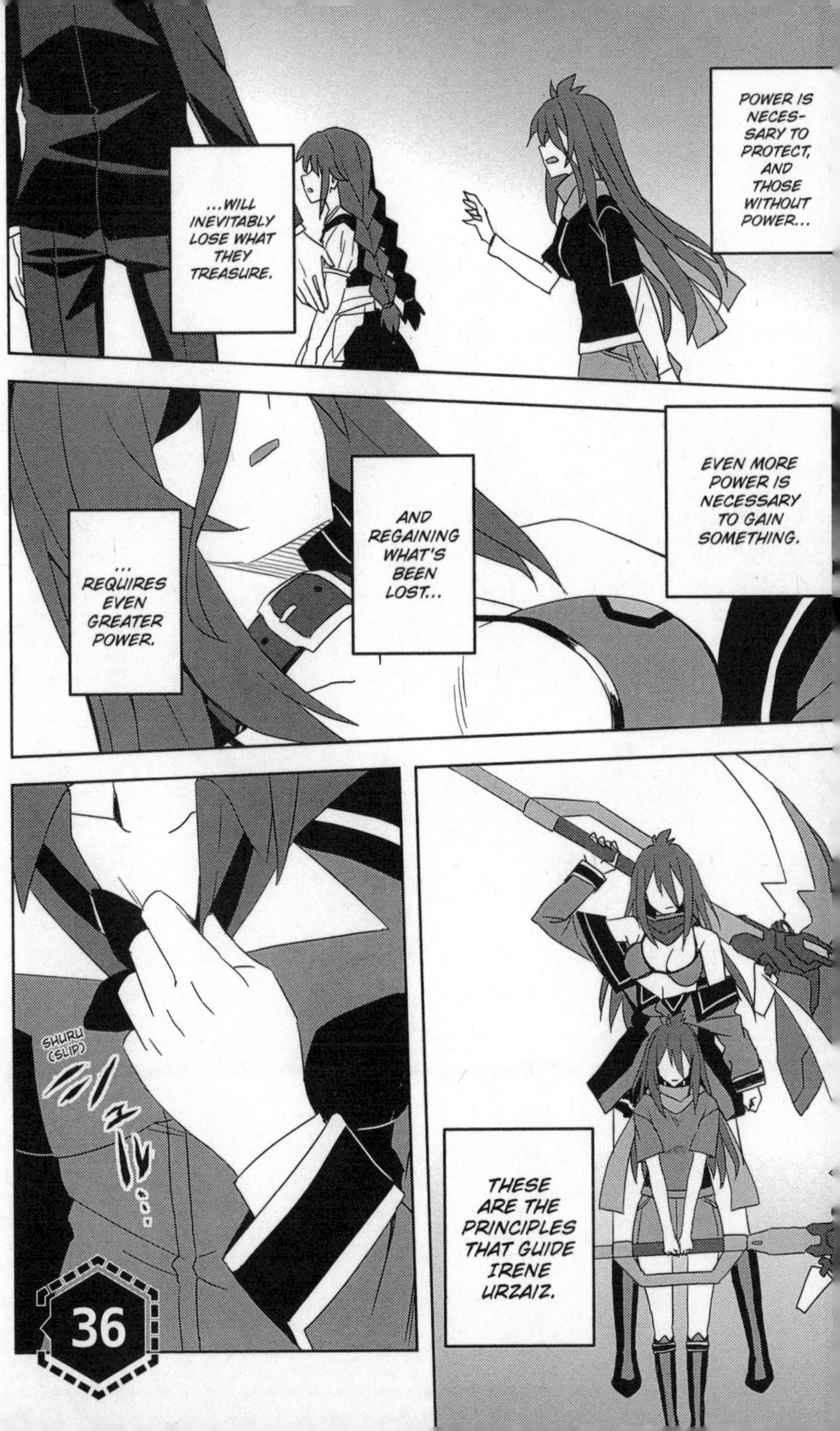
POWER IS NECES-SARY TO PROTECT, AND THOSE WITHOUT POWER...
...WILL INEVITABLY LOSE WHAT THEY TREASURE.
EVEN MORE POWER IS NECESSARY TO GAIN SOMETHING.
AND REGAINING WHAT'S BEEN LOST...
...REQUIRES EVEN GREATER POWER.
THESE ARE THE PRINCIPLES THAT GUIDE IRENE URZAIZ.
SHURU (SLIP)

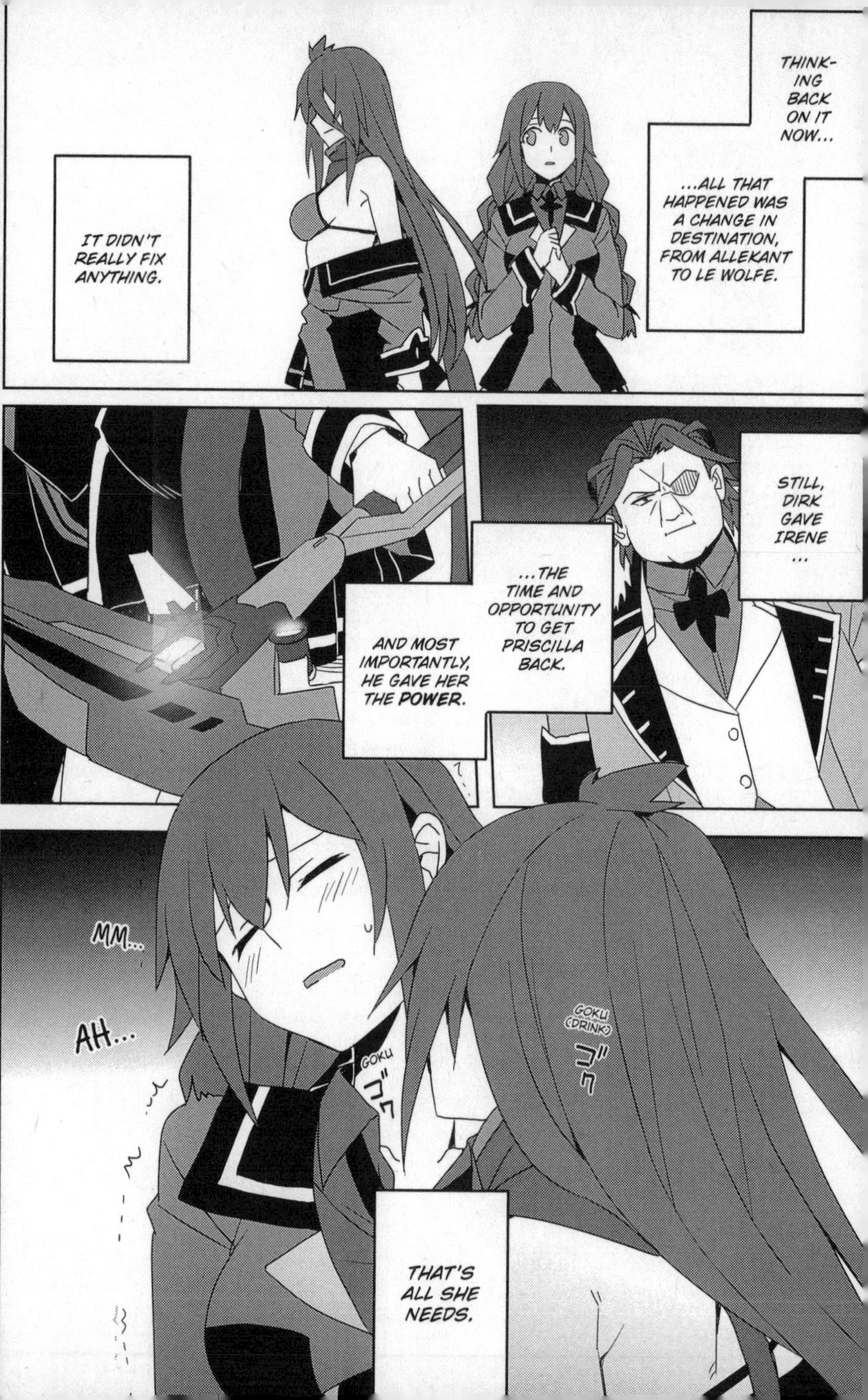
THINKING BACK ON IT NOW...
...ALL THAT HAPPENED WAS A CHANGE IN DESTINATION, FROM ALLEKANT TO LE WOLFE.
IT DIDN'T REALLY FIX ANYTHING.
STILL, DIRK GAVE IRENE ...
...THE TIME AND OPPORTUNITY TO GET PRISCILLA BACK.
AND MOST IMPORTANTLY, HE GAVE HER THE POWER.
GOKU (DRINK)
GOKU
MM...
AH...
THAT'S ALL SHE NEEDS.

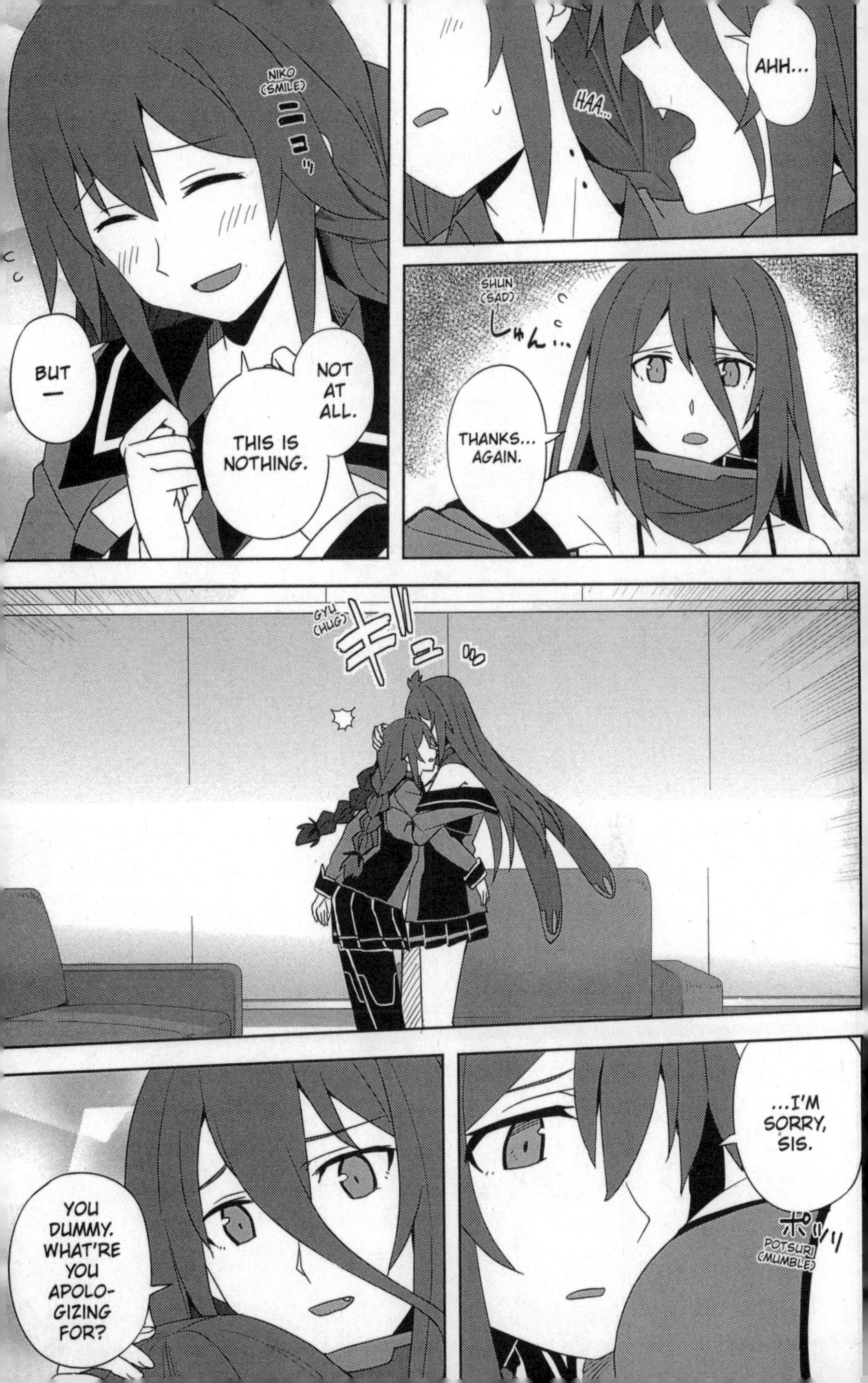
AHH...
HAA...
SHUN (SAD)
しゅん...
THANKS... AGAIN.
NIKO (SMILE)
ニコッ
NOT AT ALL. THIS IS NOTHING.
BUT —
GYU (HUG)
ギュッ
...I'M SORRY, SIS.
POTSURI (MUMBLE)
ポツリ
YOU DUMMY. WHAT'RE YOU APOLO-GIZING FOR?

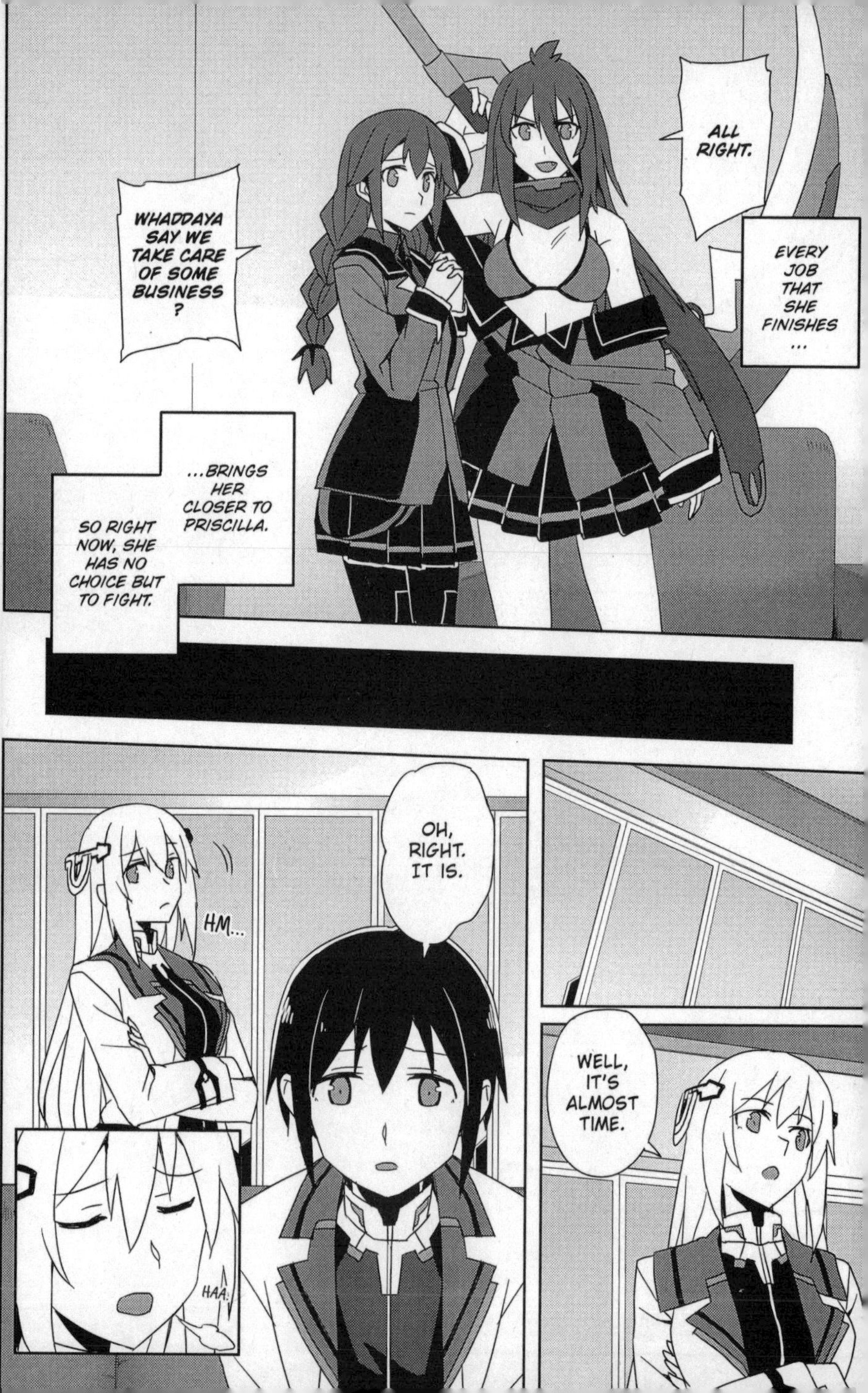
ALL RIGHT.
WHADDAYA SAY WE TAKE CARE OF SOME BUSINESS?
EVERY JOB THAT SHE FINISHES...
...BRINGS HER CLOSER TO PRISCILLA.
SO RIGHT NOW, SHE HAS NO CHOICE BUT TO FIGHT.
WELL, IT'S ALMOST TIME.
OH, RIGHT. IT IS.
HM...
HAA

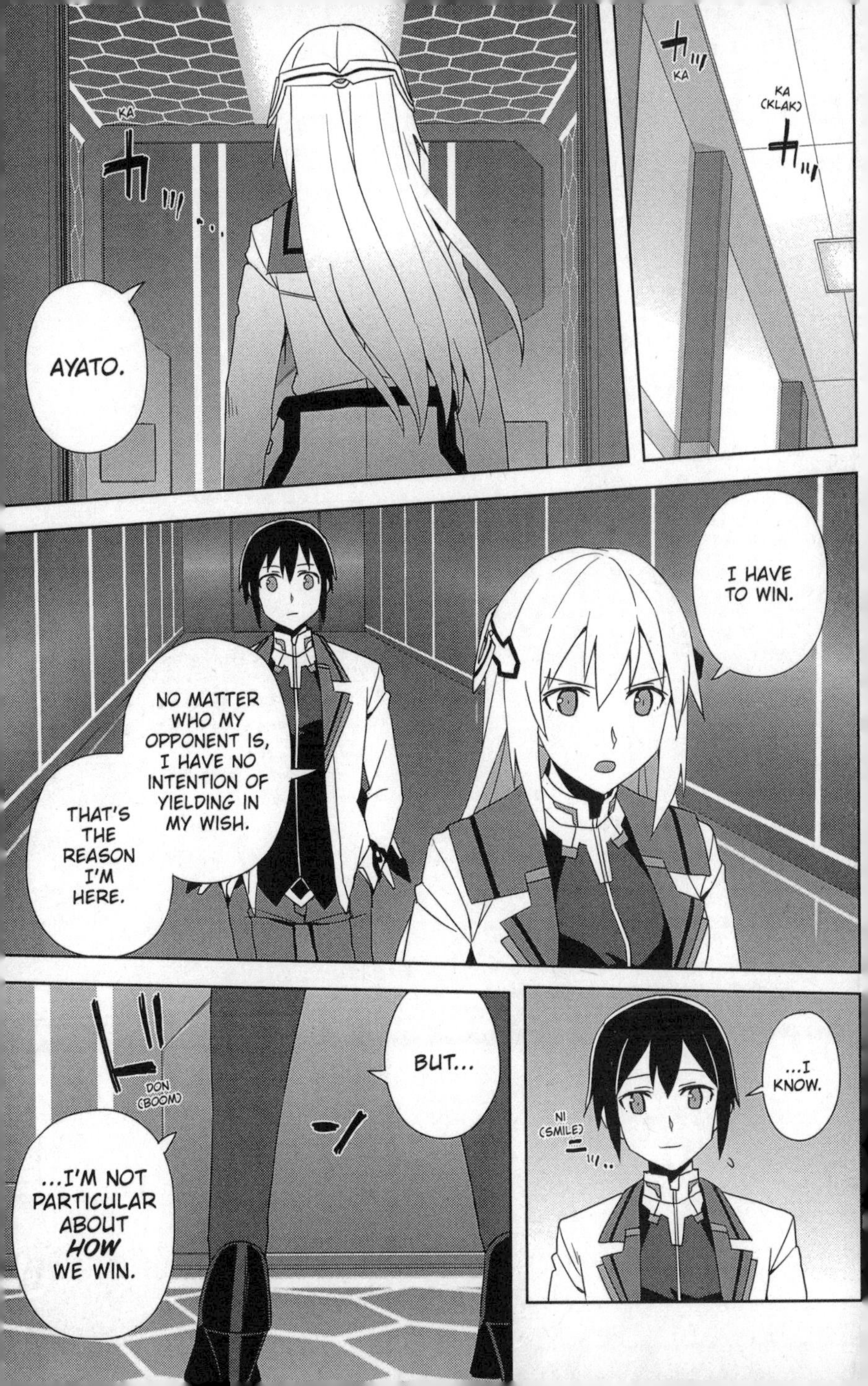
KA
KA (KLAK)
KA
AYATO.
I HAVE TO WIN.
NO MATTER WHO MY OPPONENT IS, I HAVE NO INTENTION OF YIELDING IN MY WISH.
THAT'S THE REASON I'M HERE.
...I KNOW.
NI (SMILE)
BUT...
DON (BOOM)
...I'M NOT PARTICULAR ABOUT *HOW* WE WIN.

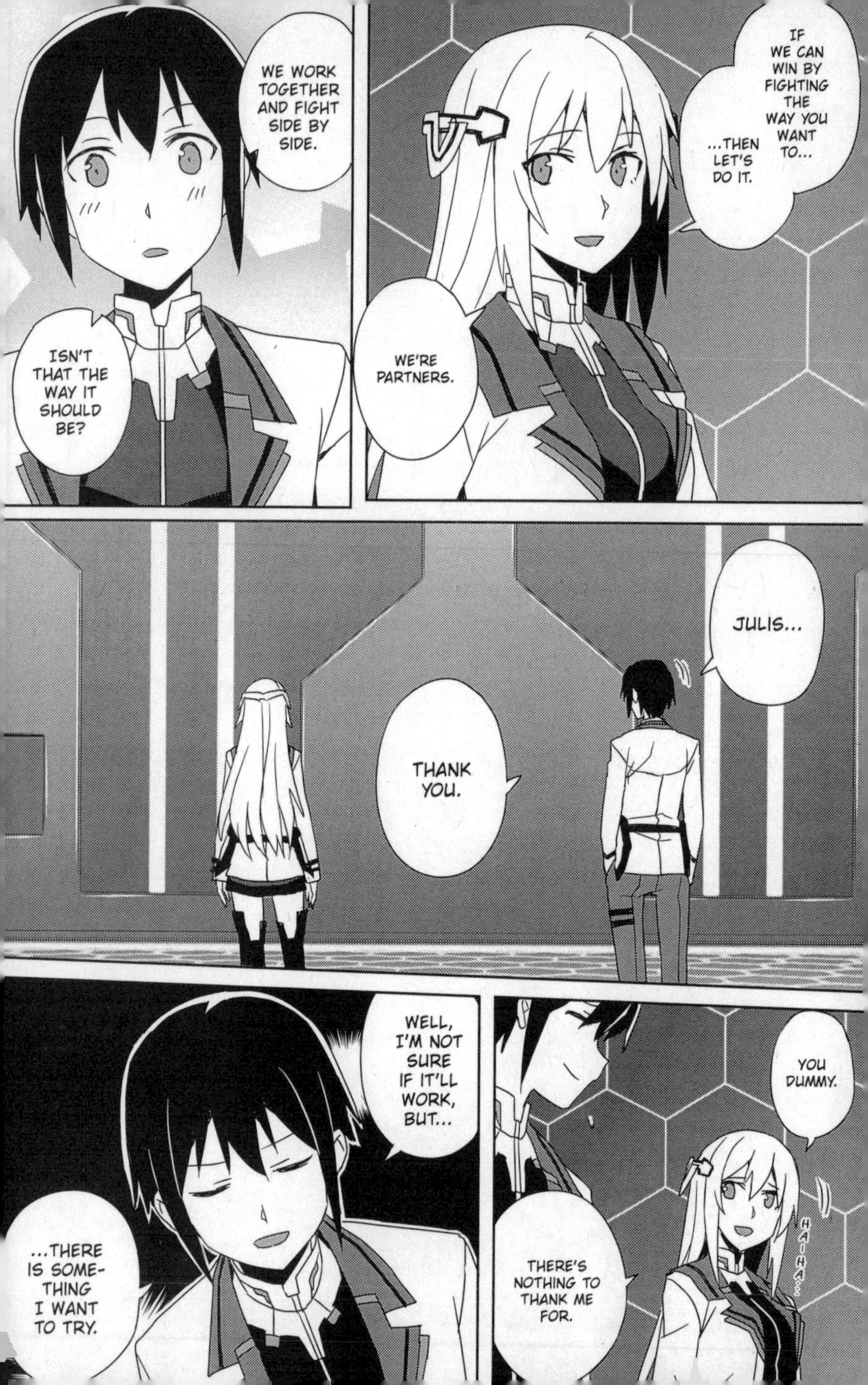
IF WE CAN WIN BY FIGHTING THE WAY YOU WANT TO...
...THEN LET'S DO IT.
WE'RE PARTNERS.
WE WORK TOGETHER AND FIGHT SIDE BY SIDE.
ISN'T THAT THE WAY IT SHOULD BE?
JULIS...
THANK YOU.
YOU DUMMY.
HA-HA...
THERE'S NOTHING TO THANK ME FOR.
WELL, I'M NOT SURE IF IT'LL WORK, BUT...
...THERE IS SOME-THING I WANT TO TRY.

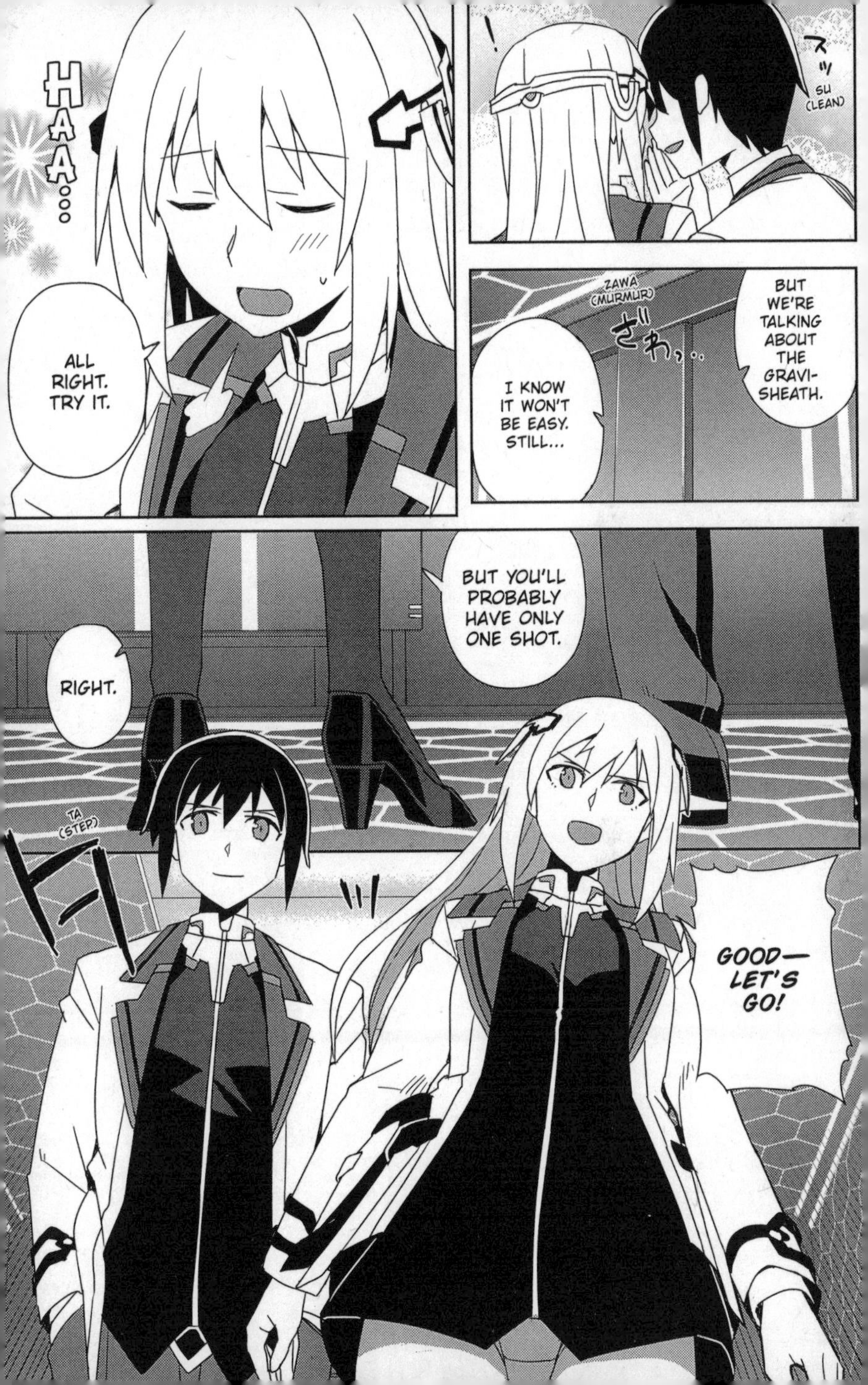
!
スッ
SU (LEAN)
ZAWA (MURMUR)
ざわ…
BUT WE'RE TALKING ABOUT THE GRAVI-SHEATH.
I KNOW IT WON'T BE EASY. STILL…
HAAA…
ALL RIGHT. TRY IT.
BUT YOU'LL PROBABLY HAVE ONLY ONE SHOT.
RIGHT.
TA (STEP)
GOOD—LET'S GO!

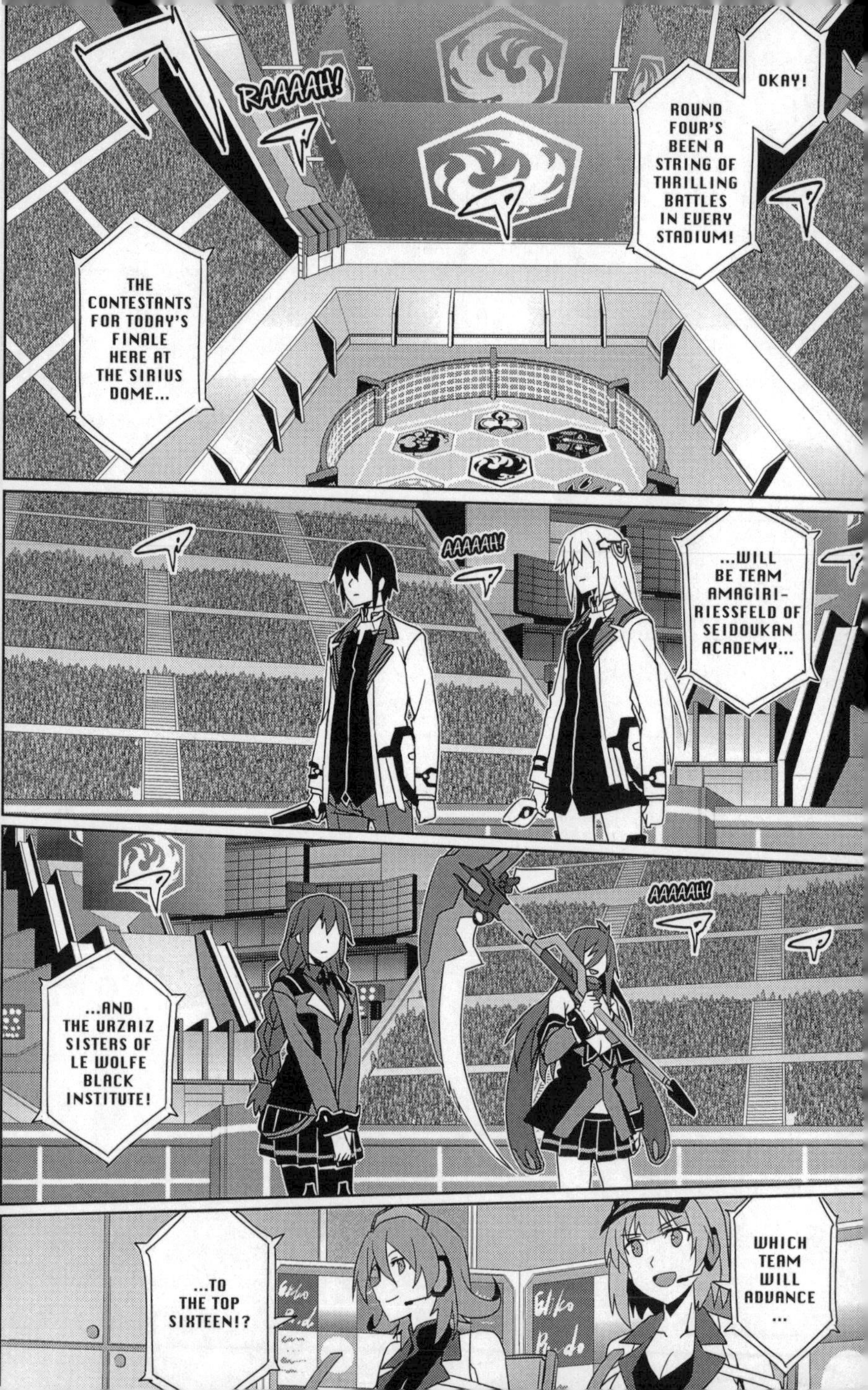
OKAY!
ROUND FOUR'S BEEN A STRING OF THRILLING BATTLES IN EVERY STADIUM!
RAAAAH!
THE CONTESTANTS FOR TODAY'S FINALE HERE AT THE SIRIUS DOME...
...WILL BE TEAM AMAGIRI-RIESSFELD OF SEIDOUKAN ACADEMY...
AAAAAH!
AAAAAH!
...AND THE URZAIZ SISTERS OF LE WOLFE BLACK INSTITUTE!
WHICH TEAM WILL ADVANCE ...
...TO THE TOP SIXTEEN!?

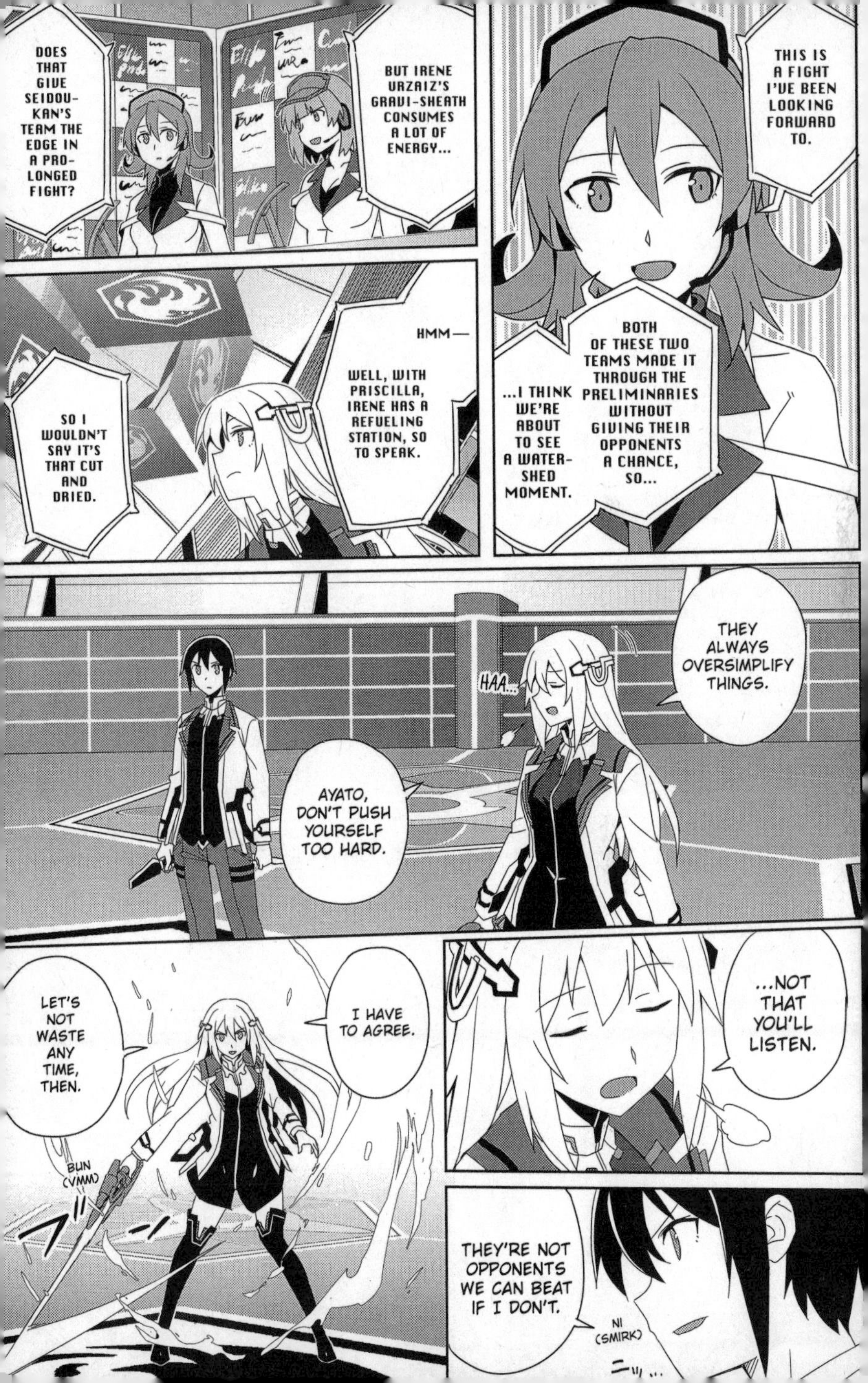
THIS IS A FIGHT I'VE BEEN LOOKING FORWARD TO.
BOTH OF THESE TWO TEAMS MADE IT THROUGH THE PRELIMINARIES WITHOUT GIVING THEIR OPPONENTS A CHANCE, SO...
...I THINK WE'RE ABOUT TO SEE A WATER-SHED MOMENT.
BUT IRENE URZAIZ'S GRAVI-SHEATH CONSUMES A LOT OF ENERGY...
DOES THAT GIVE SEIDOU-KAN'S TEAM THE EDGE IN A PRO-LONGED FIGHT?
HMM—
WELL, WITH PRISCILLA, IRENE HAS A REFUELING STATION, SO TO SPEAK.
SO I WOULDN'T SAY IT'S THAT CUT AND DRIED.
THEY ALWAYS OVERSIMPLIFY THINGS.
HAA...
AYATO, DON'T PUSH YOURSELF TOO HARD.
...NOT THAT YOU'LL LISTEN.
THEY'RE NOT OPPONENTS WE CAN BEAT IF I DON'T.
NI (SMIRK)
I HAVE TO AGREE.
LET'S NOT WASTE ANY TIME, THEN.
BUN (VMM)

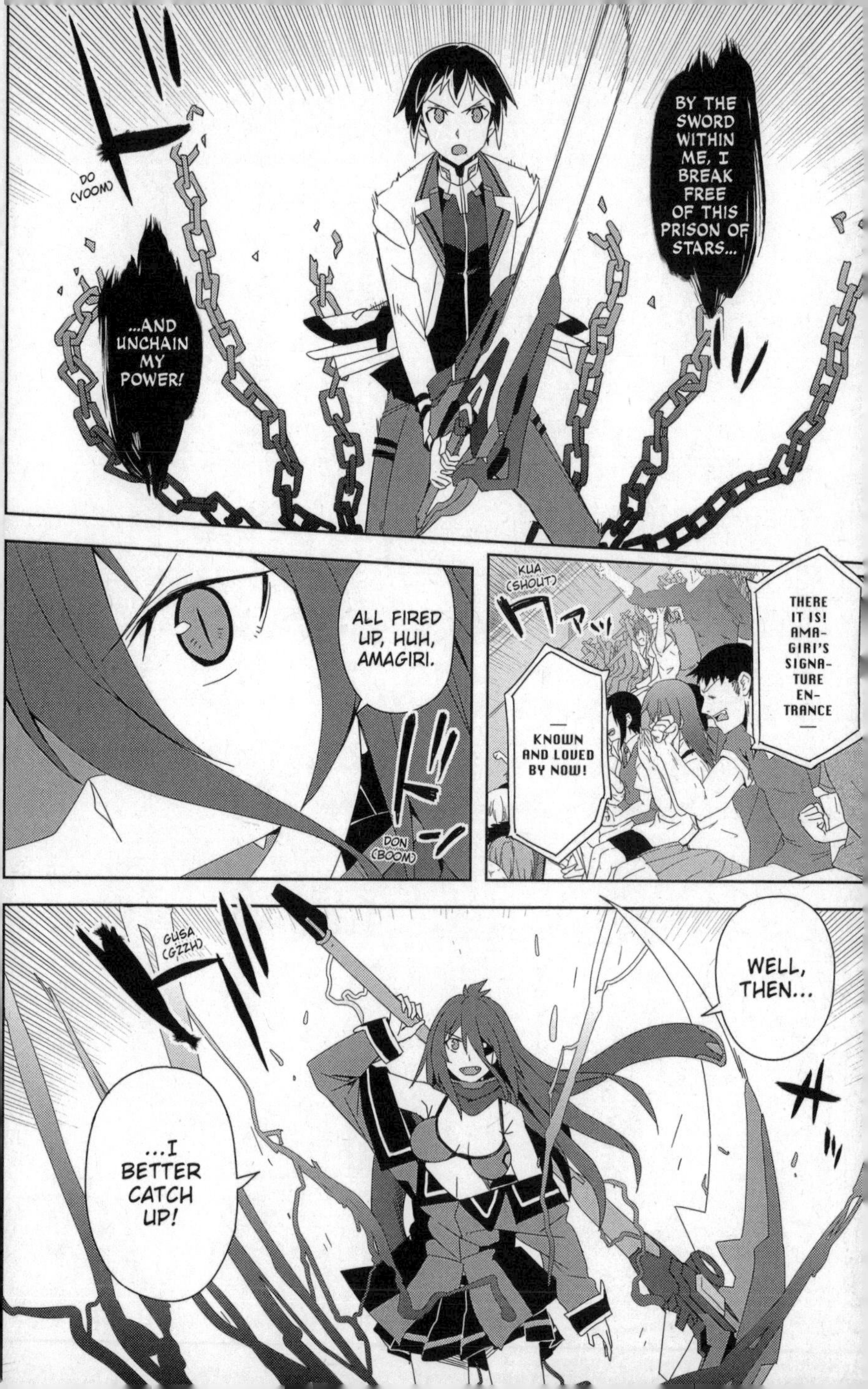
BY THE SWORD WITHIN ME, I BREAK FREE OF THIS PRISON OF STARS...
DO (VOOM)
...AND UNCHAIN MY POWER!
KUA (SHOUT)
THERE IT IS! AMAGIRI'S SIGNATURE ENTRANCE—
—KNOWN AND LOVED BY NOW!
ALL FIRED UP, HUH, AMAGIRI.
DON (BOOM)
WELL, THEN...
GUSA (GZZH)
...I BETTER CATCH UP!

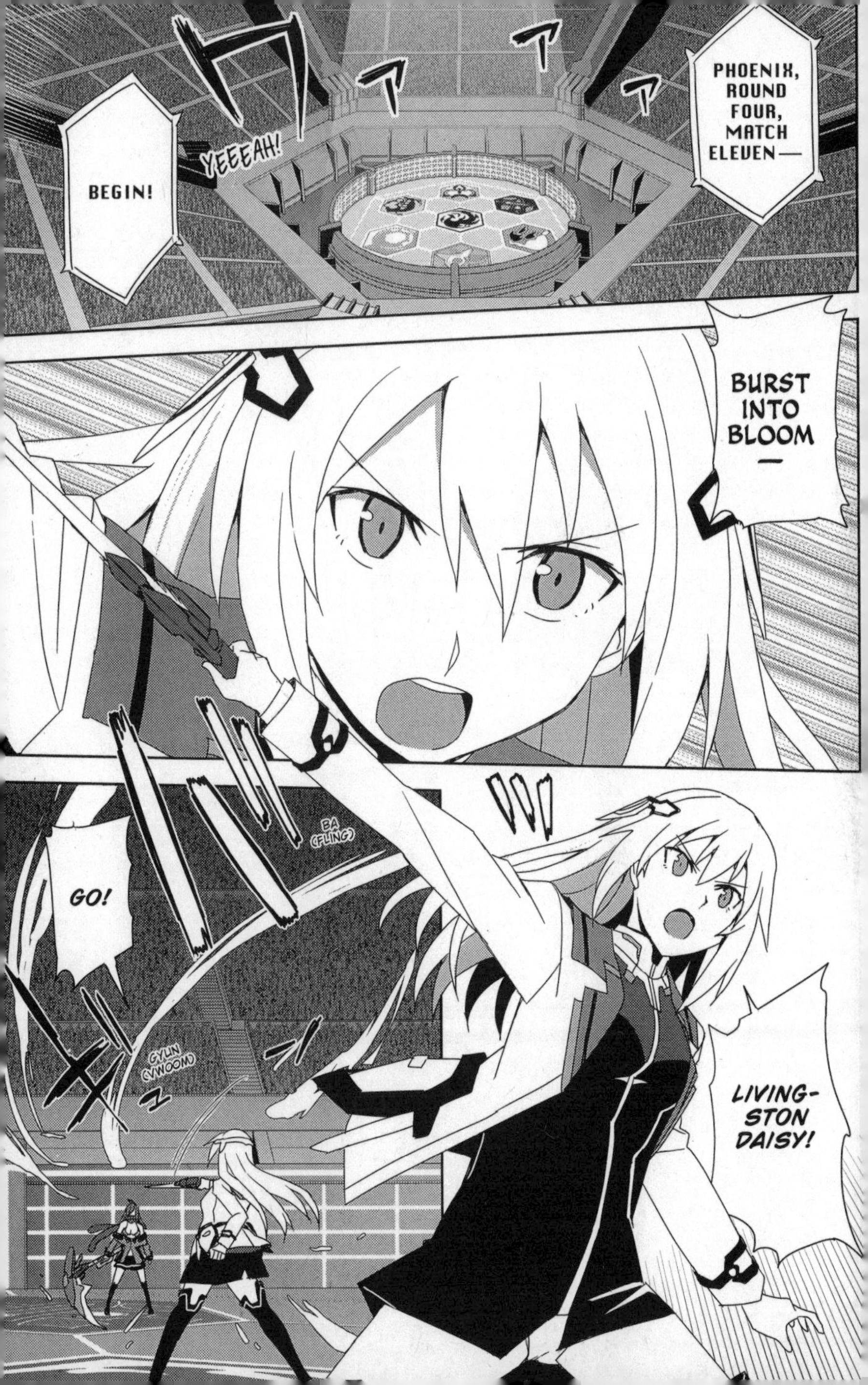
PHOENIX, ROUND FOUR, MATCH ELEVEN—
YEEEAH!
BEGIN!
BURST INTO BLOOM —
BA (FLING)
LIVING-STON DAISY!
GO!
GYUN (VWOOM)

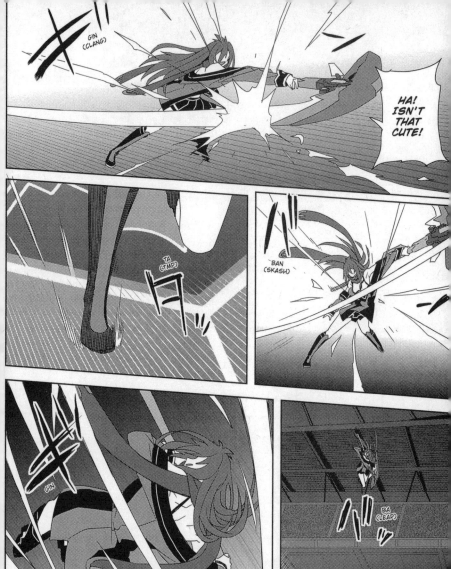

GIN
(CLANG)

HA!
ISN'T
THAT
CUTE!

TA
(TMP)

BAN
(SKASH)

GIN

BA
(LEAP)

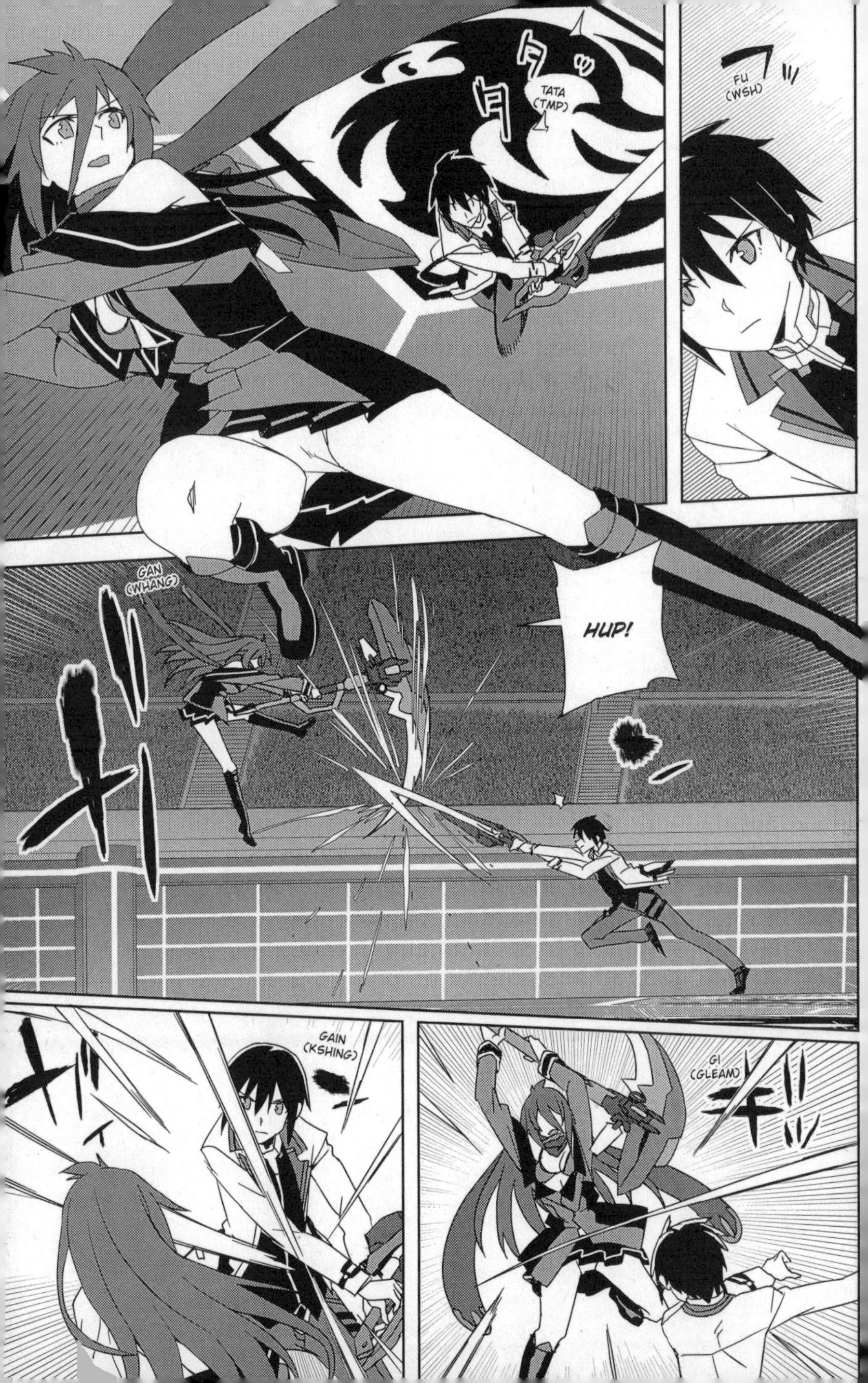
FU (WSH)
TATA (TMP)
HUP!
GAN (WHANG)
GI (GLEAM)
GAIN (KSHING)

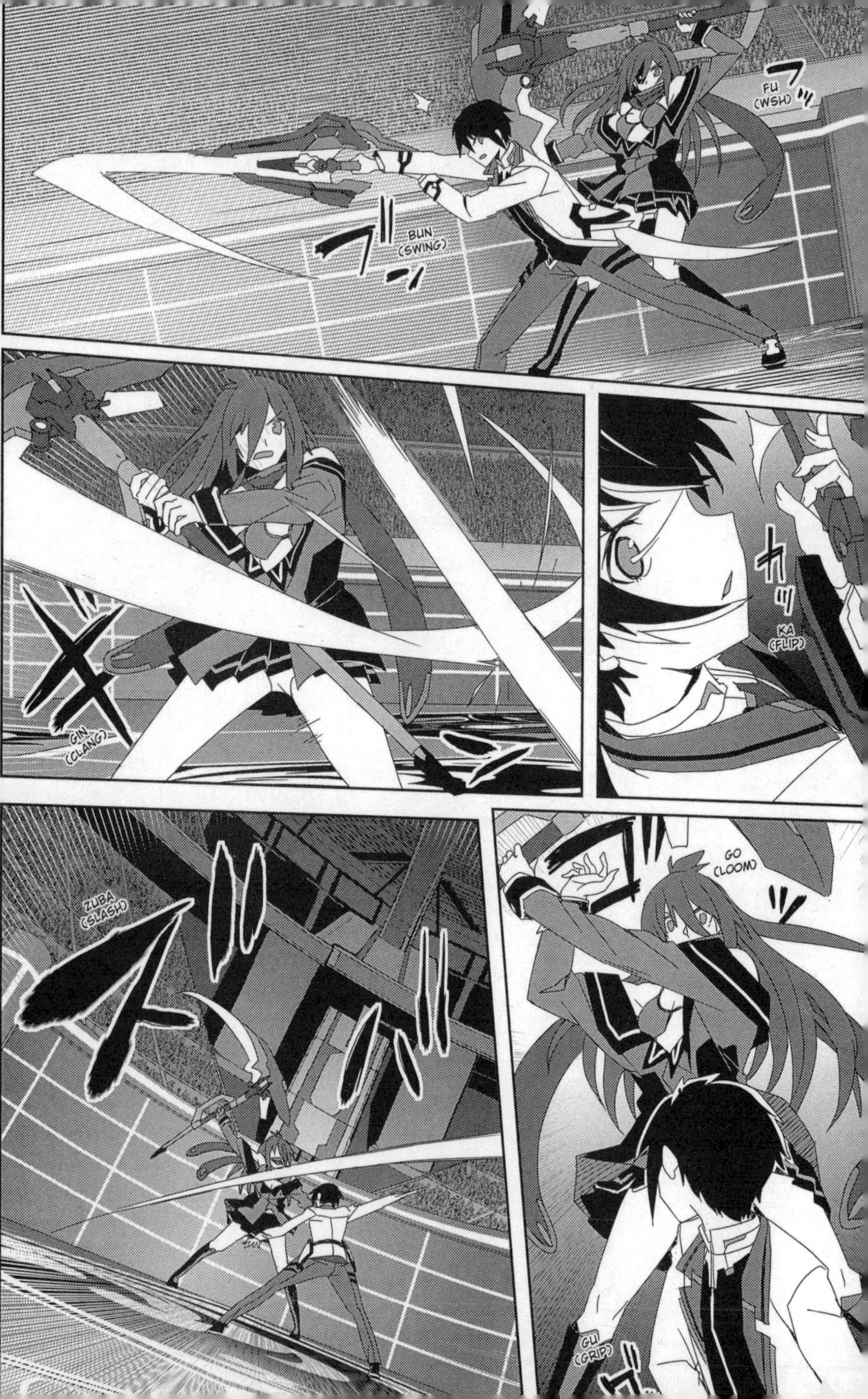
FU (WSH)
BUN (SWING)
KA (FLIP)
GIN (CLANG)
GO (LOOM)
ZUBA (SLASH)
GUI (GRIP)

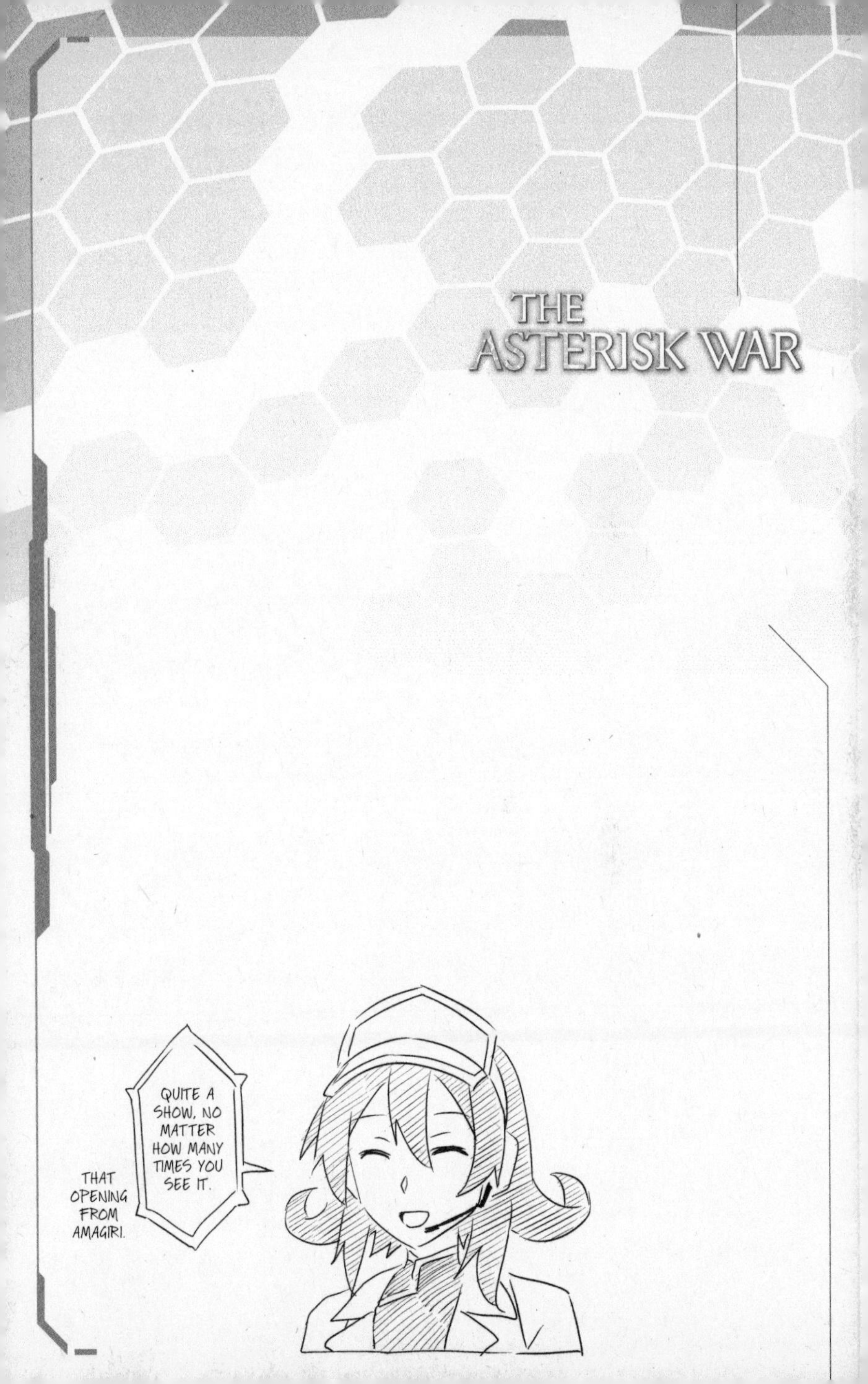
THE ASTERISK WAR
QUITE A SHOW, NO MATTER HOW MANY TIMES YOU SEE IT.
THAT OPENING FROM AMAGIRI.

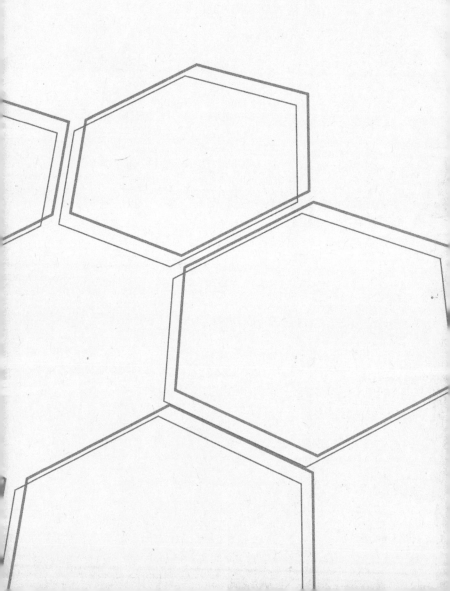

THE
ASTERISK WAR

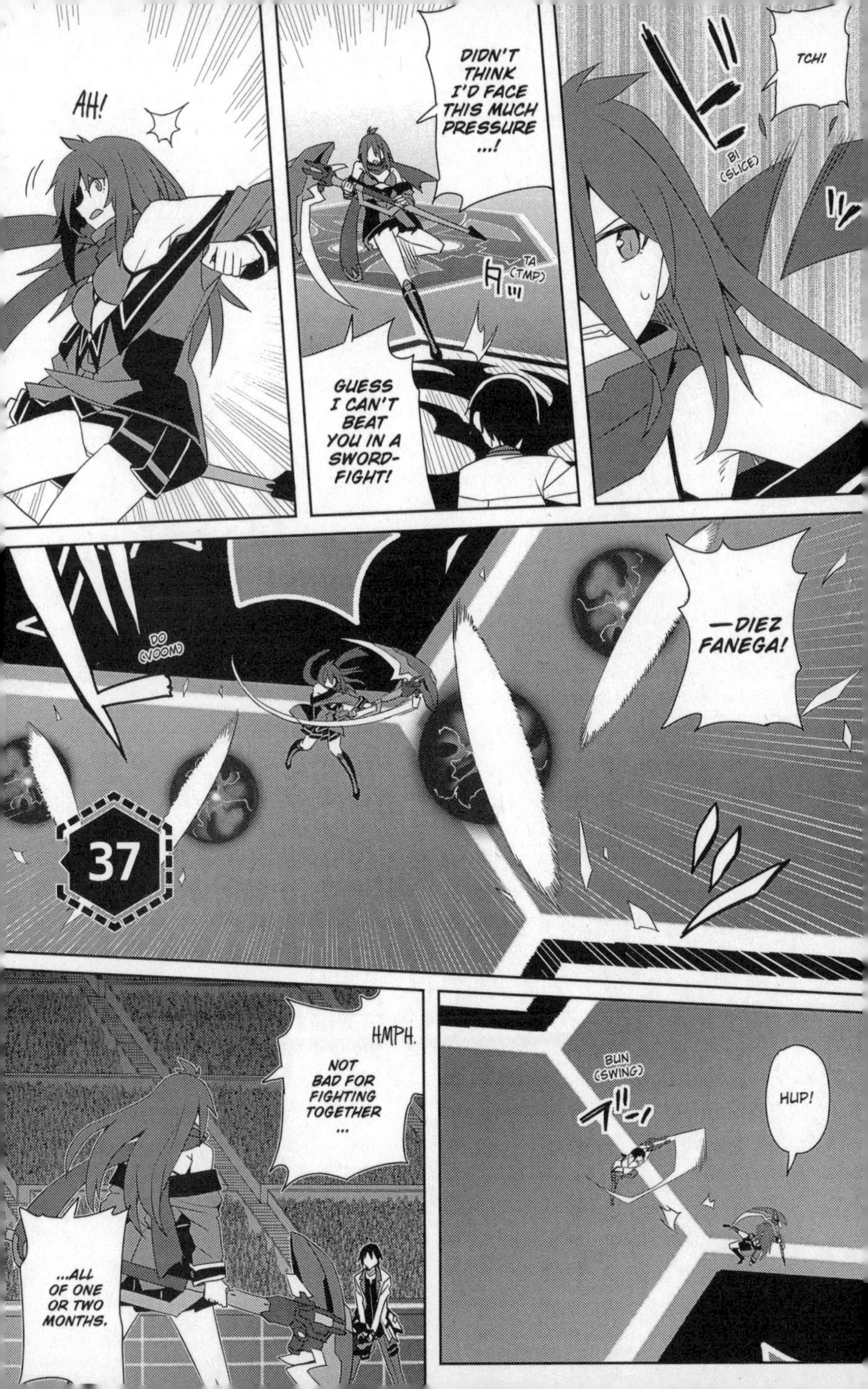
TCH!
BI (SLICE)
DIDN'T THINK I'D FACE THIS MUCH PRESSURE ...!
TA (TMP)
GUESS I CAN'T BEAT YOU IN A SWORD-FIGHT!
AH!
—DIEZ FANEGA!
DO (VOOM)
37
BUN (SWING)
HUP!
HMPH.
NOT BAD FOR FIGHTING TOGETHER ...
...ALL OF ONE OR TWO MONTHS.

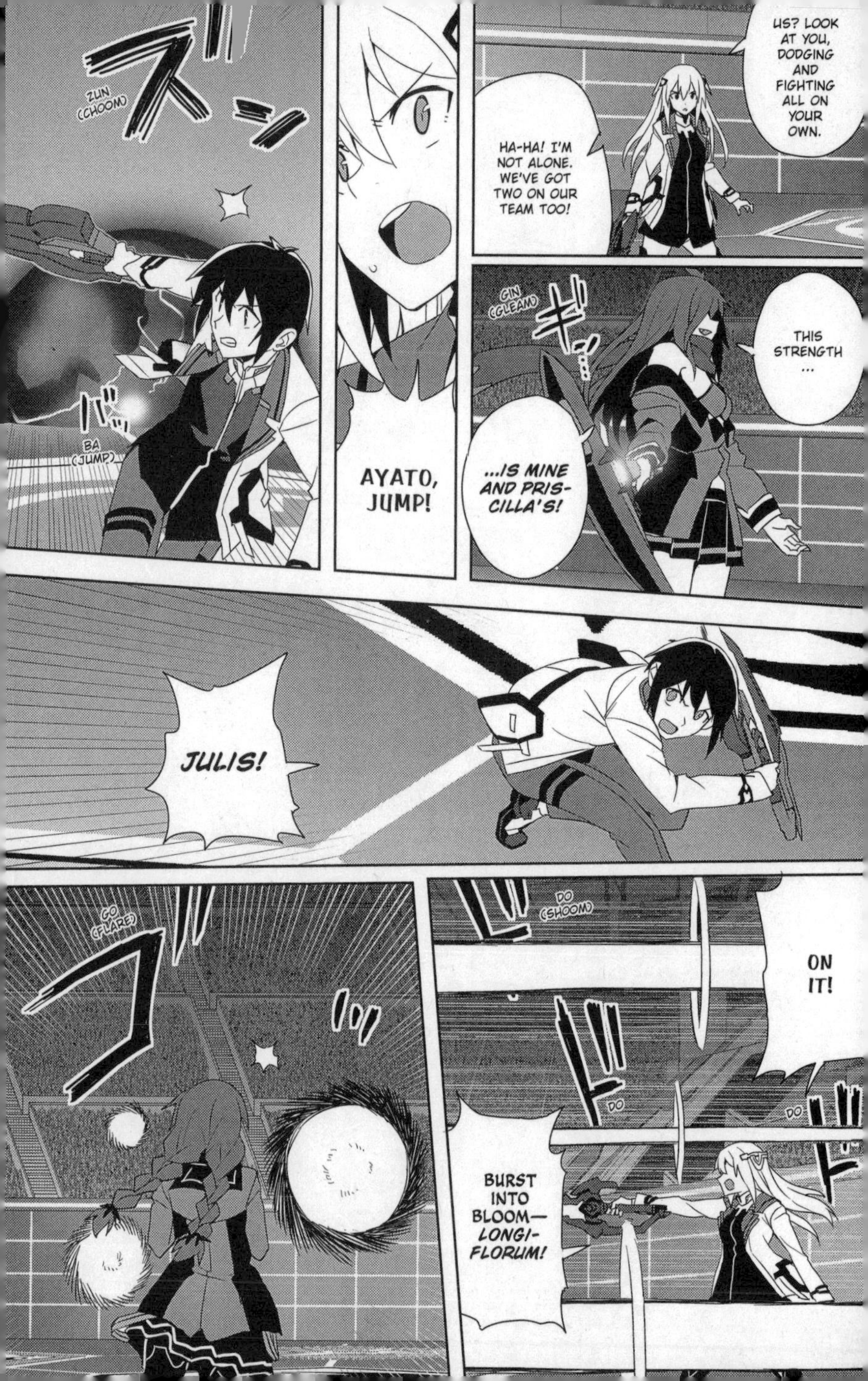
US? LOOK AT YOU, DODGING AND FIGHTING ALL ON YOUR OWN.
HA-HA! I'M NOT ALONE. WE'VE GOT TWO ON OUR TEAM TOO!
GIN (GLEAM)
THIS STRENGTH ...
...IS MINE AND PRIS-CILLA'S!
AYATO, JUMP!
ZUN (CHOOM)
BA (JUMP)
JULIS!
DO (SHOOM)
ON IT!
DO
DO
BURST INTO BLOOM—LONGI-FLORUM!
GO (FLARE)

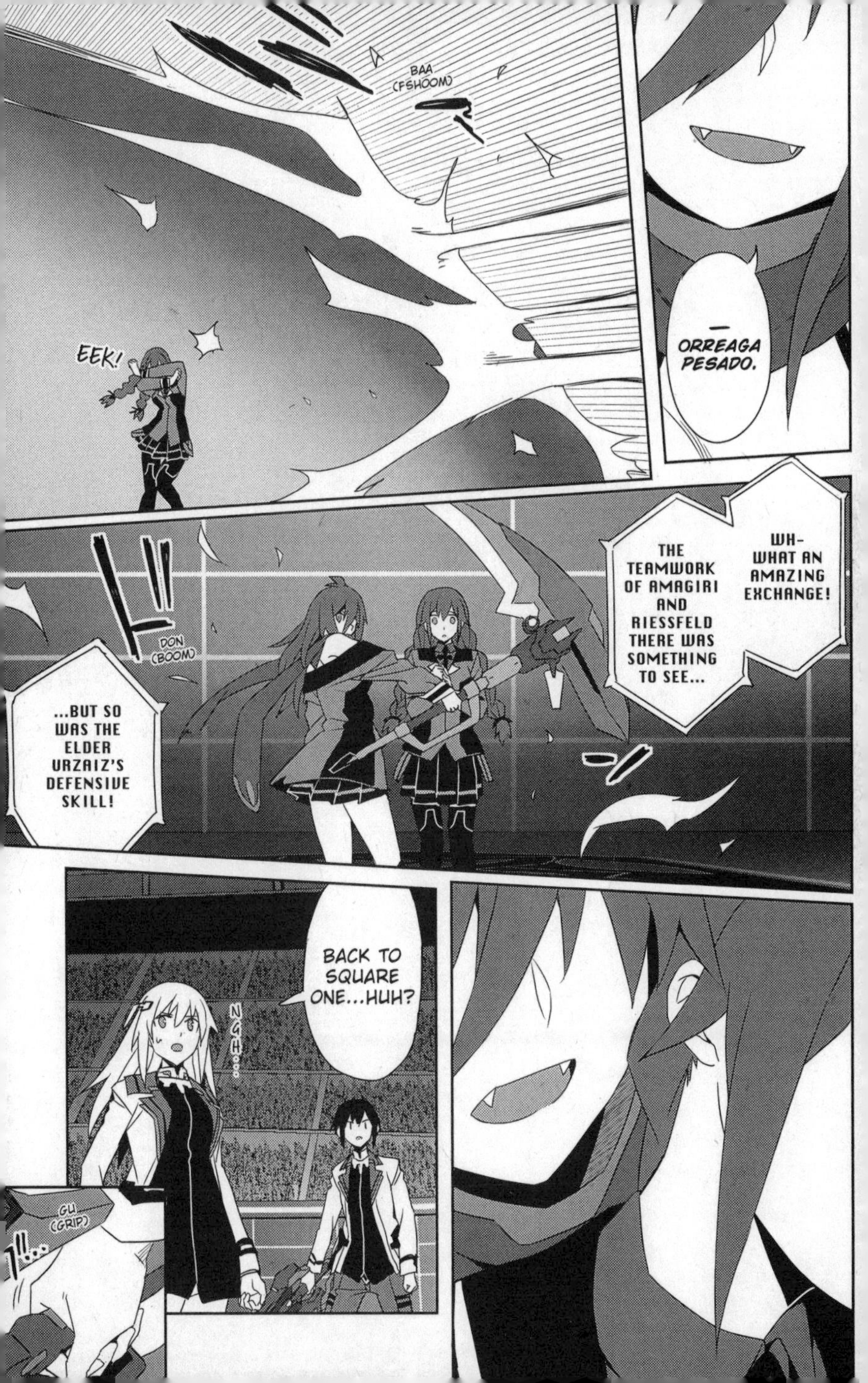
—ORREAGA PESADO.
BAA (FSHOOM)
EEK!
WH- WHAT AN AMAZING EXCHANGE!
THE TEAMWORK OF AMAGIRI AND RIESSFELD THERE WAS SOMETHING TO SEE...
DON (BOOM)
...BUT SO WAS THE ELDER URZAIZ'S DEFENSIVE SKILL!
BACK TO SQUARE ONE...HUH?
NGH...
GU (GRIP)

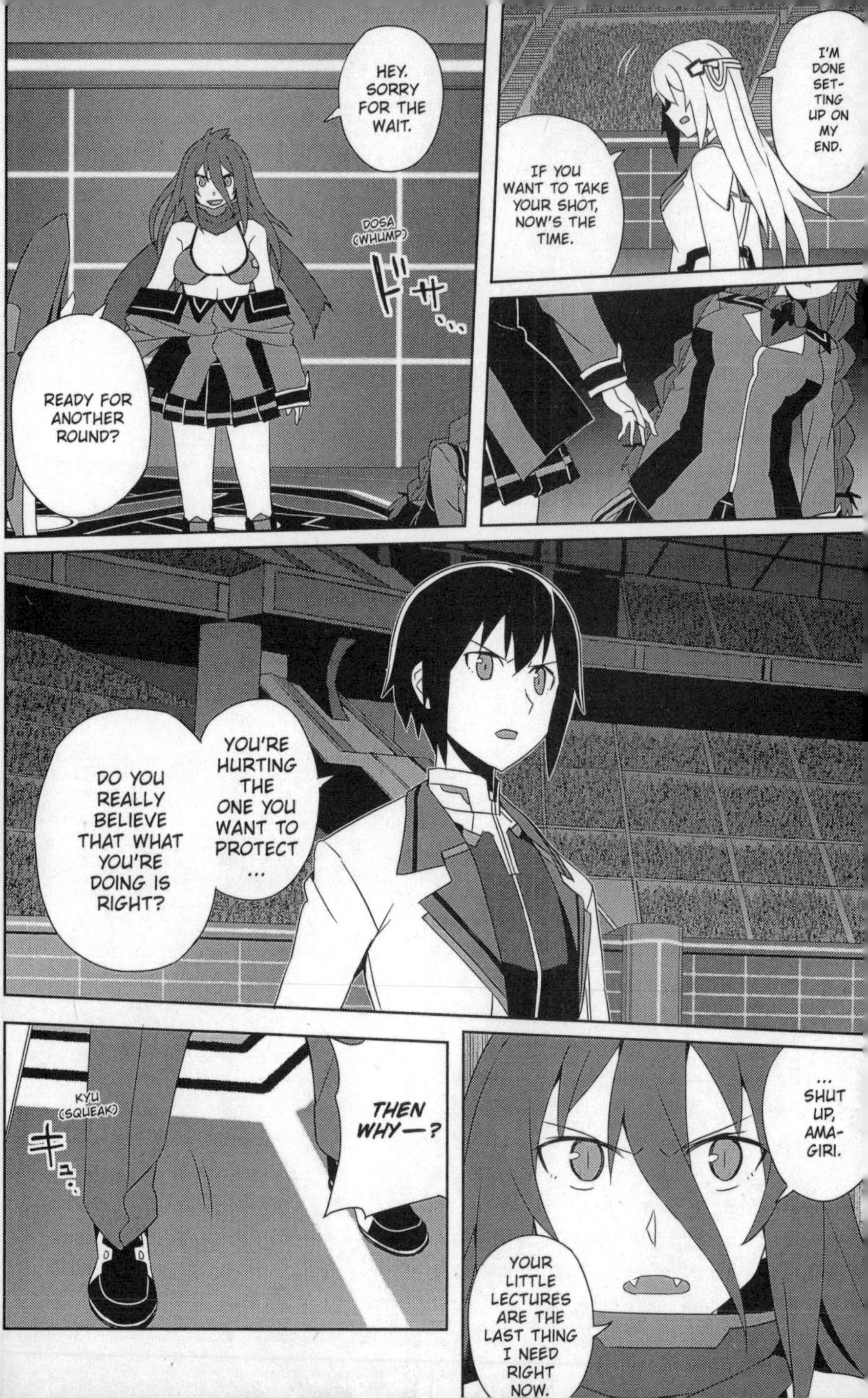
I'M DONE SETTING UP ON MY END.
IF YOU WANT TO TAKE YOUR SHOT, NOW'S THE TIME.
HEY. SORRY FOR THE WAIT.
DOSA (WHUMP)
READY FOR ANOTHER ROUND?
YOU'RE HURTING THE ONE YOU WANT TO PROTECT...
DO YOU REALLY BELIEVE THAT WHAT YOU'RE DOING IS RIGHT?
...SHUT UP, AMAGIRI.
YOUR LITTLE LECTURES ARE THE LAST THING I NEED RIGHT NOW.
KYU (SQUEAK)
THEN WHY—?

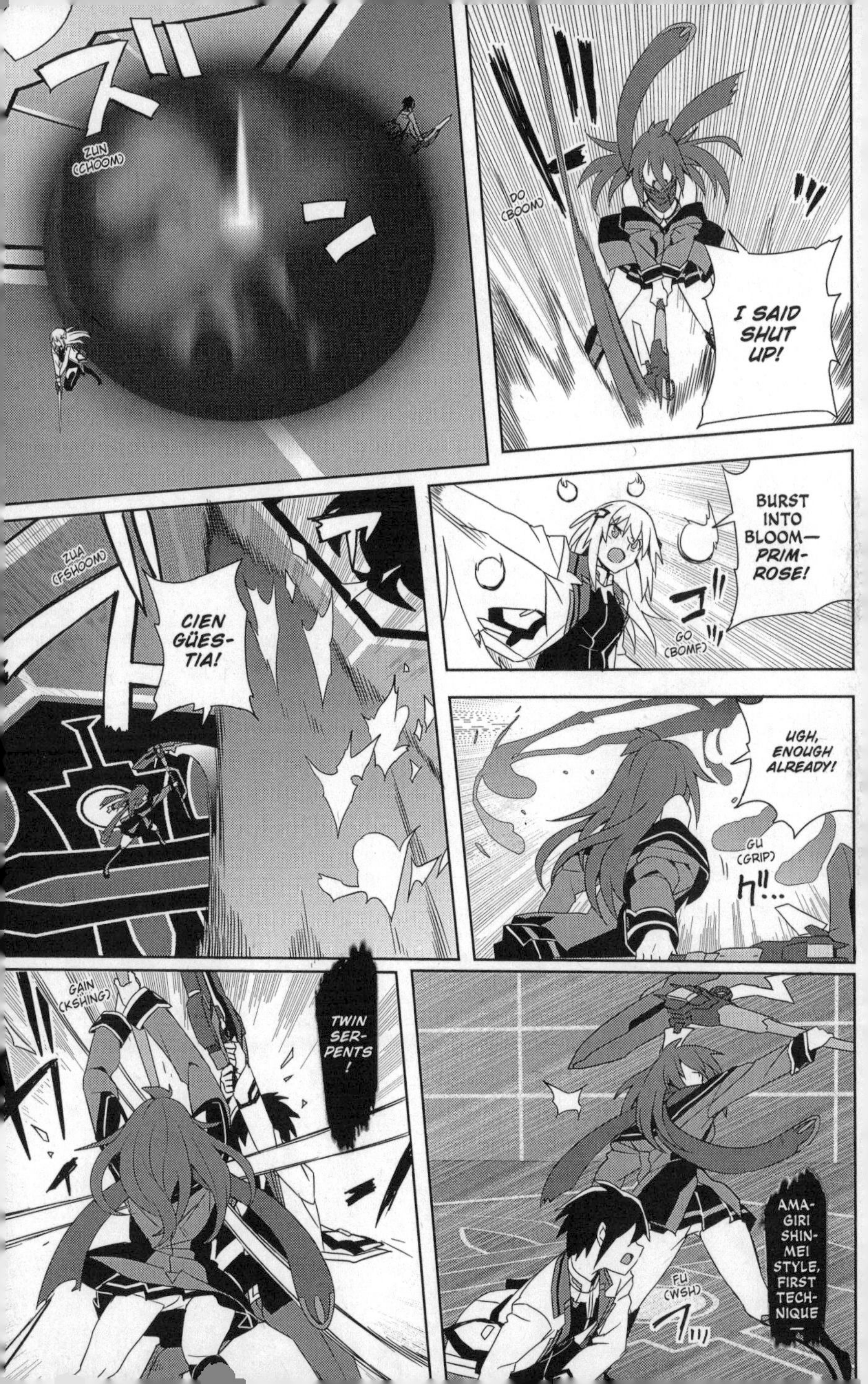
DO (BOOM)
I SAID SHUT UP!
ZUN (CHOOM)
BURST INTO BLOOM—PRIMROSE!
GO (BOMF)
UGH, ENOUGH ALREADY!
GU (GRIP)
ZUA (FSHOOM)
CIEN GÜESTIA!
AMAGIRI SHINMEI STYLE, FIRST TECHNIQUE—
FU (WSH)
GAIN (KSHING)
TWIN SERPENTS!

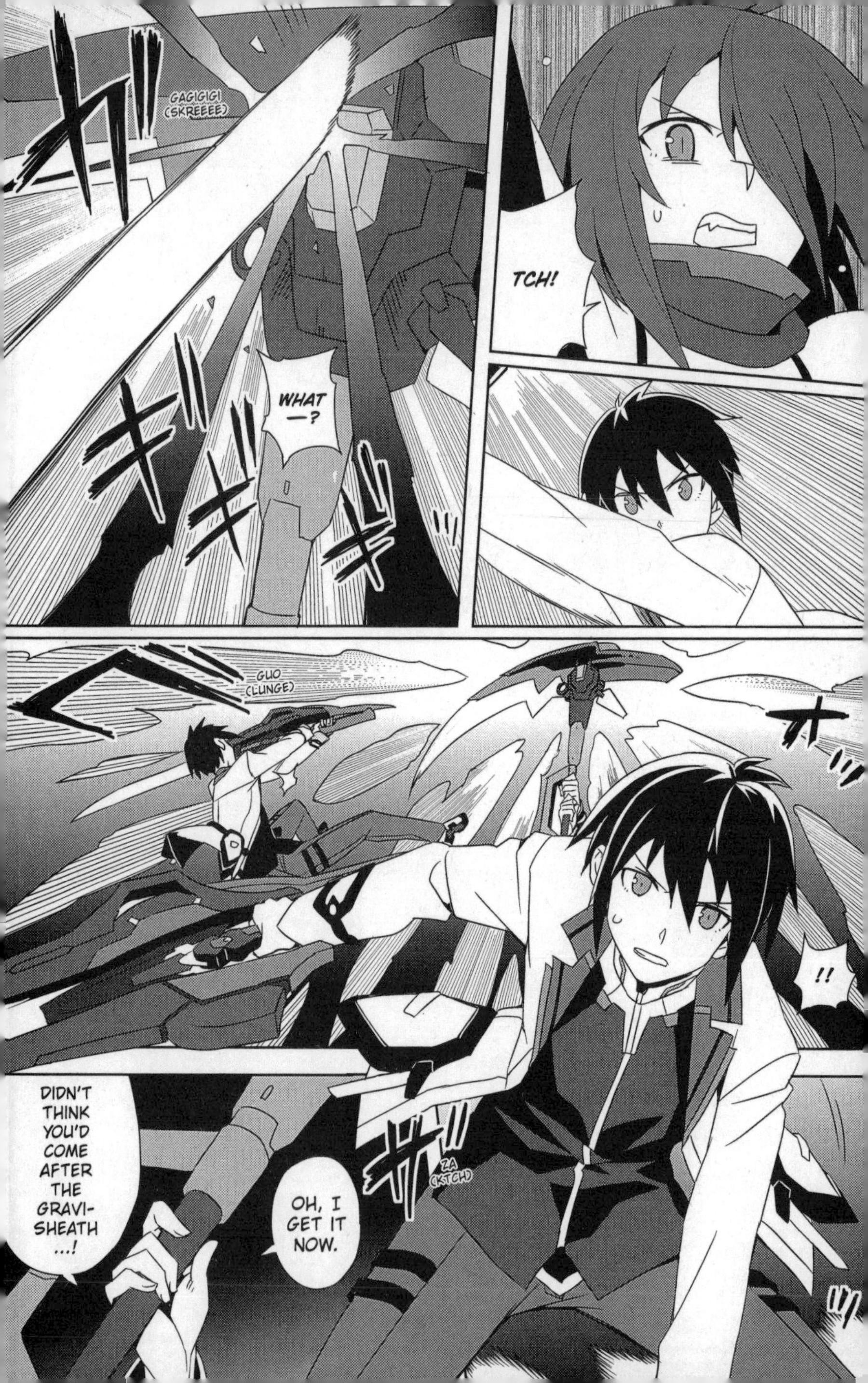
TCH!
GAGIGIGI (SKREEEE)
WHAT —?
GUO (LUNGE)
!!
ZA (KTCH)
OH, I GET IT NOW.
DIDN'T THINK YOU'D COME AFTER THE GRAVI-SHEATH ...!

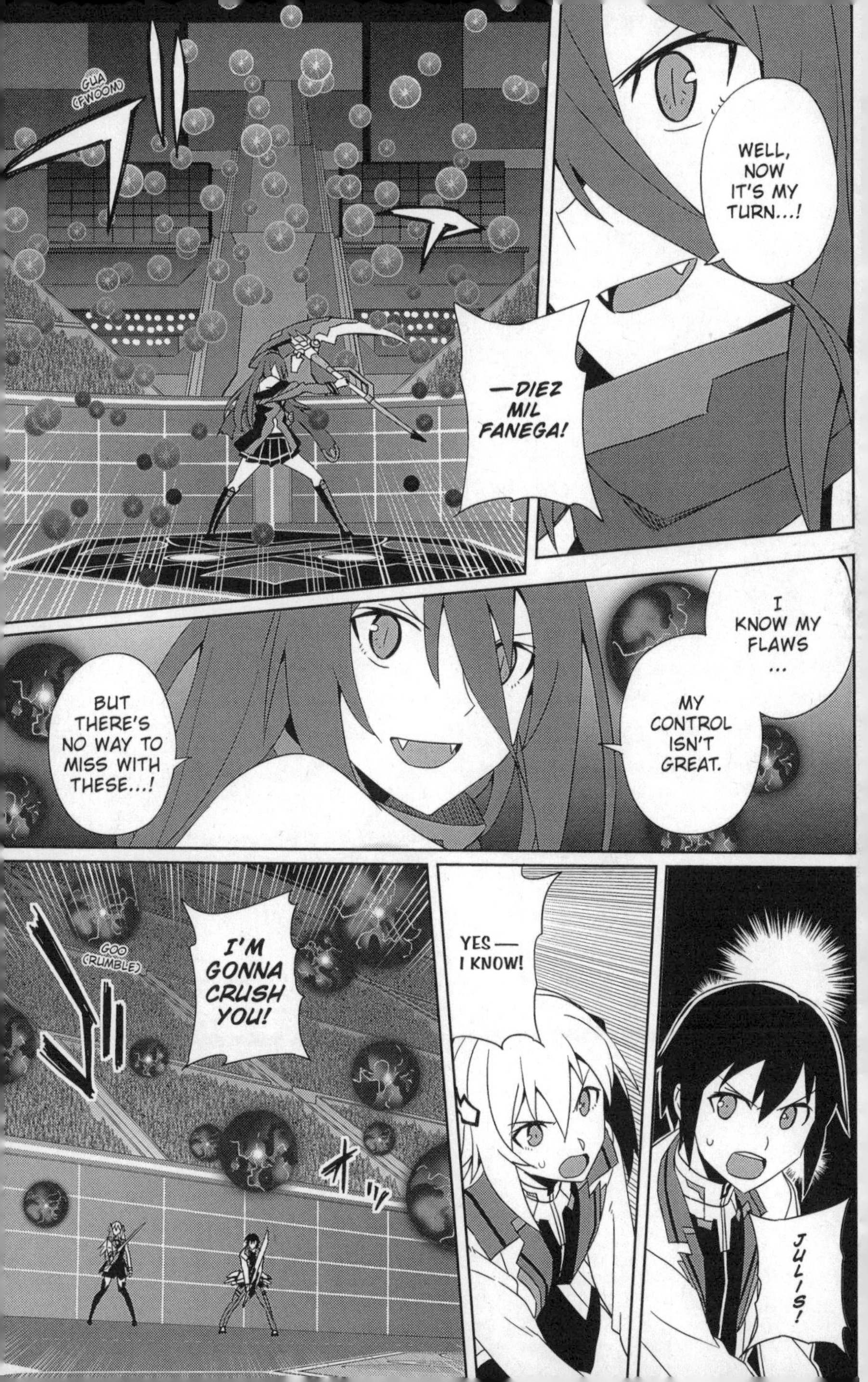
WELL, NOW IT'S MY TURN...!
—DIEZ MIL FANEGA!
GUA (FWOOM)
I KNOW MY FLAWS...
MY CONTROL ISN'T GREAT.
BUT THERE'S NO WAY TO MISS WITH THESE...!
JULIS!
YES—I KNOW!
I'M GONNA CRUSH YOU!
GOO (RUMBLE)

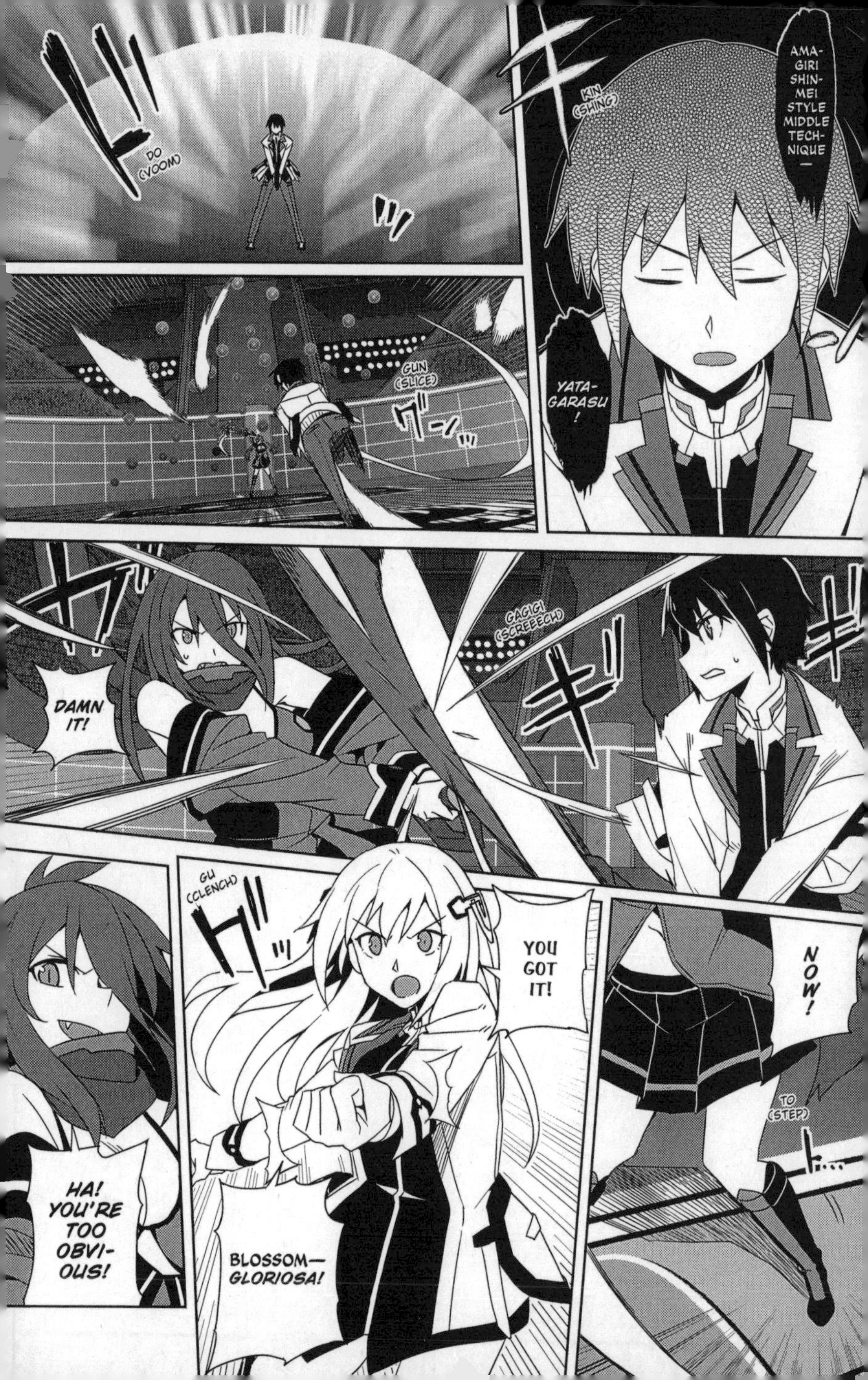
AMA-GIRI SHIN-MEI STYLE MIDDLE TECH-NIQUE—
KIN (SHING)
YATA-GARASU!
DO (VOOM)
GUN (SLICE)
GAGIGI (SCREEECH)
DAMN IT!
NOW!
TO (STEP)
YOU GOT IT!
GU (CLENCH)
BLOSSOM—GLORIOSA!
HA! YOU'RE TOO OBVI-OUS!

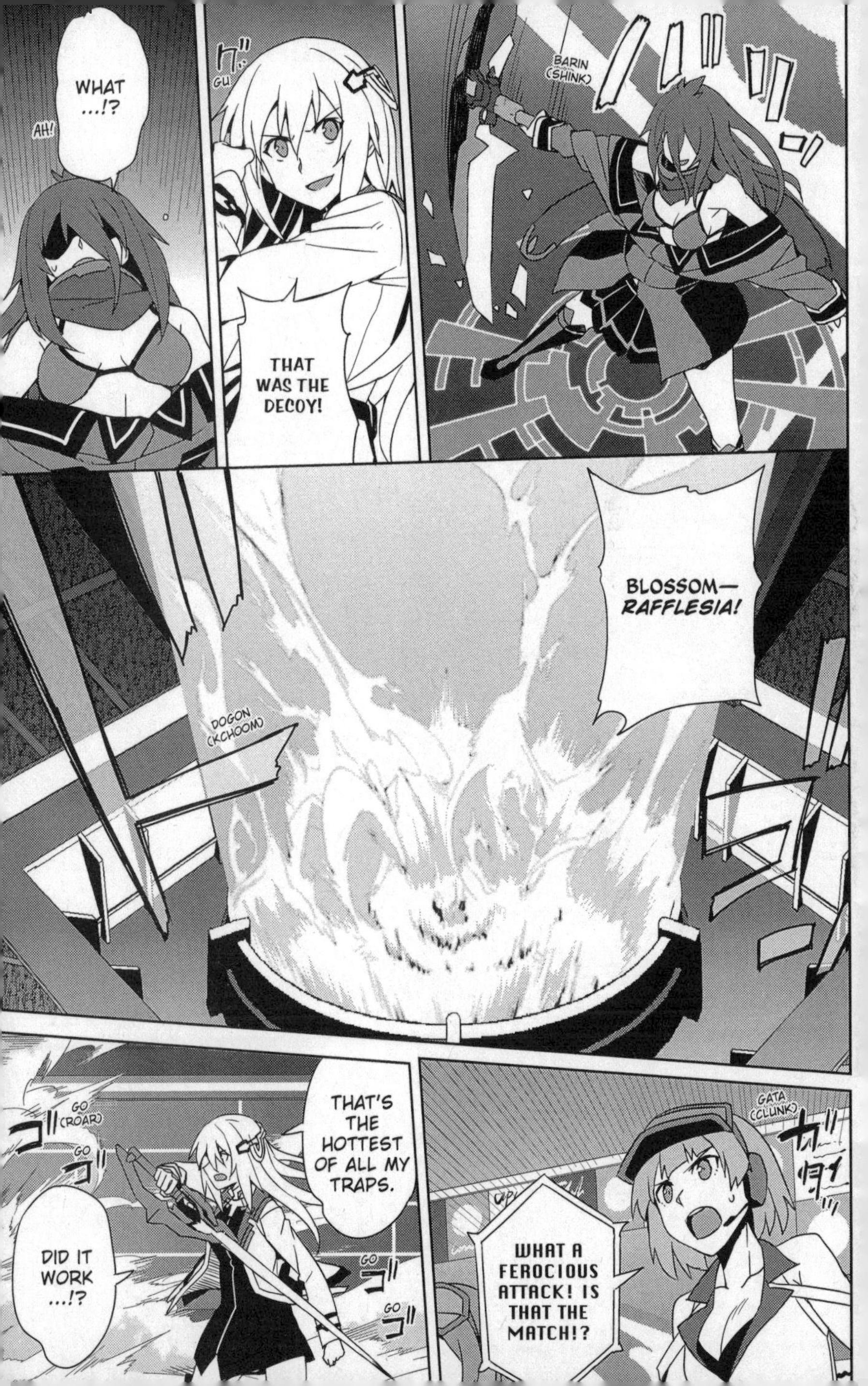
BARIN (SHINK)
GU
THAT WAS THE DECOY!
AH!
WHAT ...!?
BLOSSOM— *RAFFLESIA!*
DOGON (KCHOOM)
GATA (CLUNK)
WHAT A FEROCIOUS ATTACK! IS THAT THE MATCH!?
THAT'S THE HOTTEST OF ALL MY TRAPS.
GO (ROAR)
GO
DID IT WORK ...!?
GO
GO

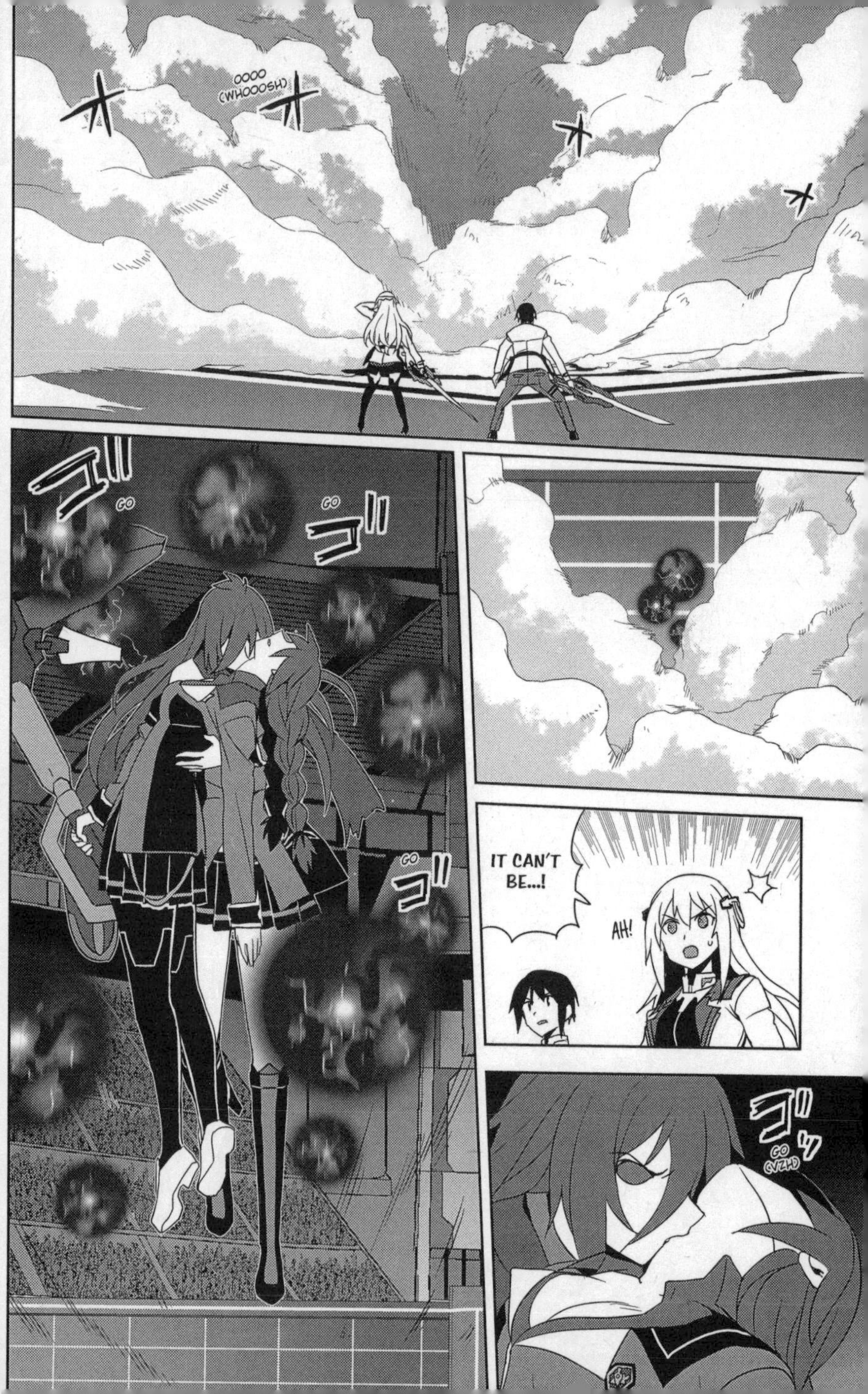

OOOO (WHOOOSH)
IT CAN'T BE...!
AH!
GO (VZHD)
GO
GO
GO

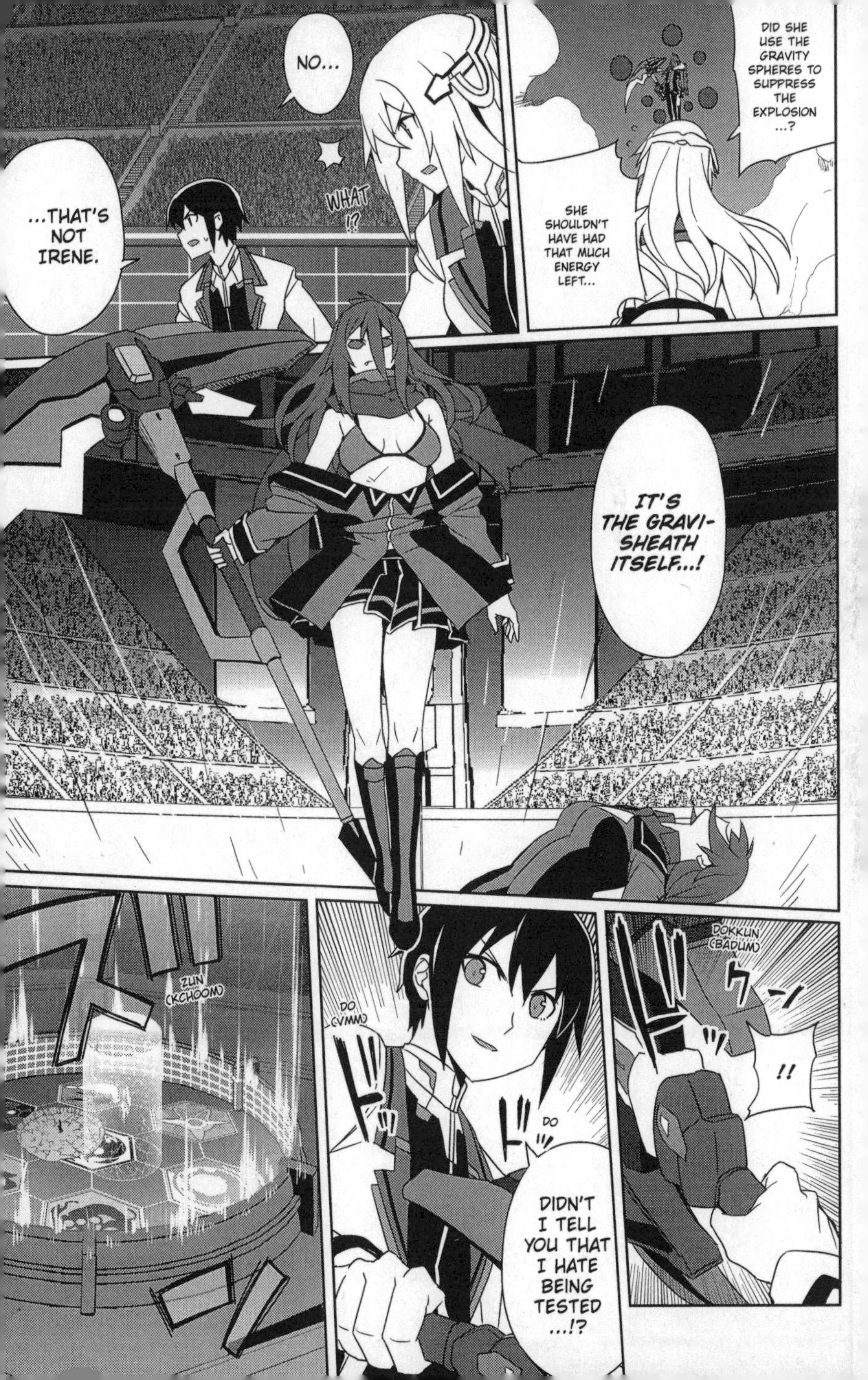
DID SHE USE THE GRAVITY SPHERES TO SUPPRESS THE EXPLOSION ...?
SHE SHOULDN'T HAVE HAD THAT MUCH ENERGY LEFT...
NO...
WHAT !?
...THAT'S NOT IRENE.
IT'S THE GRAVI-SHEATH ITSELF...!
DOKKUN (BADUM)
!!
DO (VMM)
DO
DIDN'T I TELL YOU THAT I HATE BEING TESTED ...!?
ZUN (KCHOOM)

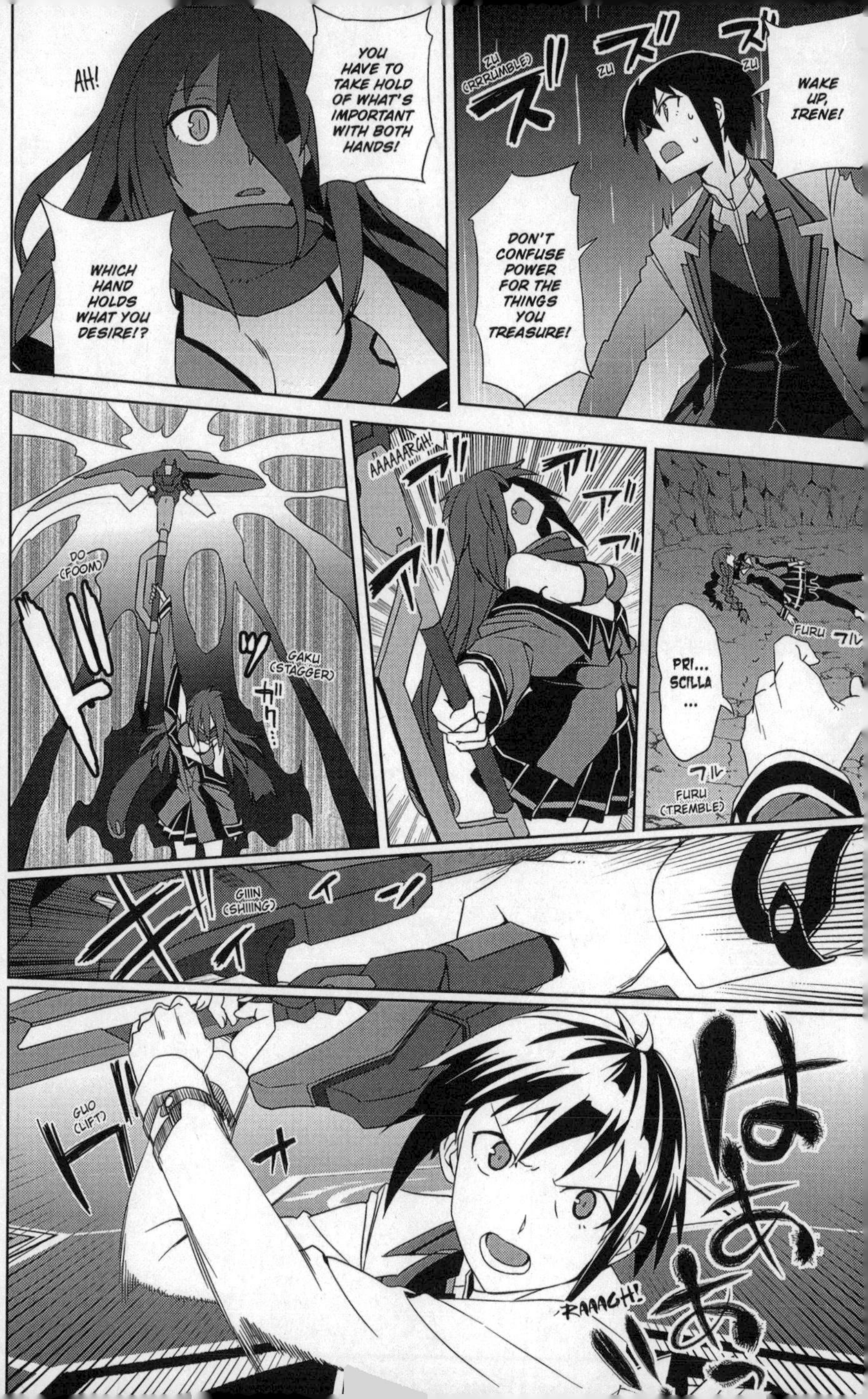
WAKE UP, IRENE!
ZU (RRRUMBLE)
ZU
ZU
DON'T CONFUSE POWER FOR THE THINGS YOU TREASURE!
YOU HAVE TO TAKE HOLD OF WHAT'S IMPORTANT WITH BOTH HANDS!
AH!
WHICH HAND HOLDS WHAT YOU DESIRE!?
FURU
PRI... SCILLA ...
FURU (TREMBLE)
AAAAAARGH!
DO (FOOM)
GAKU (STAGGER)
GIIN (SHIIING)
GUO (LIFT)
RAAAGH!

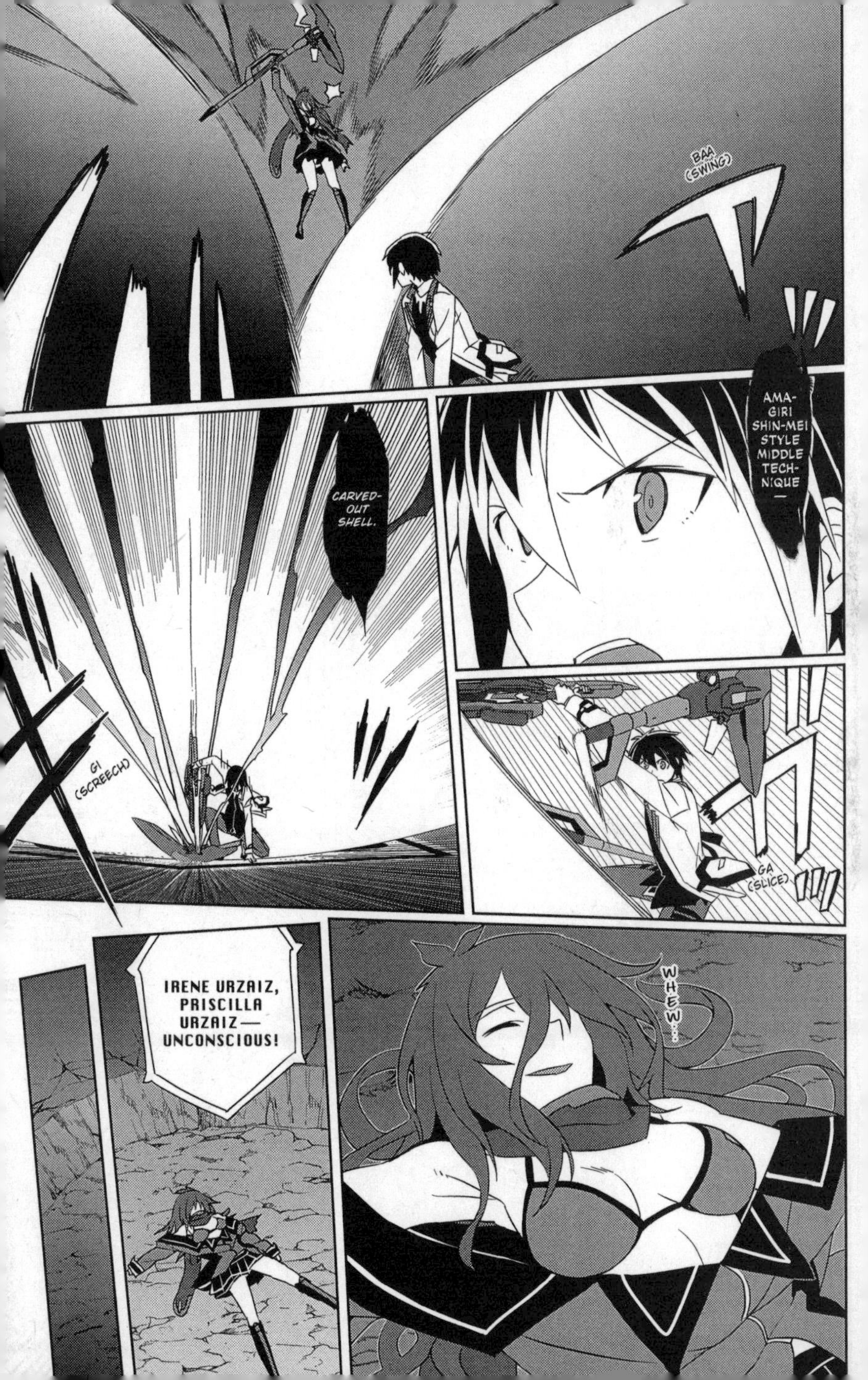
BAA (SWING)
AMA-GIRI SHIN-MEI STYLE MIDDLE TECH-NIQUE—
GA (SLICE)
CARVED-OUT SHELL.
GI (SCREECH)
WHEW...
IRENE URZAIZ, PRISCILLA URZAIZ— UNCONSCIOUS!

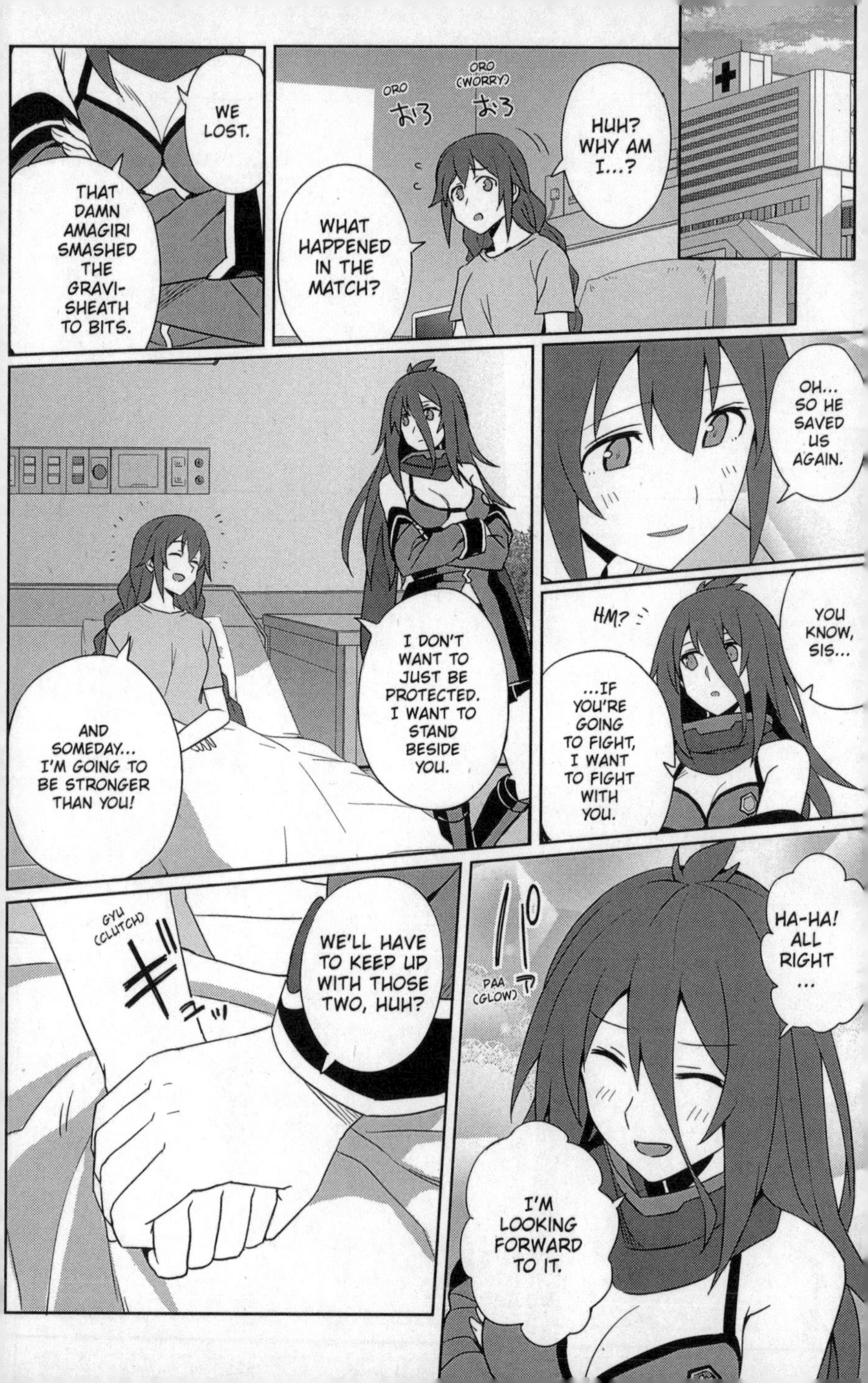
HUH? WHY AM I...?
ORO (WORRY)
おろ
ORO
おろ
WHAT HAPPENED IN THE MATCH?
WE LOST.
THAT DAMN AMAGIRI SMASHED THE GRAVI-SHEATH TO BITS.
OH... SO HE SAVED US AGAIN.
YOU KNOW, SIS...
HM?
...IF YOU'RE GOING TO FIGHT, I WANT TO FIGHT WITH YOU.
I DON'T WANT TO JUST BE PROTECTED. I WANT TO STAND BESIDE YOU.
AND SOMEDAY... I'M GOING TO BE STRONGER THAN YOU!
HA-HA! ALL RIGHT...
PAA (GLOW)
パァ
I'M LOOKING FORWARD TO IT.
WE'LL HAVE TO KEEP UP WITH THOSE TWO, HUH?
GYU (CLUTCH)
ギュッ

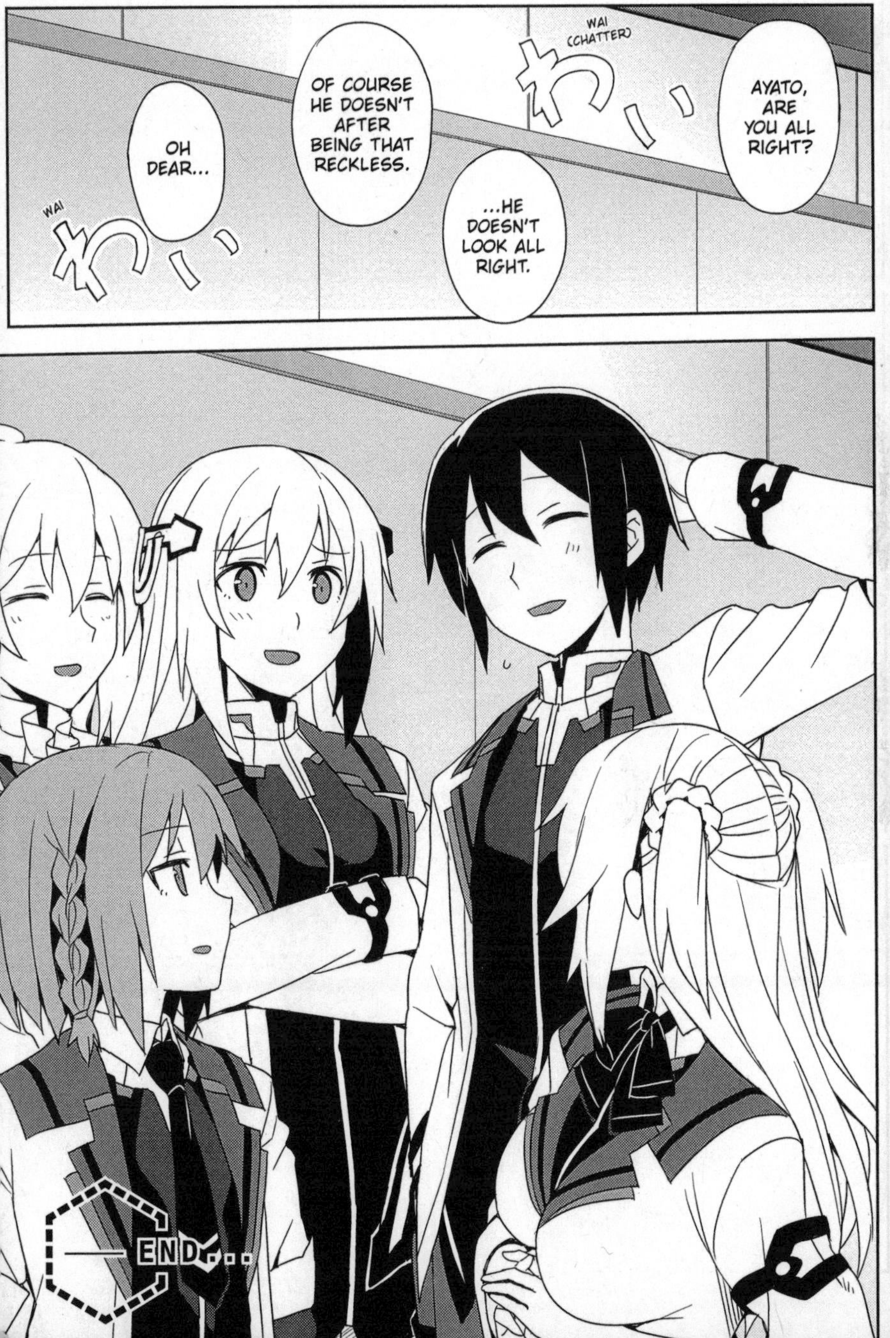
AYATO, ARE YOU ALL RIGHT?
WAI (CHATTER)
...HE DOESN'T LOOK ALL RIGHT.
OF COURSE HE DOESN'T AFTER BEING THAT RECKLESS.
OH DEAR...
WAI
END...

THE ASTERISK WAR

Afterword

Hi again. Ningen here.
Thanks to all your support, the manga adaptation of *The Asterisk War* has crossed the Volume 5 mark.

The well-received second season of the anime finished airing as well. Along with the original novels, of course, all of the adaptations make that universe so much more exciting. But the manga will stop here for the time being.
It's a little like the pause between seasons of an anime.

Thinking back on it, I've spent almost three and a half years dabbling in the world of Asterisk so intricately imagined by Mr. Yuu Miyazaki and the illustrator okiura.

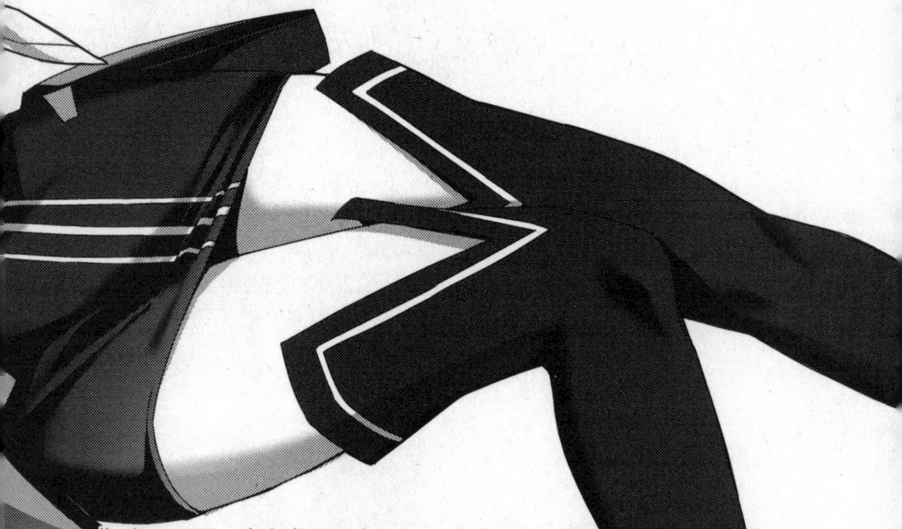

I've been constantly feeling out how much wiggle room I'd have adapting and reshaping Mr. Miyazaki's solidly structured work. I think I may have been able to touch on some things that the anime didn't get to, while the storytelling is more informal than the novels.

To me, there is no greater pleasure than knowing that fans of the novels, the anime, the game, and many others have enjoyed my work.

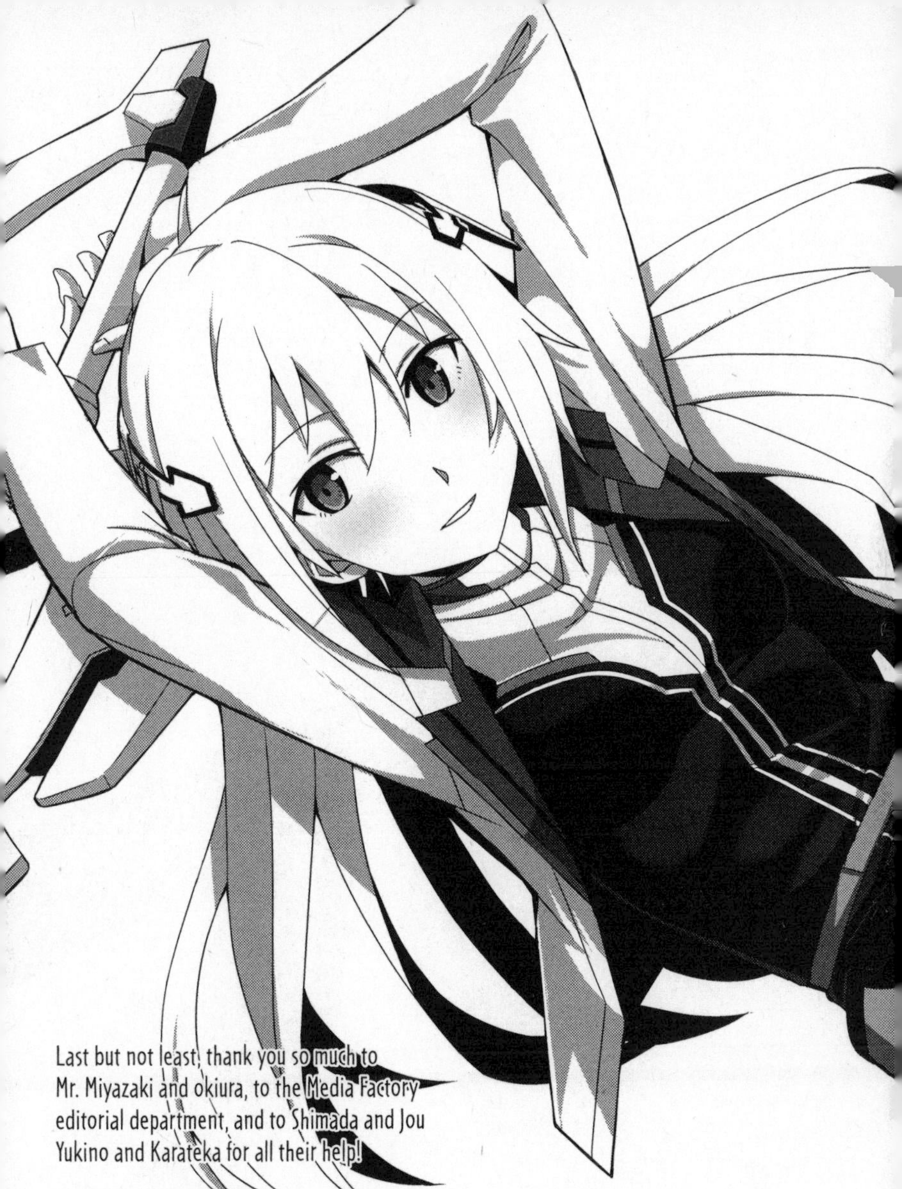

Last but not least, thank you so much to Mr. Miyazaki and okiura, to the Media Factory editorial department, and to Shimada and Jou Yukino and Karateka for all their help!

Until we meet again!

Ningen

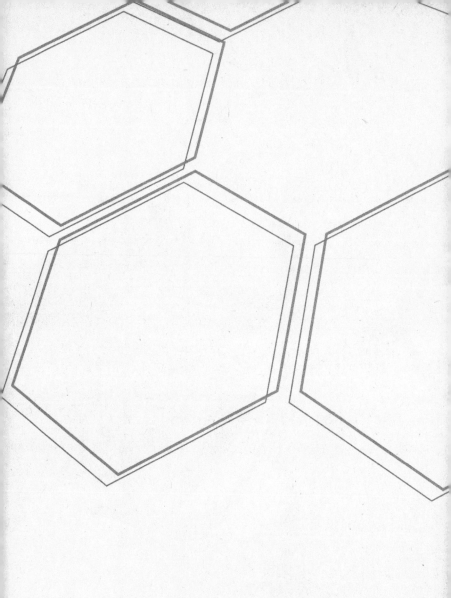

THE
ASTERISK WAR

IN THIS FANTASY WORLD, EVERYTHING'S A GAME—AND THESE SIBLINGS PLAY TO WIN!

No Game No Life © YUU KAMIYA
KADOKAWA CORPORATION

A genius but socially inept brother and sister duo is offered the chance to compete in a fantasy world where games decide everything. Sora and Shiro will take on the world and, while they're at it, create a harem of nonhuman companions!

No Game No Life, Please! © Kazuya Yuizaki 2016 © Yuu Kamiya 2016
KADOKAWA CORPORATION

LIGHT NOVELS 1–6 AVAILABLE NOW

LIKE THE NOVELS?

Check out the spin-off manga for even more out-of-control adventures with the Werebeast girl, Izuna!

Yen Press

PRESENTING THE LATEST SERIES FROM
JUN MOCHIZUKI

THE CASE STUDY OF
VANITAS

**READ THE CHAPTERS AT
THE SAME TIME AS JAPAN!**

**AVAILABLE NOW WORLDWIDE
WHEREVER E-BOOKS ARE SOLD!**

www.yenpress.com

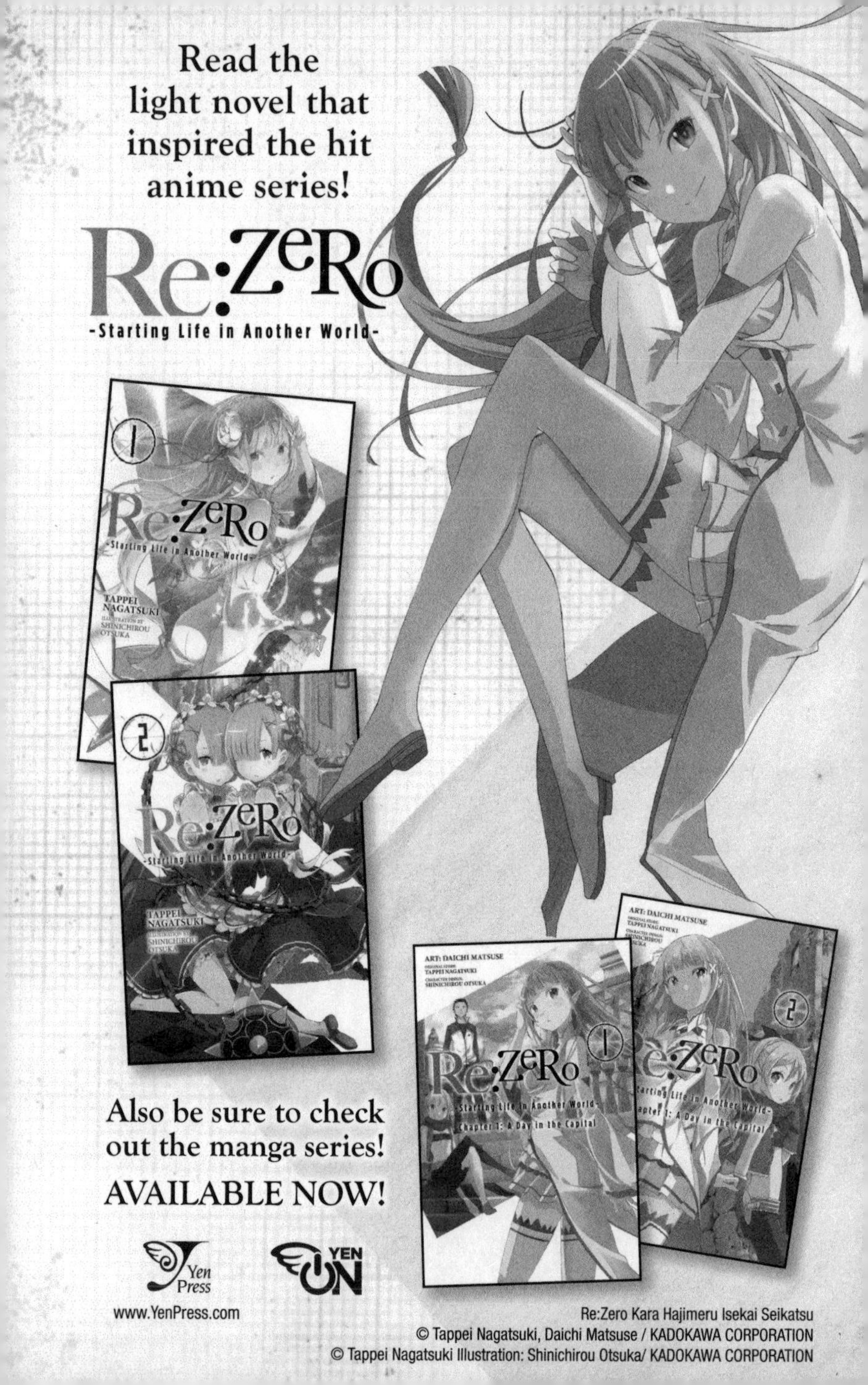
Read the light novel that inspired the hit anime series!
Re:ZeRo
-Starting Life in Another World-
Also be sure to check out the manga series!
AVAILABLE NOW!
Yen Press
YEN ON
www.YenPress.com
Re:Zero Kara Hajimeru Isekai Seikatsu
© Tappei Nagatsuki, Daichi Matsuse / KADOKAWA CORPORATION
© Tappei Nagatsuki Illustration: Shinichirou Otsuka/ KADOKAWA CORPORATION

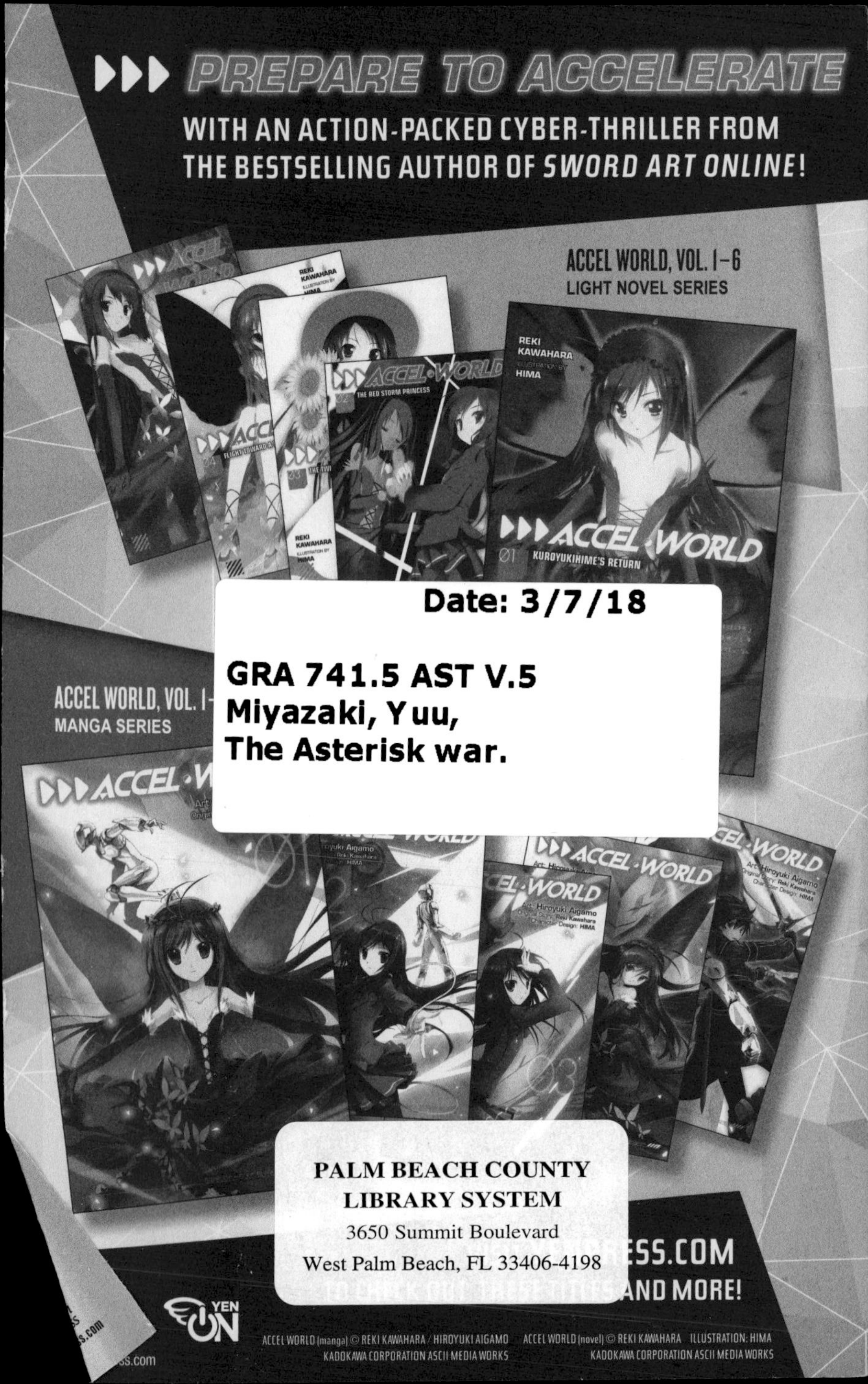
PREPARE TO ACCELERATE
WITH AN ACTION-PACKED CYBER-THRILLER FROM THE BESTSELLING AUTHOR OF *SWORD ART ONLINE*!
ACCEL WORLD, VOL. 1–6
LIGHT NOVEL SERIES
REKI KAWAHARA
ILLUSTRATION BY HIMA
ACCEL WORLD
THE RED STORM PRINCESS
01 KUROYUKIHIME'S RETURN
ACCEL WORLD, VOL. 1-
MANGA SERIES
ACCEL WORLD
Art: Hiroyuki Aigamo
Original Story: Reki Kawahara
Character Design: HIMA
ESS.COM
AND MORE!
YEN ON
ACCEL WORLD (manga) © REKI KAWAHARA / HIROYUKI AIGAMO KADOKAWA CORPORATION ASCII MEDIA WORKS
ACCEL WORLD (novel) © REKI KAWAHARA ILLUSTRATION: HIMA KADOKAWA CORPORATION ASCII MEDIA WORKS

THE ASTERISK WAR 05

Ningen
Original Story: Yuu Miyazaki
Character Design: okiura

Translation: Melissa Tanaka   Lettering: Phil Christie

THE ASTERISK WAR
© Ningen 2016
© Yuu Miyazaki 2016
First published in Japan in 2016 by KADOKAWA CORPORATION, Tokyo.
English translation rights arranged with KADOKAWA CORPORATION, Tokyo,
through TUTTLE-MORI AGENCY, Inc., Tokyo.

English translation © 2017 by Yen Press, LLC

Yen Press
1290 Avenue of the Americas
New York, NY 10104

Visit us at yenpress.com
facebook.com/yenpress
twitter.com/yenpress
yenpress.tumblr.com
instagram.com/yenpresss

First Yen Press Edition: September 2017

Yen Press is an imprint of Yen Press, LLC.
The Yen Press name and logo are trademarks of Yen Press, LLC.

Library of Congress Control Number: 2016936539

ISBNs: 978-0-316-47342-2 (paperback)
       978-0-316-47344-6 (ebook)

10 9 8 7 6 5 4 3 2 1

BVG

Printed in the United States of America